INDIAN ENGLISH WOMEN'S FICTION

A Study of Marriage, Career and Divorce

INDIAN ENGLISH WOMEN'S FICTION

A Study of Marriage, Career and Divorce

D. Murali Manohar

ATLANTIC
PUBLISHERS & DISTRIBUTORS (P) LTD

Published by
ATLANTIC
PUBLISHERS & DISTRIBUTORS (P) LTD
7/22, Ansari Road, Darya Ganj, New Delhi-110002
Phones : +91-11-40775252, 23273880, 23275880, 23280451
Fax: +91-11-23285873
Web: www.atlanticbooks.com
E-mail: orders@atlanticbooks.com

Branch Office
5, Nallathambi Street, Wallajah Road, Chennai-600002
Phones : +91-44-64611085, 32413319
E-mail: chennai@atlanticbooks.com

Printed in India at Nice Printing Press, A-33/3A, Site-IV,
Industrial Area, Sahibabad, Ghaziabad, U.P.

DEDICATED TO

Lord Krishna
Who Has Given Me All

Contents

Acknowledgements

I have been fortunate to receive help and guidance from a large number of persons in completing the present literary work. I would like to acknowledge first and foremost my Research Advisor Prof. Alladi Uma who has been supporting and encouraging me right from my student days to the present as a student colleague in the department. She has been my "true" teacher.

Dr. M. Sridhar and Dr. K. Suneetha Rani have been my close friends in the department, sharing the pinch of my research, giving suggestions and making this book what it is.

My colleagues from other departments, namely K.Y. Ratnam, B. Nagarjuna, Tirumal, Rajasekhar, Sumant Dutt, and Ramulu have been encouraging me to complete my book as early as possible.

I would like to thank the University of Hyderabad for sanctioning me study leave for two years, of course, with the great help and support of my own colleagues.

Prof. Mohan Ramanan, Prof. Sudhakar Marathe, Prof. Sachidananda Mohanty, Prof. Syed Mujeebuddin, Dr. Hoshang Merchant and Dr. Afeefa Banu have been very much concerned about my completing the work as early as possible. I thank them for their concern.

I would like to thank Dr. Anand Mahanand from CIEFL for providing me all sort of help and emotional support whenever I needed.

I thank Mr. Nagarajan and Mr. Anand for guiding me in using computer. I also thank Suresh for every help and support he has given me.

I am thankful to the following libraries: Indira Gandhi Memorial Library, Hyderabad, C.I.E.F.L Library, Osmania University Library, City Central Library, and State Central Library, Hyderabad.

I am indebted to Sahitya Akademi, New Delhi for sending me the book Shevantibai M. Nikambe's *Ratanbai* in a short period of time, as this was one of the primary texts for my introductory chapter. My sincere thanks to Prof. Meenaksi Mukherjee for giving me the information about this book and its publication details.

I openly admit that this book would not have been possible had I not received full cooperation and encouragement from my wife D. Mamtha. She has always been with me in my work wholeheartedly. Also, no less is D. Vijaya Sai's, my son, cooperation. His naughty games have always provided me with much needed relaxation and a pleasant recreation.

Lastly, I would like to thank all those people who have directly or indirectly helped me in completing this task, but have not been particularly acknowledged here.

D. MURALI MANOHAR

Preface

Education has always been a tool for social, political and economic changes in any/our country, especially with regard to change in women's social position. Education is a stepping-stone for alertness, readiness, confidence and independence, to mention only a few. I have chosen Hindu characters who are educated formally right from primary education to the doctoral level. I do not include women who are not educated formally because the task will be unwieldy. One can argue that life itself/personal experiences of a woman can be considered "education". But my focus in this project is only on women obtaining a formal education and how they respond to real-life situations and alter their lifestyles according to their own choices. The basic problem is that most educated people fail to understand that education is linked with real life. Education is not an end in itself. In other words, I have not chosen uneducated women who appear in the novels. My observation is only about educated women from a Hindu background. What are the problems of these educated women? Educated women are supposed to be different from uneducated women, doing something different from uneducated women.

I think I have narrowed down my topic to make my book feasible. For instance, in the broader category of Indian Writing in English, I have chosen fiction as the genre. Further, it is fiction written originally in English by women. The translated novels from various Indian languages into English do not find a place for analysis in my book. Furthermore, most of the novels that I have chosen are mostly canonical though there are a few exceptions. The period that I have taken is from the Post-Independence era, i.e., from 1947 to 1999. The novels that are published from 2000 onwards are not taken into account. I must also mention that it has not been possible for me to consider every novel written by Indian English women novelists from 1950s to 1990s. I may have omitted some either because of their unavailability or because they are not immediately relevant to my study.

The reasons for which I have opted this topic are as follows: I have been observing women who are educated. Some of them get educated in order to get a qualified husband. Some of them get educated to achieve something in their lives. Quite a lot are helpless even if they want to educate themselves as their parents may not allow them to do so either due to financial constraints or due to the fear that men may not marry highly qualified women. Some of them get educated in order to fall in love with a boy and marry him. These are some of the observations I have made about educated women. However, the main person who made me think of educated women is none other than my only sister. She happens to be next to me in my family of six brothers and one sister. Her life is a source of inspiration for this literary work. Later on, I began observing my own wife. And the observation continues in real life as well as in characters in Indian English women's fiction. This area has been giving me utmost satisfaction, as I find the educated women dealing with the issues of "marriage", "career" and "divorce". It is interesting to deal with educated women characters in the novels that I have chosen. At the same time it is very difficult to make a list of all the educated women, keeping in mind their qualifications. However, I have read all the novels of the period and shortlisted those novels that have educated women characters. My concern herein is only with educated women and how they change themselves or try to change other educated or uneducated women. The women they try to change may be their own sisters, cousins, mothers, daughters, nieces, friends or neighbours.

On the other hand, there is a reason why I have chosen to look at the issue of "marriage" first, followed by "career" and "divorce". One of the main problems for educated women is marriage. Most of their problems are related to marriage. When the woman is a school going or college going girl, the parents always worry about their daughter. They wish their daughters would not be victims of eve-teasing, violence, black-mailing etc. They wish their daughters would not choose boy-friends and sleep with guys before marriage. They wish that their girls do not come home late. They wish that their girls do not go to pubs and restaurants with friends without informing them. Many educated women who are married think about a career. But whether they should continue their career/job is determined by the bridegroom or the in-laws. If women are consulted then this problem does not arise. Of course, of late some of the bridegrooms or in-laws want women to be employed so that the income of the family may increase. If the women are not consulted and do not have a role in the decision-making, then problems will arise. Women feel that questions of career should be left to them. In some cases, there are no problems until a child is born. Once the child enters the family there are chances of conflict. These conflicts may lead to divorce. This does not imply that it is the only reason for divorce. There may be different reasons as well.

We have to understand clearly the difference between job/employment and career. A woman having a job is not necessarily a career-oriented woman. She may have a job to earn some extra money. The money may be useful to her family. One man's income may not be sufficient for a family in the corporate, liberalised and privatised scenario. She may be doing the job not for her own satisfaction but for the needs that have to be met in the materialistic life. As long as the women/wives work and earn money there is no problem for the husband. There may still be petty problems that need to be resolved. At the same time, the problem may arise if the woman/wife is career-oriented. A career-oriented woman has some goal to achieve in her life. For this woman, earning money is secondary. A sense of self-fulfilment, achievement, name and fame are of primary importance. Once she is established in her career, automatically money also comes in. Moreover, a career woman can become a workaholic. If the career woman becomes a workaholic, there may be objections either from her husband or from her in-laws or from both sides. If the husband is mature enough and broad-minded, then she has no problem. If he understands that she is target-oriented or goal-centred, he will not create problems for her. Otherwise, she may have to give up either her career or her marital life. Marital life and career-oriented do not go always together. For a marriage to work, the couple should have mutual and broad understanding.

This book would be of great help to those educated women particularly who are groping in the dark and may provoke them and sharpen their education-tool to change themselves and to recharge their inner power in order to overcome the problems that they face in the stiff and tough competitive world. It is hoped that the present book will answer all the queries that usually arise in educated women's mind, such as:

- Is marriage necessary for educated women?
- How does society look at an educated unmarried woman?
- Do educated women believe in chastity?
- What is the right age for marriage?
- Do educated women have choice in their marriage?
- If women make a choice of their own, are such marriages successful?
- How do we look at educated women who rely on their parents' consent for their life partners?
- What marriage would educated women like to have—arranged or love or love-cum-arranged marriage?
- Would educated women like a joint family or a nuclear family?
- Do educated women have problems either with educated in-laws or uneducated in-laws?
- How do educated women perceive pre-marital and extra-marital relationships?
- How do educated women respond to a second marriage?
- Are caste and religion barriers for women's education?
- What are the career options for educated women?
- Do educated women choose their career on their own?
- Do educated women seek opinion of a teacher, parent and friend before choosing a career?
- At what level do educated women determine their career?
- What, according to educated women, is a sustainable career?
- Are educated women forced to choose certain kinds of career such as film acting, modelling and business to mention only a few?
- Is there any connection between the qualification and the career that the educated women choose?
- What is a challenging career for educated women?

- Are men and educated women treated as equals in a career?
- Is there any fixed career for educated women?
- How do we view creative writing as a career for educated women?
- Why is modelling for educated women gaining ground?
- Why do educated women go in for divorce?
- Are the husbands or in-laws responsible for divorce?
- Are divorce cases increasing as far as educated women are concerned?
- Does divorce happen due to domination of either sex?
- Does divorce take place because of extra-marital relationships?
- Love marriages are supposed to be successful marriages. Why are they not successful and why are they leading to divorce?
- Are career women in the forefront in going for divorce, especially because of their financial independence?
- Is divorce a threat/challenge to the institution of marriage?
- Under what circumstances should educated women go in for divorce?

It is hoped that this book will be found extremely valuable by all readers in general and educated urban women in particular. It is an eye-opener for all those who still live in a world where women are considered subordinate to men.

D. MURALI MANOHAR

1 Introduction

Education has been an important aspect of human beings. It is especially so with women because they can then widen their knowledge. It is obvious that without the struggle for education in the early nineteenth century we would not have had Indian English women's fiction at all. Let us see how women have acquired education in early nineteenth century. According to P. S. Balasubramanian, "By the beginning of the nineteenth century women in India were hardly educated" (71). Moreover, there was "a superstitious feeling" among the majority of Hindu families that if a girl was educated she "will soon" "become" "a widow." This was according to a report of William Adam on the state of Education in Bengal in 1836. Perhaps this was the reason why women themselves "enforced the prohibition against female education" (Forbes 33). The British government "was also apathetic towards educational activities for girls in the beginning" (Balasubramanian 71). The progress of women's education in India during the British period was extremely slow, as the British government did not encourage women's education. It was the same in England too in Valerie Hey's view:

> The historical development of education in England in nineteenth century traces the role of ideologies of femininity and their contestation. [...] Educational provision was initially restricted to the aspirant sons of the upper class. This practice confirmed the scholarly clerical tradition of Oxbridge. Despite capitalist expansion stimulating the demand for education, middle and upper class women and their working-class sisters were variously denied access. The subsequent history of education traces numerous challenges to this exclusion. (67)

Women's movement was thus a result of the denial of education to women across the globe. One of the "challenges" was to see why women were excluded in the history of education.

Coming back to India, according to Sahab Deena:

> [...] in 1819[1] Christian missionaries opened girls' schools. But many families did not send their children to these schools. The first step in giving a modern education to girls was taken up by the missionaries in 1821, but these efforts were marred by the emphasis on Christian religious education. The Bethune school had great difficulties in securing students. The young students were shouted at and abused and sometimes even their parents were subjected to social boycott. Many believed that girls who had received western education would make slaves of their husbands. (63)

Thus, the parents were hesitant to send their girl children to school. In addition to this, the fact that parents were subjected to "social boycott" shows that something like the caste system existed then. There was yet another opinion that those girls who "received" "western education" would make their "husbands slaves."

The missionary schools had spread to all parts of the country. For example, "The Church Missionary Society was more successful in South India where it opened its first boarding school for girls in Tirunelveli in 1821" (Forbes 39). However, in North India "female education was encouraged by the Arya Samaj, a reformist Hindu sect which followed the teachings of Swami Dayanand Saraswati. By the end of nineteenth century, progressive Arya Samajists recognized the importance of involving women in their reform efforts" (Forbes 44). According to Sahab Deena, in the western part of India "in 1848 several educated young men formed the students' literary and scientific society, which had two branches, the Gujarati and the Marathi. One of the aims of the society was to start schools for the education of women" (63). This was a welcome step by the young men. As has been already indicated, "The Bethune school, founded in Calcutta in 1849, was the first fruit of the powerful movement for women's education that arose in the 4th and 5th decade of the nineteenth century. While the education of women was not unknown in India, a great deal of prejudice against it existed" (Deena 63). The "Wood's Despatch in 1854 was the first official proclamation pleading for the encouragement of women's education" (Balasubramanian 71). According to Mehtab Giri, "No schools were supported before 1854. Only after 1854 was official/governmental support given in the form of grants-in-aid. The Brahmo Samaj too contributed towards women's education in Bengal" (80).

The main hurdle for the growth of women's education in the nineteenth century was the role religion played. Yes, religious Hindu parents were not in favour of sending their girls either out into the world or to schools. Hindu society was a kind of closed society. As opposed to this, Christian Missionaries were in favour of education for women and they did play a role in educating women. The missionaries were aware of the lacuna in the education of women in India. Thus they took up the cause of educating women.[2] Just like the missionaries, the Indian religious reform movements too made some efforts towards encouraging education of girls as can be seen from the following:

> [W]anting to present a juxtaposition to the sweeping popularity of christianity in Indian society, [they] tried to do everything they could to match Christian missionaries. They tried to develop parallels to missionary action. The education of women was an area which Indian reformers handled with singular success. By the middle and the end of the nineteenth century the Brahmo Samaj, the Prarthana Samaj, the Arya Samaj etc. were all actively engaged in the education of women. About this time, around 1860-1870 European liberalism was beginning to have a strong impact on Indian thinking. (Chitnis 61)

The historical fact is that "In 1883, two Bengali Brahma Samaj women became the first Indian women from Bethune College" (Giri 80).

Mehtab Giri gives us "the old maxim": "'When you educate a man, you educate an individual, but when you educate a woman you educate a family and a nation' is not an exaggeration" (79). I agree with Mehtab Giri as it is generally believed that women take great care of children's education. So it is better to provide education first to girls, then to the family, the village, the town, the district and the state. Thus the country will have better citizens. Superstitious beliefs, ignorance and economic reasons were responsible for the absence of systematic female education at the beginning of the nineteenth century. Moreover, the social evils of child marriage and the purdah system were also responsible for not sending the girls to educational institutions. However, some Christian missionaries and social reformers like Swami Dayanand Vidyasagar and P.C. Benerjee attempted to educate girls during this period.

Susanne Greenhalgh in her article "Growing Up" presents the argument about girls of eighteenth and nineteenth centuries remaining restricted either to home or to employment. As a result, they were deprived of education and were married off. They, thus, did not constitute the category "youth":

> During the eighteenth and nineteenth centuries a gendered way of viewing youth was reflected and developed in novels and other writing. Youth came to be seen as a period of restless experimentation, a journey of rebellion and self-discovery which ended in acceptance of the demands of society, usually in the form of marriage (Moretti, 1987). Such stories of adventures in search of a "sentimental education" away from home were essentially boys' stories, however. A girl's growing up, based in the home of her family or employers until marriage, largely excluded from education, and often rigorously protected from sexual encounters, did not take the same form, either in fiction or in fact. To a large extent girls were not seen as part of this new category of "youth." (20)

This confinement to home denied them any exposure to the outside world:

> This historical association of girls with home also made them less prominent in public, on the streets, where they were out of place and even at risk. As a result girls were thought of as less of a public problem than boys. Indeed the term "youth" came to have predominantly masculine and delinquent connotations and adolescence, viewed as a phase of achieving a separate, individual identity, often through rebellion against family or social conventions, came to be typified by the sort of teenage boy played by James Dean in 1950s films such as *Rebel Without a Cause*. For girls, however, such adolescent attempts to take charge of their sexuality and other aspects of their lives conflicted with the socially preferred feminine goals of being carers, dependents and sex objects (Lees, 1993: 15, 17, 21). (Greenhalgh 21)

These views are relevant in the case of India too. That is why I feel education is a must for all girls irrespective of their nation and country. They should not be brought up in the above manner. They have to be given education in order not to be "carers", "dependents" or "sex objects."

In the Indian context, "Pandita[3] Ramabai was truly remarkable as a pioneer in women's education and as a rebel and champion of women's rights. Her father supervised her education and allowed her to remain unmarried. When her father and mother died, Ramabai was sixteen years old, unmarried, and able to read Sanskrit" (Forbes 46). She wrote a book entitled *The High Caste Hindu Woman* (1888). This book is a critique of Hindu customs and traditions of women in terms of caste, marriage, children, duties of a wife and widowhood. In the book she also appeals to all men and women who have sympathy for the high-caste Hindu women to help them by making them aspire for "self-reliance" (Ramabai 100) and providing them "education" (Ramabai 102) and "Native Women Teachers" (Ramabai 105) in order to improve the condition and status of Hindu women in India. It is important to note that "[t]en thousand copies of this book were sold before Ramabai had left America. In

1887, Boston admirers set up a Ramabai Association to support her work in India" (Forbes 47).

According to the *Status of Women in India: A Synopsis of the Report of the National Committee of the Status of Women (1971-74)* (New Delhi: ICSSR, 1988), the nineteenth century social reformers' "aim [...] was to use education to make women more capable of fulfilling their traditional roles as wives and mothers and not to make them more efficient and active units in the process of socio-economic or political development. The colonial authorities generally supported this limited view of women's education" (88). "Education started" according to Alladi Uma "on a large scale in the late nineteenth century, but at that time it was designed to develop in a woman those qualities that were seen as essential to making her a good housewife—reticence in speech, subservience of manners, fortitude, and consciousness" (8). Although the "aim" was limited in its scope, it was a stepping-stone for women to get educated. In Madras, the Theosophical Society did encourage female education. "Speaking as a leader of the society, Annie Besant (1847-1933) asserted that in ancient times Hindu women were educated and moved freely in society. She urged women to return to this "golden age" (Forbes 43).

According to K.A. Kunjakkan:

> More education gives more intelligence, reasoning power, more I.Q., and such an individual is able to understand and comprehend things around them. They acquire an inquisitive mind and thus able to question things. This is however opposed to Indian view of life, where women are expected to be obedient, disciplined, submissive, chaste and docile. All these womanly qualities are believed to be evaporated (sic) on attaining excess education by women. The feminists say that this misunderstanding is due to the popular notion that women are to be a wife and a mother. Nothing more. (371)

I strongly agree with Kunjakkan views about education giving more intelligence, reasoning power, more I.Q., and an ability to comprehend things but I do not agree with the later part of Kunjakkan's ideas about women being expected to be obedient, submissive, and docile. In fact my work is based on the assumption that "education" can make women more intelligent and comprehend things in a better fashion.

After this brief historical and sociological background to the question of education, let us move on to how education for women has been viewed in the literary world in the nineteenth century. Before I proceed, let me make a statement about my choice of the novels for study in this dissertation. I am dealing only with selected novels originally written in English from the 1950s to the 1990s by women writers and not translations. This is only for the purposes of convenience and to make the study focussed. I also need to define what I mean by "educated" women. I consider any woman with a formal education (from the primary level to the doctoral) an "educated" woman. Moreover, I have not considered those novels that have no "educated" women characters at all. The novels that I have not considered for instance in the present study are: Kamala Markandaya's *A Silence of Desire* (1960), *A Handful of Rice* (1966), *The Golden Honey-comb* (1977), and *Pleasure City* (1982); Anita Desai's *The Village by the Sea* (1982) and *Baumgartner's Bombay* (1988); Nayantara Sahgal's *Mistaken Identity* (1984); Gita Mehta's *A River Sutra* (1993); Githa Hariharan's *The Ghosts of Vasu Master* (1994) and *When Dreams Travel* (1999).

I have considered only "educated" Hindu women characters and not considered those with a different religious or cultural background like Roshan Merchant in Kamala Markandaya's *Some Inner Fury* (1955), Caroline in Kamala Markandaya's *Possession* (1963), Helen in Kamala Markandaya's *The Coffer-Dams* (1969), Sarah in Anita Desai's *Bye-Bye Blackbird* (1971), Miss Mendoza in Kamala Markandaya's *Two Virgins* (1972), Nell and Lydia in Nayantara Sahgal's *A Situation in New Delhi* (1977), Anna Hansen and Stella in Nayantara Sahgal's *Plans for Departure* (1985), Rose in Nayantara Sahgal's *Rich Like Us* (1985), Roxanne Lamba in Namita Gokhale's *Gods, Graves and Grandmother* (1994), Rahel and Margaret

Kochamma in Arundhati Roy's *The God of Small Things* (1997). In other words, I will be dealing with characters with an Indian Hindu background, who are "educated" and who live in India.

I will deal with these "educated" women in terms of "Marriage", "Career" and "Divorce." These three issues are not independent but are inter-connected. Moreover, by dividing my dissertation into five chapters chronologically, I will analyse the novels to see if different decades have any effect on the issues discussed. The final concluding chapter will sum up my findings.

There are a few novels written originally in English and published in the late nineteenth century. I consider these novels to provide the historical background and in order to place Indian English women's fiction in the Post-Independence Era. The novels that are written in the late 19th century are: *Bianca* (1878) by Toru Dutt, *Kamala* (1894) and *Saguna* (1895) both by Krupabai Satthianadhan, and *Ratanbai* (1895) by Shevantibai M. Nikambe.

Toru Dutt "is the first Indian woman novelist in English and the first woman novelist of India" (Mund 25). Although Bianca in Toru Dutt's *Bianca: Or The Young Spanish Maiden* is not a Hindu woman character, I would like to discuss her, as she is the first woman character in Indian English women's fiction. In this novel we have Bianca, an "educated" woman, rejecting a marriage proposal on the ground that the man who proposed was already in love with her sister Inez. Although he proposed to Inez when she was alive, he claims that he is in love with Bianca too. She tells him that he cannot change his mind of having loved her sister like that and propose to any family member of Mr. Alanzo Garcia. He has to be reasonable in his proposal. Moreover, his logic is not adequate. Thus, she rejects his proposal. Later she falls in love with Henry Montague Moore. This is her true love. However, initially her father Mr. Alanzo Garcia resists this marriage proposal. Later on he agrees. Henry's mother wants her son to marry Miss De Wilton and not Bianca. The reason is that she can bring fifty thousand pounds as dowry. Henry's mother is interested only in the dowry and is not concerned about the mind or choice of her son. Moreover, Henry is strongly in love with Bianca and turns down his mother's proposal. Henry's sister Maggie supports her brother and is interested in her brother marrying Bianca. Henry's mother says this about Bianca to her daughter Maggie: "She is not at all like what an English young lady ought to be" (Dutt *Bianca* 91). Also Henry's mother wants her daughter-in-law to be like an English girl. Her daughter says: "But mamma, if Henry marries her, we can polish her up in a few days, and make her a little more English!" (91)

Another interesting thing about Bianca living in Indian culture is that although she is not an Indian she feels as though she has committed a sin when Henry kisses her without her permission. In the later novels discussed in this study we find even having pre-marital sex is not considered a sin. There is lot of change in the perspective of "educated" women in the later novels.

Even as *Bianca* was the first published novel by an Indian woman, the editor of *Kamala*: *The Story of Hindu Life* (1894), Chandani Lokuge claims that "[...] Krupabai Satthianadhan holds the distinction of being the first Indian woman author to fictionalize in English, the life of an upper-caste Hindu woman" (1). Lokuge in the introduction to *Saguna*: *The First Autobiographical Novel in English by an Indian Woman* says that "while Indian women were contributing to the genre during the late nineteenth century in various Indian languages, Krupabai Satthianadhan pioneered that tradition in English" (1) with her autobiographical novel *Saguna*. But I feel that Toru Dutt is the pioneer of Indian English woman novelists as her novel *Bianca Or The Young Spanish Maiden* was not only written in 1878 but also dealt with "Indian" themes (I have indicated one such instance in my previous paragraph.) [See M.K. Naik's *A History of Indian English Literature* (New Delhi: Sahitya Akademi, 1982) and K.R. Srinivasa Iyengar's *Indian Writing in English* (Bombay: Asia Publishing House, 1962) who have also argued that *Bianca* is the first novel.]

In Toru Dutt's *Bianca,* we have a possibility of love marriage but the marriage does not take place. Bianca is betrothed to Henry who is only able to put a ring on her finger but has to leave for war. On the one hand love marriage is not successful and on the other hand, in Krupabai Satthianadhan's *Kamala* there is an arranged marriage in the form of a child marriage. In those days, in orthodox Hindu families, child marriages were quite common. Chandani Lokuge rightly says, "Kamala has no voice in the selection of her partner; the marriage has been arranged in her infancy by elders" (4). During those days parents used to think that they arranged marriages for the bright future of their daughters. And it was true that they were also responsible for any unfortunate incident that may happen in their marriage. Although Kamala is not formally educated, her educated husband Ganesh "introduces her to the basics of education. She is seen to blossom under his tutelage. However, Ganesh is too weak to oppose traditional Hindu opposition to female education, and withdraws from the experiment" (7). Men like Ganesh were ready to help girls/women by educating them. But the tradition was so rigid that it would not allow any male member to undertake reforms in female education at an individual level.

In the late nineteenth century itself the nuclear family emerges, breaking out from the joint family system. Perhaps, this allowed for the woman's individual self to emerge. As Chandani Lokuge says:

> Satthianadhan provides Kamala with the opportunity of expressing her latent feminism when she transfers Kamala and Ganesh from Ganesh's parents' residence to a house of their own in the city. By granting them this independence, Satthianadhan also enables them to transcend the traditions of the joint or extended family. (11)

Kamala "transcend[ing] the traditions of the joint or extended family" as far back as the late nineteenth century will have some kind of a bearing on the later novelists. While the nuclear family may have its positive effect on Kamala, it enables Ganesh to entertain his lover Sai in his home. Perhaps, this is one of the drawbacks of the nuclear family. In the joint family system, a person like Ganesh would not have dared entertain his lover, as he would have been afraid of his parents and family members. At the same time Kamala shows her authority in her home. Chandani Lokuge says:

> [H]er awkward selfhood cannot be contained now and develops subversively and when Ganesh begins to entertain his lover [Sai] in their [Kamala's and his] home, it asserts itself. One of the most memorable moments of the novel occurs when the unfailingly humble *pativrata* (husband-worshipper) militantly stands up to her husband and to his mistress. "It was an unusual thing for a woman to behave in this fashion," the author herself admits as she records how Kamala literally drives Sai out of her house. Indeed, it was quite against the norm: Kamala's speech and behaviour mark a momentous and historic step forward for India's upper-caste Hindu womanhood. Kamala, by this assertion of the rights of individualism, crosses the traditional threshold. Kamala's rebellion is the culmination of Satthianadhan's feminist stance in the novel; at least fictionally, she has liberated the upper caste Hindu women from the bondage of mute husband-worship. (Lokuge *Kamala* 11-12)

Kamala has literally driven her husband's lover Sai "out of her house" and has asserted her "right" and her "individualism" over her husband and her house. In the traditional sense it is "against the norm" of decorum. Kamala's "speech and behaviour" remain a significant and historical lesson for any Indian Hindu womanhood not just for "upper caste Hindu womanhood." This "rebellion" and "liberation" of "upper caste Hindu women from the bondage of mute husband-worship" may be seen in Hindu women of other castes also. As far as Sai is concerned she is educated and she misuses this advantage. She tries to interfere in the life of Ganesh and Kamala and even disturbs their married life for some time. Ganesh is also a party to Sai becoming his mistress. He is aware that he is married and has a child to look after. How then could he have a relationship with Sai and bring her home? He has a wife and a son at home. Due to Kamala's bold steps Sai has to leave Ganesh. One cannot but appreciate Kamala's boldness in claiming that it is her house as she is the daughter-in-law of the house. Sai "[...] is shown up as a vile and amoral opportunist. Unorthodox female education and female liberation are held responsible for the destruction of her moral sensibility" (Lokuge *Kamala* 16). Sai misuses education in trying to snatch Kamala's legal husband.

Sai, an unmarried woman, tries to have sex with Ganesh. She knows very well that Ganesh is married; yet she tries to keep Ganesh to herself. Sai even goes to the extent of breaking Ganesh's relationship with Kamala by creating false ideas in his mind. She finds out, first of all, information from Ramchanderpunt about the purpose of his visit and takes him to a place where she can show Kamala talking to Ramachanderpunt who has come there only to inform her about her father's deteriorating health condition. Thus she creates misconception in Ganesh's mind about a non-existent affair between Kamala and Ramachanderpunt.

After *Bianca* and *Kamala* we have Krupabai Satthianadhan's *Saguna: The First Autobiographical Novel in English by an Indian Woman* (1895). Before I proceed to discuss *Saguna* I would like to justify the use of this work for this study. Krupabai was one of "the first converts to Christianity in the Bombay Presidency (an administrative unit of the colonial government)" (Tharu and Lalita 275). I mention this fact here because this is an autobiographical novel. She is a Hindu woman but her family had converted to Christianity. During those days converting to Christianity had many benefits like access to western education, freedom from several orthodox rituals and scope for earning money. Hindu society was a closed society. So the conversion. In spite of conversion, her mother hinders her education. Her mother is of the following opinion: "What a girl you are to go and trouble your head with books! What is the use of learning for a girl? A girl's training school is near the *chool* (the fire over which everything is cooked), and however learned a girl may be she must come to the *chool*" (Satthianadhan *Saguna* 21). I do not agree with Saguna's mother's view about her daughter troubling her head with books. It is with the help of learning that there will be a change for girls in the future. At the same time we cannot blame Saguna's mother having that kind of an opinion. She is part of a patriarchal set-up. However, Saguna is clever enough and is passionate about learning. She says: "I generally managed to seat myself beside them with a pencil and a slate and pretend to be very busy and quite [...] I tried to pick up little snatches of knowledge, and employed my time in working out the sums on which my brothers were engaged, and in setting their lessons by heart" (Satthianadhan *Saguna* 21). If the girl like Saguna has this kind of a passion for studies, one has to appreciate her interest. She also questions the society at large about gender discrimination.

Prema and Harni who are friends of Saguna are educated women. Saguna's mother has been helpful in making Saguna visit Prema and Harni quite often. Perhaps Saguna's mother wants her daughter to mingle with Prema and Harini so that she may get interested in studies. Saguna claims:

> They regarded me as a younger sister, and let me hold their hand and stand by them while they chatted with others after the service. [...] Prema, my first friend, to whom I have only made a cursory reference, was tall, and had a peculiar sweetness of face and manner. [...] She talked English as her mother tongue, for she went to a European school. She was fond of telling me of her school, where the teacher wore a train and belt and a flower, and where she expected soon to be a teacher; for she was in the highest class. (Satthianadhan *Saguna* 79)

In the late nineteenth century, the age for marriage was approximately fifteen. The girls were also conscious of their marriageable age. Prema tells Saguna:

> "It is only girls of my age that know what it is. When a man offers his hand in marriage, the young lady accepts it. Then she is engaged and a ring is put on her finger."

> "And shall I be engaged too?" I said.
>
> "Oh! Not all girls are engaged. When they are young ladies, you know, like me. They must be fifteen and you are only twelve." (Satthianadhan *Saguna* 84)

Prema explains to Saguna at what "age" "girls" are married as though she is aware of all these details. But Saguna's mother has now changed her opinion that a girl's training is not near the *chool* but at the school, and she is keen on educating her daughter. She herself takes her daughter along and says:

> "My daughter is alone at home. She learns a little too much, so I have brought her here to be more like other girls, to learn a little and to play a little; but you will have to give her a room to herself, and let her be free from the rules of the school at first. Let her join the classes or not as she likes; for she is delicate. I will pay all extra charges." (Satthianadhan *Saguna* 125-126)

Perhaps Saguna's mother being a home-maker has experienced loneliness "at home." Therefore, she wants her daughter not to face the same loneliness "at home" as she had faced, whether it is before marriage or after marriage. Thus, she wants her daughter to be "more like other girls," learning and playing at school. However, Saguna's mother requests that she be provided a separate "room" and not be forced to join classes. The reason for not making Saguna attend classes compulsorily is due to her "delicate" nature and she is ready to "pay all extra charges" for those facilities.

Saguna is so bright that the teachers are amazed. She seems to be a gifted child. The teacher even recommends Saguna to move on to a higher class. One of the teachers tests her and says:

> "Well," said the teacher, "you can afford not to see, you can sit where you like."
>
> Several other subjects followed, in which I found myself far ahead of the girls, but in passing I came to a standstill. (Satthianadhan *Saguna* 129)

Saguna proves that if parents encourage their daughters they can prove their talents and intelligence to society. Saguna is given an option to "sit" in whichever class she would "like" to sit. She has been tested in several "subjects." In whichever subject she is tested, she has been "far ahead" of all "the girls" in the school. I feel it is because of her mother's sense of adventure, that too in the late nineteenth century, in admitting her in a school that makes Saguna do exceedingly well. Furthermore, looking at Saguna's intelligence and sharp brain Mrs. T. encourages her to do medicine. She says:

> "[...] You had better learn medicine."
>
> "Medicine?" Oh I wish I could," I said, quite taken aback by the proposal [...] I felt bewildered, and turned inquiringly to Mrs. T. "She is the lady doctor, you know," she said in answer to my look, "and it is very good of her to take an interest in you. Could you learn medicine?"
>
> "Anything" I said impetuously, now quite beside myself with joy. (Satthianadhan *Saguna* 130-131)

When Mrs. T. wants to send Saguna to England to do her medicine, there are complaints against Saguna that she is not religious enough to go to England. Saguna ought to be religious as she is sponsored by the British. She is questioned for she "do[es] not read [...] Bible, or pray" (133). She too questions them: "How do you know?" (133). She says she does pray but is not a pretender.

The important point to be noted is that given a chance any girl will be able to do any kind of course. Saguna has been identified as a genius and she has been asked to take up medicine. So the career in medicine had started as early as in the late nineteenth century for "educated" women.

Having seen Bianca, Kamala and Saguna, the last character in the late nineteenth century I would like to look at is Ratanbai in Shevantibai M. Nikambe's *Ratanbai: A Sketch of a Bombay High Caste Hindu Young Wife* (1895). Ratanbai undergoes child marriage as it used to be the tradition in those days. However, she is sent to school as long as she is with her parents. Her school going stops once she goes to her in-laws. She has no encouragement from her mother Anandibai, her aunt Kakubai and her mother-in-law. Her father Vasudevrav Kashinath Dalvi is a strong advocate of women's education. Even Ratanbai's husband Prataprao has no problem in his wife being sent to school. Ratanbai's mother Anandibai has to do what Ratanbai's mother-in-law asks her to do. When Anandibai asks her whether she has any objection to sending Rantanbai to Goa in order to stop her schooling, she says:

> "Send her anywhere, but not send her to school." It was, then, thus settled, but Ratanbai was kept in ignorance of her being removed from school. She was told to go to school and take two months' leave, to pay the fees for those months, and to tell the Bai that she was going to Goa with her aunt. Ratan obeyed sadly and reluctantly, and the teachers and the girls were very sorry indeed to lose her, though they were led to suppose, for a time only. (Nikambe *Ratanbai* 64)

Though such an attitude of the mother-in-law may have to be condemned, we may wonder whether we need to understand why she does so, coming from the background she does. Here it is Ratanbai who is being stopped from attending school. She asks Ratanbai's mother to "send" their daughter "anywhere" but not to "school." This is ridiculous. She has been doing exceedingly well in school. She is just like Saguna, doing exceedingly well in school. Why should her schooling be stopped? Moreover, Ratanbai "has been kept in ignorance" about "being removed" from school. On the other hand, she has been asked "to take two months' leave" from school and "pay her school fees for those months" and "tell the Bai that she was going to Goa with her aunt." Ratan "obeyed sadly and reluctantly." But her teachers feel "very sorry" about losing her, even for a short time. In fact the decision is taken for her entire life.

But, later on, her husband helps her by encouraging and allowing her to attend school, despite his failing in his examinations. He is broad-minded unlike his mother. He is just like his father-in-law who supports women's education. In this novel those who create problems for girls' education are women themselves whereas the male characters are for women's education. For example, take the case of Vasudevrav and Rambhao talking about sending Ratanbai to school again. Vasudevrav says:

> When [...] Mr. Rambhao (Kamala's father-in-law) came to Mr. Vasudevrav, the latter said, "I am sorry to say my daughter is not in my hands. If you can persuade her mother-in-law and the other lady, Kashinathpant's wife, nothing will give me more pleasure, for I am in favour of our girls and women being educated. If some lady were to open a class for the married ladies, I would be the first one to send Anandi. I am thinking, however, of getting a native lady to come to my house and teach her. If Ratan were in my charge, I would send her to school to-day. I would not have allowed her to be kept at home at this early age, when she was getting on nicely, too; but our girls are not ours when married!" (Nikambe *Ratanbai* 72)

One can easily understand Vasudevrav feeling sad that Ratan is "not" in his "hands." He is in "favour of girls and women being educated." He would have "sent" his daughter "to school" if she were to be unmarried. According to Eunice de Souza in her introduction to the book, "Ratanbai's father [Vasudevrav], a lawyer, is an interesting character, full of contradictions. He insists on Ratan being educated, but the constant pressure of his women-folk makes him give in. His progressiveness does not extend to meal-times, when he is served before the others. Shevantibai does not comment on this, ironically or otherwise. It is merely stated as a fact" (*Ratanbai* 7). However, Vasudevrav is willing to send his wife Anandi to the class "if some lady were to open a class for the married ladies." At the same time we can question Vasudevrav himself. If he is so interested in his daughter's education, he would not have got Ratan married at such an early age. But in those days, child marriage was practised and so he perhaps had to go along with society. This argument does not stand as he plans to educate his "wife" with a tutor. He also comments on the tradition of fathers losing the right over their daughters after they are "married."

In conclusion, based on the socio-cultural values as evident from books on women's education and on literary texts, we can say women had to struggle in order to get educated and be called "educated" women. There were traditional women, patriarchal males, orthodox religious preachers, political institutions etc., that were denying education to women as we have seen from our readings of the views of some historians, sociologists and educationists. However, there were a few men who were all for women's education. There were women novelists who were trying to raise some of the important questions about "education", "marriage", "separation" (that may or may not lead to divorce) and "career" in their works written in the late nineteenth century. These women writers showed the path to the Indian English women novelists in the twentieth century.

WORKS CITED

Balasubramanian, P.S. "Women's Education." *Quest for Gender Studies: A Critique of the Status of Women in India*. Madras: T.R., 1991. 69-77.

Chitnis, Suma. "The Sociology of Women's Education: Two Different Issues." *Women's Studies in India: Some Perspectives*. Ed. Maithreyi Krishna Raj. Bombay: Popular, 1986. 59-66.

Deena, Sahab. *Mourya Women in India*. Allahabad: Chugh Publications, 1988.

De Souza, Eunice, ed. Introduction. *Ratanbai: A Sketch of a Bombay High Caste Hindu Young Wife*. By Sevanthibai M. Nikambe. 1895. New Delhi: Sahitya Akademi, 2003. 1-14.

Dutt, Toru. *Bianca Or The Young Spanish Maiden*. 1878. Ed. Subhendu Mund. New Delhi: Parachi, 2001.

Forbes, Geraldine. "Education for Women." *The New Cambridge History of India. IV.2: Women in Modern India*. Cambridge: CUP, 1996. 32-63.

Giri, Mehtab. "Women's Education: National Policies and Development." *Women's Development: Problems and Prospects*. Ed. Shain Aleem. New Delhi: APH, 1996. 79-92.

Greenhalgh, Susanne. "Chapter 2: Growing up." *An Introduction to Women's Studies*. Ed. Beryl Madoc-Jones and Jennifer Coates. Oxford: Blackwell, 1996. 16-37.

Hey, Valerie. "Chapter 4: Girls and Schooling." *An Introduction to Women's Studies*. Ed. Beryl Madoc-Jones and Jennifer Coates. Oxford: Blackwell, 1996. 62-83.

Kunjakkam, K.A. "Women's Issues verses National Perspective." *Feminism and Indian Realities*. New Delhi: Mittal, 2002. 364-373.

Lokuge, Chandani. Introduction. *Kamala: The Story of a Hindu Life*. By Krupabai Satthianadhan.1894. New Delhi: OUP, 1998.1-16.

Mund, Subhendu. Introduction. *Bianca Or The Young Spanish Maiden*. By Toru Dutt. 1878. New Delhi: OUP, 1998. 1-28.

Nikambe, Shevanthibai M. *Ratanbai: A Sketch of a Bombay High Caste Hindu Young Wife*. Ed. Eunice De Souza. New Delhi: Sahitya Akademi, 2003. Rpt. of London: Marshall, 1895.

Saraswati, Pandita Ramabai. *The Hindu-Caste Hindu Woman*. Philadelphia: Jas Rodgers, 1888.

Satthianadhan, Krupabai. *Kamala: The Story of a Hindu Life*. Ed. Chandani Lokuge. 1894. New Delhi: OUP, 1998.

——. *Saguna: First Autobiographical Novel in English by an Indian Woman*. Ed. Chandani Lokuge. 1895. New Delhi: OUP, 1998.

Seshadri, Vijayalakshmi. *The New Woman in Indian-English Women Writers Since the 1970s*. Delhi: B.R., 1995.

Tharu, Susie and K. Lalita, eds. Introduction to Krupabai Satthianadhan. *Women Writing in India: 600 B.C to the Present Volume I: 600 B.C to the Early Twentieth Century*. Delhi: OUP, 1993. 275-276.

Uma, Alladi. *Woman and Her Family: Indian and Afro-American—A Literary Perspective*. New Delhi: Sterling, 1989.

Zelliot, Eleanor. *From Untouchable to Dalit: Essays on the Ambedkar Movement*. New Delhi: Manohar, 1992.

NOTES

1. Eunice de Souza in her introduction to Shevantibai M. Nikambe, *Ratanbai: A Sketch of a Bombay High Caste Hindu Young Wife* (1895) (Rpt. New Delhi: Sahitya Akademi, 2003) gives the picture of education for women. Schools were established in order to promote women's education in India in the nineteenth century, starting from 1819 up to 1889. The

following information helps in coming to know about people's involvement in female education in India:

> Concern for the education of women in India began early in the 19th century. In 1819, the Calcutta Female Juvenile Society under the patronage of the Baptist Mission was established to promote female education. Jyotiba Phule and his wife Savithribai opened the first school for girls in Poona in 1848 while John Elliot Drinkwater Bethune and Ram Gopal Ghosh established the Hindu Female School, later called Bethune College in Kolkata the following year. Faiz-unnessa Chaudhurani set up an English medium school in Bengal in 1873, while Pandita Ramabai set up the Arya Mahila Samaj in 1882 and Sharada Sadan in 1889. (10-11)

2. Vijayalakshmi Seshadri in her book *The New Woman in Indian-English Women Writers Since the 1970s* says: "But there were strong prejudices against schools run by missionaries and the upper caste Hindu families did not 'condescend' to send their girls to such schools. Only converts from Harijan and the lower classes sent their daughters to these schools" (38). Eleanor Zelliot also says in *From Untouchable to Dalit: Essays on the Ambedkar Movement*: "His [Jyotiba Phule] schools for Untouchable children in Poona in the 1850s were among the earliest non-missionary efforts on behalf of the Depressed Classes (45). She further says: "Phule backed his preaching with such concrete action as a school for Untouchables and one for women, and seems to have been the first to use the word *dalit* in connection with caste in the term *dalitodhar* (uplift of the depressed)" (271). I mention these facts to point out that if the upper class and upper caste Hindu women were struggling to get education in those days, could the lower caste, lower class women think of getting education?
3. The first name of Pandita Ramabai is not "Pandita" but it is "Pundita." The original book refers to the name as follows: Pundita Ramabai Saraswati. The title of her book is *The High Caste Hindu Woman*, New Delhi: Inter-India Publications, 1888 and reprinted in 1984.

"Trembling Silence": The 1950s

2

In this chapter I will be dealing with "educated women" characters such as Rukmani from Kamala Markandaya's *Nectar in a Sieve* (1954), Mira and Premala from her *Some Inner Fury* (1955) and Kusum and Devaki from Nayantara Sahgal's *A Time to Be Happy* (1958) to examine the issue of "marriage" and Veena for that of "career."

Let us first of all see how the question of marriage is portrayed in these novels. Jasbir Jain makes a very interesting and relevant point about marriage and the way the literary and media projections help us evaluate it:

> Marriage, home, the claims of the family are traditional goals set for the female child. It is only by examining and exploring the restrictive aspects of this value system that any change can be affected. Formal education does not equip women for this kind of self or social analysis—but literary and media projections are likely to be of greater relevance. (69)

I do not however agree with Jain when she says, "formal education does not equip women for [...] self and social analysis [...]." If the women are serious about formal education, they can utilize its tools for self and social analysis. Also women with a formal education may be in a better position to produce literary texts.

Marriage has been considered sacred in a human being's life. "From ancient times," as V.V. Prakasha Rao and V. Nandini Rao say, "marriage is considered as a ritual and a sacramental union. Marriage is an indispensable event of

Hindu life and the person who is unmarried is considered unholy" (14). In Hindu epics like the *Ramayana* and the *Mahabharata* too we have the concepts of both arranged and love marriages. In India, it is often believed that arranged marriages are the most effective. However, due to the literacy rate and education, the scenario has changed with regard to marriage. Qualities like independence, democracy, rights, self-reliance, self-respect, self-assertion, economic freedom, employment aptitude etc., have been the most significant reasons for the changing scenario. V.V. Prakasha Rao quotes Gore's study:

> Education was considered a major differentiating factor in the attitudes of respondents toward arranged marriages [...]. He found that 73 per cent of the respondents without a formal education as against 9 per cent with graduate education hold to the traditional arrangement of marriages by elders. That means the more educated a respondent is, the more likely he is to give more freedom to the boy or girl concerned. In summary, he concludes that high education and urban residence are directly related to the attitudes of the respondents in regard to the freedom of choice of the parties to the marriage concerned. (20)

The alternative to arranged marriage is love marriage. The reason is that education helps them think and question their parents' attitude and adamant behaviour. However, in India, as Aileen D. Ross puts it, "love was not necessary prelude for testing the relationship" (251). Prakasha Rao says:

> Love was regarded as an uncontrollable and explosive emotion which makes a young person blind to reality, reason and logic. The family's stability may even be jeopardized since the emotions might lead one to marry an unsuitable person not only to his temperament but to the entire joint family. [...] [T]he Hindu system regarded mate selection by self choice as undesirable and feared that freedom of choice might upset the process of adjustment of the bride in her new family. (16)

In spite of the above statement about Hindus regarding love as an "uncontrollable and explosive emotion" and emphasizing that love is "blind to reality, reason and logic," the "educated" women feel that they have their own desires, aspirations and dreams about married life. If women do not like the proposal that the parents bring, they cannot be forced to accept the proposal. At the same time, the parents' point of view cannot be ignored. Girls/women may not be mature enough to take a decision about marriage, as they do not have enough experience. It could be just infatuation or lust, but sometimes they may mistake it for love and think they are capable of selecting their own life partners. Kalidasa, the Indian poet, remarked that "[y]oung people seek pleasures."[1] Sometimes it may work out very well and sometimes it may not. Let us now see how the "educated" women in the novels in the 1950s choose between arranged marriages and love marriages.

Rukmani in Kamala Markandaya's *Nectar in a Sieve* (1954) is not formally educated. She is from a rural background. In spite of being from a rural background and from a poor family, she had been "educated" by her father. Had she been in an urban middle class family, she would have done a marvellous job both at the family and at the social levels. Yet her rural, economic, social barriers could not stop her from achieving a little education with her father's help. She is thus able to read and write. She has three elder sisters and one elder brother, all of whom are married. She is the fourth and the last daughter of her parents. Her parents have chosen a tenant farmer Nathan as her husband. Rukmani has this to say about the match:

> Our relatives, I know, murmured that the match was below me; my mother herself was not happy, but I was without beauty and without dowry and it was the best she could do. "A poor match," they said, and not always quietly. How little they knew, any of them! (2)

In an arranged marriage the problem is often with the "relatives." They come to the wedding and comment on the couple. They call it "a poor match." Of course in this case Rukmani herself is not happy with the match. Her parents cannot afford better, having already got three daughters married. She is very realistic and practical in her approach towards life. Moreover, Rukmani realizes that she is "without beauty and without dowry." Rukmani is able to recognize her own physical handicap and her family's economic conditions. Her parents have no more money left to get her a better husband. The positive aspect of this arranged marriage is that the bride is content with her husband and is sympathetic, mature and broad-minded enough to understand her parents' problems. Moreover, there is no question of career for Rukmani. However, she does some menial job later on in the face of utter poverty.

Like Rukmani, Premala's marriage to Kitsamy in Kamala Markandaya's *Some Inner Fury* (1955) is an arranged one. This marriage is seen as a marriage without love. The couple is not happy in the marital life. Although Premala is from an urban background and upper class family, there is no happiness in her marriage. This is in contrast to Rukmani who hails from a rural, lower class background but has no problem with her married life, except for the economic conditions. Moreover, Rukmani does not have much education as compared to Premala. This is what happens in an arranged marriage like Premala's if the couple does not like each other. Unlike this couple Mira and Richard in the same novel love each other but do not get married. There is Govind who spoils the mind of Kitsamy. Premala showing affection and love towards Govind hurts Kitsamy. Furthermore, Kitsamy has an inclination towards western culture and expects his wife to become westernised too. On the contrary, Premala believes in the "true" Indian culture. This is the main reason why there is no understanding between the couple. Another reason for the misunderstanding is that of Premala showing and "assert[ing] [her] individualit[y] [...] by adopting a child against Kits[amy]'s wishes [...]" (Srivastava 22). Premala is trying to fulfil her desire to have a child even if it were through adoption. Moreover, she does not feel that she needs to take permission from Kitsamy. She has no children and therefore adopts a child.

Mira who is in love wants her parents' approval. She has been asked to wait for marriage for some days: "Her [Mira's] rich Hindu background and exposure to western life style equip her with the knowledge to select the best from both Indian and British culture" (Jacob 109). Though she does not marry Richard, they behave as husband and wife. Mira belongs to a highly rich family. She has no barriers of traditions that prevent her from living with Richard without formal marriage. Though, the marriage does not take place in the course of the novel, we can definitely see that they desire to marry each other. There is a positive attitude towards marriage. Initially, when they want to marry each other, Mira's mother asks them to wait till she attains the age of marriage. Later on there is no reference to marriage. However, Mira goes away on a holiday to spend some time with Richard. Jacob says: "Despite their deep and lasting love for each other she is mature enough to understand the hindrances to their union"(109). A girl who is not married going away on a holiday with her lover especially in the 1940s makes us ask an important question. Are the socio-economic and urban background of the female character and her higher "education" reasons for such a step being taken? Can such a thing happen in a case like that of a Rukmini? No, never can such a thing happen to a person from a rural and lower class background. Mira may have felt that as they were getting married there was no problem in having an affair or pre-marital sex. Richard creates a situation so that he can have intercourse with Mira:

> "I fevered for you so long," he said, "It became a permanent ache. Can you understand that?"
>
> "Yes," I said.
>
> "I'm still in a fever for you," he said, kissing me; and his lips on mine were without gentleness, and his body against me was no longer passive. Obeying some obscure instinct, I struggled away, moving away from him, his urgency, striving to sit up.
>
> "Not here," I said, Not——"
>
> "Yes, here. Now."
>
> "No," I said breathless, "It's ——"

> "We're alone," he said, holding me still. "Quite alone," and the skies were empty, the sands were bare, I listened and there was only the sound of the sea.
>
> "You see," he said softly, "There is nothing and no one. No one but us."
>
> Slowly my senses awoke and responded, the buds of feeling swelled and opened one by one. In the trembling silence I heard the blood begin its clamour, felt its frantic irregular beat; then the world fell away, forgotten in this wild abandoned rhythm, lost in the sweep and surge of love. (Markandaya *Some Inner* 168-169)

It is Richard who expresses a desire to have an intercourse with Mira before marriage. He says that he has been longing for intimate moments with Mira. He also tells Mira that it is his "permanent ache" and asks her to "understand." Mira agrees to his wishes. He again reiterates his feelings even after she has agreed to fulfil his "permanent ache." He starts "kissing" Mira and expressing his longing and continuing "fever." The moment Richard moves against Mira's body there is "some obscure instinct obeying" his desire, at the same time trying "to move away" from him reluctantly. The reason for moving away is not to resist or prevent him from advancing but due to the impropriety of the place. Had the place been different, she would not have minded. However, Richard is particular about the place as it is a lonely and conducive place. He gives reasons such as they are "alone", "skies were empty", "sands were bare", "nothing", "no one." Mira too is convinced. As a result her "senses awoke" and "responded" the "buds of feeling swelled and opened one by one." There is no reference here to show that Mira does not want to marry or that her parents are unwilling or have protested against the marriage.

Unlike Rukmani and Premala, Devaki in Nayantara Sahgal's *A Time to Be Happy* (1958) has a love-cum-arranged marriage with Girish. I think this is the best match if the couple is in love and gets the consent of the parents from both sides. Girish is a businessman and employed in the Calcutta office of James McDermott Ltd. Girish gets angry when any one calls his marriage an arranged marriage:

> Devaki was both decorative and efficient, an altogether suitable wife for a young businessman employed in the Calcutta office of James McDermott Ltd. It was Rohan Masi who, with unerring instinct for matchmaking, had drawn Lakshmi's attention to the girl one summer in Mussoorie. Devaki's parents had hoped for a son-in-law in the I.C.S., Rohan had informed Lakshmi privately, but Girish's charm and his family's considerable income, backed by Rohan's own determined manoeuvres, had won them over. Girish would have protested had anyone suggested it was an arranged match. He had fallen in love with Devaki, he said; it was a marriage of choice. It was a marriage of choice, all right—Rohan's choice—and she was delighted with the outcome. (72)

The marriage of Devaki and Girish ends on the happy note—all is well that ends well. Devaki finds Girish a "suitable" match for Girish is in love with her. He has no pride about his job. He is happy to marry Devaki. Moreover, he does not want his marriage to be considered an "arranged marriage." He will even "protest" if anyone calls their marriage "an arranged marriage." Devaki's parents are also happy with Girish's "charm and his family's considerable income." Rohan, the unnamed narrator's aunt and a family friend of Girish, has played a crucial role in the "delighted outcome" of his "manoeuvres."

Kusum in the same novel has a love-cum-arranged marriage with Sanad. Sanad is in love with Kusum and he proposes to her. The marriage is fixed without any difficulty and "a year later, in February 1947, Sanad and Kusum were married" (*A Time* 203).

After discussing the issue of marriage, it is logical to discuss the issue of career, as career and marriage are inter-related. Before I proceed further, I would like to define what "career" means to me. One has to be very clear about the difference between a "career" and a "job." In my view one takes on a career with "passion" and "enthusiasm" and is completely involved in the work. This motivation has to come from "within," and cannot be forced from outside. One should not choose a career based on someone's advice. On the other hand, one does a job either out of one's own choice or out of compulsion. It could be to earn one's own livelihood. There is no passion or enthusiasm. It is only a mandatory, routine work.

Since the issue we are discussing is related to "educated" women, we have to look at it from the women's point of view. Is every career the same for men and women? Are there any careers that are male or female specific? Is there any change in anyone's perception regarding career? Does the career prospect reduce once women get married? How do "educated" women deal with this kind of a situation? What happens when a woman is asked to give up her career after marriage? Does she still hold on to her career and give up her marriage or wait for a person who can allow her to continue with her career? The issue of marriage has a dominant role to play in terms of career. The conflict of marriage and career may lead to divorce. This is one of the main arguments of the thesis and will be discussed at length in the next few chapters. There may be some women characters who are not married but have careers in their respective fields.

I feel that no "educated" woman should give up her career for the sake of marriage. A marriage can wait but a career will not wait for a woman. Marriage can be sidelined but not career. The tragic part is that marriage can completely undermine career. There are many problems for career women. Some of the problems for these "educated" career women are as follows:

Marriage can be one of the biggest problems for a career woman who wants to lead a happy married life. The man should be broad-minded and should be able to understand the importance of career in the life of his wife. If he understands the importance of his wife's career, then that particular woman is lucky and fortunate. Otherwise her life will be hell.

Second, if both husband and wife are in different fields and different places, they will have unresolved problems. This will affect their children adversely, if they have any.

Third is the problem of getting or finding a suitable and well-educated husband. India is full of customs and traditions. In addition to these there are castes, religions and inter-state problems.

In the 1950s, though marriage is a significant theme in the novels, there are no "educated" women who have a career. Veena in Nayantara Sahgal's *A Time to Be Happy* has a job as an announcer in All India Radio, Delhi. Perhaps Veena doing a job itself is something unusual. There are not many cases of career women found in the novels of this period. Educated women themselves are not many. As a result the issues of career and divorce do not arise. There are in fact no cases of divorce in these novels. Therefore, let us move on to the 1960s.

WORKS CITED

Gore, M.S. *Urbanization and Family Change*. Bombay: Popular, 1969.

Jacob, Asha Susan. "Victims and Survivors: Kamala Markandaya's Indian Women Protagonists." *Post-Independence Indian English Fiction*. Ed. Rajeswar Mittapalli and Alessandro Monti. New Delhi: Atlantic, 2001. 103-116.

Jain, Jasbir. "The Feminist Perspective: The Indian Situation and Its Literary Manifestations." *Other Englishers: Essays on Commonwealth Writing*. Ed. Niaz Zaman et.al. Dhaka: University Press, 1991. 66-75.

Markandaya, Kamala. *Nectar in a Sieve*. 1954. Bombay: Jaico, 1996.

——. *Some Inner Fury*. 1955. Bombay: Jaico, 1957.

Rao, V.V. Prakasha Rao and V. Nandini Rao. *Marriage, The Family and Women in India*. New Delhi: Heritage, 1982.

Ross, Aileen D. *The Hindu Family in its Urban Setting*. Toronto: U of Toronto P, 1961.

Sahgal, Nayantara. *A Time to Be Happy*. 1958. New Delhi: Sterling, 1975.

Srivastava, Ramesh K. "Love and Death in Kamala Markandaya's *Some Inner Fury*." *Indian English Literature Since Independence*. Ed. Ayyappa Paniker. New Delhi: IAES, 1991. 14-26.

NOTES

1. Quoted in V.V. Prakasha Rao and V. Nandini Rao, *Marriage, The Family and Women in India*, New Delhi: Heritage, 1982. 16. Prakasha Rao and Nandini Rao take the quotation from the book entitled *Daily Life in Ancient India* (New York: Macmillan, 1965. p.176) written by Jeannine Auboyer and use it for their argument.

"Standing Up for the Rights": The 1960s

3

In this chapter I will look at the "educated" women characters from the 1960s' novels. Maya and Leila from Anita Desai's *Cry, the Peacock* (1963), and Monisha from *Voices in the City* (1965), Nita, Uma, Rashmi from Nayantara Sahgal's *This Time of Morning* (1965), and Saroj, Leela, Gauri and Tamara from *Storm in Chandigarh* (1969) will be considered keeping in mind the issue of "marriage." Leila from Anita Desai's *Cry, the Peacock* (1963), and Amla from *Voices in the City* (1965), Nita from Nayantara Sahgal's *This Time of Morning* (1965) and Tamara from *Storm in Chandigarh* (1969) will be discussed in terms of the issue of "career." Nila from Anita Desai's *Cry, the Peacock* (1963) and Rashmi from Nayantara Sahgal's *This Time of Morning* (1965) will be examined to see how the issue of "divorce" is dealt with.

Maya in Anita Desai's *Cry, the Peacock* (1963) obeys her father as far as her marriage is concerned. Gautama is her father's friend. Maya says: "[M]y father's proposal [was] that I marry this tall, stooped and knowledgeable friend of his, one might have said that our marriage was grounded upon the friendship of the two men, and the mutual respect in which they held each other, rather than upon anything else" (40). Raisahib has asked his daughter to marry Gautama, his friend who is knowledgeable. What have friendship and knowledge got to do with Maya's marriage? In fact, Maya is a victim of their friendship as her marriage is an arranged one. Raisahib and Gautama may have mutual respect but that does not mean Maya must marry Gautama. Moreover, her father does not take her opinion but suggests that she marry him. One of the problems of arranged marriages is that parents decide without taking their daughters into confidence. The boy may be good to the father. He may behave according to the wishes of the father. But the girl may not like that kind of a behaviour. Parents imposing their likes on their daughters is not justified. Marriage is a life-long journey. The girl must have a role to play while consenting to the match. I agree with M. Rajeshwar's opinion that Maya's father Raisahib has made a mistake in getting his daughter married to Gautama:

> On Maya's attaining marriageable age he creates what appear to be the ideal circumstances for Maya to develop tender feelings towards Gautama, his protégé. Gautama is perhaps only the other soul that Maya is exposed to for any significant length of time and allowed to be on intimate terms with. And surely she finds in him some of the best qualities—intelligence, understanding—that her father has in plenitude apart from the similarity in age. It therefore comes as no surprise that Maya should meet with "quickening passion,"(40) her father's proposal to marry Gautama. But what intrigues us is: why in the first place does he propose Gautama's match? Gautama has none of the things that he admires. Gautama's financial position is anything but enviable (he always comes riding a bicycle; one remembers Raisahib's angry disapproval of Arjuna's buying a bicycle). To add to this, Gautama's life-style and circumstances of his family are just the opposite of what Raisahib cherished all his life. Gautama's father was a freedom-fighter and mother is a social worker. Yet Raisahib just cannot tolerate Arjuna's similar concerns. That Raisahib and Gautama hold each other in mutual respect itself cannot be a plausible explanation for his preference of Gautama as his son-in-law. (46)

Since Maya's model is her own father, she cannot enjoy her married life with Gautama, especially because of his family background. It is Raisahib's fault that has created chaos in Maya's life and ruined not only her life but also Gautama's. M. Mani Meitei comments:

> Lack of mutual concern leads to apathy which causes the total breakdown of husband-wife relationship. In this case, it is Gautama who is solely responsible for this breakdown. Maya's is a kind of forced marriage in which her father's interest rather than her own is served. Such a marriage is an institution intended to exploit women socially and sexually. It never considers women's freedom and liberty; it leaves them chained in their husbands' home. (46)

Maya has neither a career nor does she take divorce from her husband.

In the same novel we have Leila who has married for love. She has eloped with her lover without her parents' permission. She loves the boy even though he suffers from tuberculosis. They love each other until death. The narrator, Maya feels touched by the fact that the couple is fighting the disease with strong will power. Maya says: "When I saw her hand him a glass of medicine, or lift his body into comfortable positions, I saw in her movements an aching tenderness subdued, by a long sadness, into great beauty and great bitterness" (*Cry*, 57). She is surprised to see no hatred in Leila towards her husband. To Maya, this is a very touching and sad scene. Prabhat Kumar Pandeya says: "Leila's marriage is a love marriage and she had eloped with her lover who is a consumptive. She is an ascetic wearing neither bangles nor jewellery. She is an exact contrast to Pom in this respect. She was detached and worked tirelessly in college and at home nursing her husband whom she had married knowing that he is a consumptive" (40-41). Leila has chosen a career as a college lecturer in a girl's college. Unfortunately, her husband suffers from tuberculosis. Maya wants to see Leila:

> Today I longed to see her. I even prepared to go out and meet her. Then I recalled that she would not be at home, but in the girls' college where she taught Persian literature to a handful of girls who, while waiting, coyly, for suitable marriages to be arranged for them, read allusions to sly and underhand sex in every romanticism, and yawned at the smallest sophistries. (Desai *Cry* 57)

Maya is angry with Leila's husband because he criticizes Leila's parents for not coming and seeing him, his wife and their daughter. Maya says:

> Sometimes I thought of him as an animal, a ferocious and wild beast that had allowed itself to become a house pet for its own reasons, and he accepted the food and drink she earned for him, as his due, even teasing her about her parents who had not seen her, written to her, or in any way communicated with her since the day of her elopement. (Desai *Cry* 58)

Leila and her husband have been suffering due to their problems; yet their life goes on.

Having looked at the issues of "marriage" and "career" in *Cry, the Peacock*, let us now look at the issue of divorce. My opinion on divorce is that it should be the last resort if both the husband and the wife find it extremely difficult to adjust to each other. I completely agree with what Shakuntala Devi has to say:

> Both the husband and the wife have to develop self-control and a high sense of responsibility. They have to realize that human nature being what it is, temperamental differences are bound to arise now and then in daily life, and they cannot be got rid of by divorce and a second marriage. Happiness in family is possible only if the husband and the wife are prepared to make great sacrifices in order to accommodate themselves to each other. Divorce should be the last remedy in very exceptional cases. (133)

After reading the novels I have found some reasons why "educated" women go in for divorce. They are (a) incompatibility, (b) extra-marital relationship, (c) age disparity, (d) physical assault, (e) the husband asking the wife to sleep with his boss, (f) patriarchal attitude of the husband, (g) wife's working career, and (h) mental deficiency. There is a study done by J.N. Chaudhary on the causes for divorce and he states the following reasons and causes for divorce:

> Role-conflict (or authority), poverty and non-support, physical assaults, Family structure (very large family and inadequate home life), Illicit relations, Wide age disparity, Chronic diseases calling under Factors endogenous to Family; Secondly, Dowry, Wife's working career, calling under Factors exogenous to family; thirdly, Domineering nature, Impotency, Barrenness, Lethargic nature, Irritative nature, Mental deficiency under Personality factors. (51)

Not just studies on the causes for divorce, there have also been studies on the consequences of divorce like the one conducted by Judith S. Wallerstein and Joan B. Kelly which has been reported by Andrew J. Cherlyn in his book, *Marriage Divorce Remarriage* (Cambridge: HUP, 1981):

> With the results of this national survey in hand, there are still no firm estimates of the proportion of children who experience harmful psychological effects from parental divorce. But taking into account the little that is known from recent studies, we might conclude that: (1) almost all children experience an initial period of great emotional upset following a parental separation; (2) most return to normal development within one or two years following the separation; and (3) a minority of children experience some long-term psychological problems as a result of the separation. (79)

As the above study reveals, it is not so easy for the couple and their children to adjust, and coming to a normal state will take time. Therefore, it is suggested that divorce should be the last and final resort keeping the above implications on children. However, this study does talk about the effect on a couple who takes divorce before having children.

Nila in Anita Desai's *Cry, the Peacock* (1963) divorces her husband. This is perhaps the first ever case of divorce in Indian English women's fiction. Prithvi Nath Tikoo in his book *Indian Women: A Brief Socio-Cultural Survey* quotes Jawaharlal Nehru's views in his chapter "Pro-feminine Reforms" that are very relevant to divorce:

> During the debate on Special Marriage Act in the Lok Sabha, Prime Minister Jawaharlal Nehru said, "You will find women standing up for the rights of divorce though some men may challenge it because men happen to be in a dominant position. I hope they will not continue in that dominant position for all time. These different standards of morality cannot be maintained. Therefore, the approach is to bring about a certain measure of equality between them; it is a question of custom, education and basically the economic position of individuals." (105)

Jawaharlal Nehru also emphasizes the importance of "education" and "economic position" of women in order to attain "equality." He also suggests that the "dominant position" of men is not "for all time." Nila proves that with economic independence she can claim equality and can ask for a divorce from her husband. She is the sister of Gautama. She seeks her brother Gautama's help in getting a divorce but, though a lawyer, he refuses to undertake his own sister's divorce case. The reason is that he does not think what his sister is doing is right. When Maya asks her husband to take up the divorce case, he says:

> "Nila," I said, and pressed her hand. She smiled, and tossed the black hair out of her long eyes. She had come to consult Gautama regarding her divorce. Gautama had refused, in a noisy family conference, to have anything to do with it. "Why Gautama?" I was shocked. "What does she take me for—one of those two-rupee lawyers that squat under the banyan tree outside the courts, waiting for clients low enough to consider them—prostitutes and petty swindlers? I haven't time to waste on a case like hers—the mess she makes by being too bossy and self-willed and bullying." (Desai *Cry* 161-162)

Nila comes with great expectations hoping to get a divorce without any problem, as her brother himself is a lawyer. Surprisingly, her brother "refuses" to fight on her behalf. Nila thus finds another lawyer to file a case for divorce:

> And in high indignation Nila had found herself another lawyer, on her own. "You went *alone* and spoke to him?" "And why not?" she was wryly amused. "After ten years with that rabbit I married, I've learnt to do everything myself." "Except lead a sensible life," said her mother, tartly, very tartly for her, for she hated this matter of a divorce in the family, and children going fatherless. But I was admiring, and "Nila" I said, pressing her hand in wonder. (Desai *Cry* 162)

There are mixed opinions about Nila's initiative to divorce her husband. Maya is surprised when she comes to know that Nila went alone to talk about her divorce case with a lawyer. Nila does not consider it anything wrong to go "alone" to meet a lawyer and file a case. At this moment Nila comments on her "married" life of ten years and calls her husband a "rabbit" and wants a divorce. This comment proves that they are incompatible. Moreover, she claims that she has "learnt" to do "everything" by herself. However, Nila's mother is not in favour of the divorce and calls her daughter insensible. Nila's mother does not want to see her daughter take a "divorce" and make the "children fatherless." For Nila her life is more important than the life of her children. Maya admires Nila for seeking divorce and as a sign of appreciation she presses Nila's hand in "wonder."

Nita in Nayantara Sahgal's *This Time of Morning* (1965) has been engaged at the age of 17. According to T. Ashoka Rani, "Nita resents arranged marriages and when she is engaged to Vijay, she is unhappy. She feels withdrawn with no prospect of fulfilment" (125). Moreover, Nita is involved in pre-marital relationship[1] with Kalyan Sinha, a minister. Nita is not responsible for this act. Nita's parents force her to get engaged to Vijay who she does not want to marry. Moreover, she does not want to marry at the age of 17. She wants to have a job. Kalyan Sinha, a minister, offers her a job, something her parents cannot refuse. She works in his office. She does not want to leave the office. She even refuses to go home and openly expresses her love for Kalyan:

> "But don't make me go."
>
> He rose from his chair, "Nita..."
>
> She got up, too, and came like a sleepwalker into his arms, clinging to him.
>
> "Don't make me go, please don't make me go."
>
> He took her by the hand and then to his room. (152)

Kalyan is a fatherly figure to Nita. Yet she has pre-marital sex with him. There is an age gap between Nita and her fiancé Vijay. Also, she does not like the boy she is going to marry. Such a girl like Nita may indulge in pre-marital sex. Who is to be blamed for this kind of relationship? Are her parents responsible for Nita's lost chastity? She may have believed in chastity but her parents by bringing her a proposal that makes her unhappy may have perhaps led to her not wanting to retain her chastity. T.R. Dash comments:

> [T]he new-found emancipation that has come Nita's way changes her whole mental outlook and turns her against the traditional ideal of arranged marriages. The western way of getting to know the prospective life partner over a period of time influences her so much that the usual match-making appears too hasty a beginning for a lifelong liaison. From this point of view her sexual inclination for Kalyan seems but natural. She displays no conscious love for Kalyan. Through this relationship, she rebels against the accepted norms and conventions of a traditional social system. (99)

Nita goes in search of a job. However, she does not get the job by herself. The job she secures is through influence. But, Nita's interest in having a job is a fact. In fact, she wants to work so as to delay the wedding with Vijay. Kalyan is a minister without portfolio. Kalyan encourages Nita, an educated girl, to take up a job. He says:

> "Narang," he [Kalyan] repeated the name. "Your father is the doctor, isn't he?"
>
> "Yes he is."
>
> "And what do you do? Are you studying?"

> "I've done my B.A.," she told him, and stumbling bravely on, "I'd like to do something, some work, I mean."
>
> "Is that such a problem? Do your parents object?"
>
> "Well, not exactly," she had never felt so young and foolish. "I mean not since Rakesh spoke to them."
>
> "Ask Rakesh to bring you round some time. I see no reason why an intelligent, educated young woman should not have a job." Her nervousness vanished and she looked at him with pure joy. "It's so kind of you. But I couldn't think of taking your time. I know how busy you are."
>
> He cut her short. "Come round with Rakesh." She found Rakesh. "He noticed me, *me!* He's going to give me a job!" (Sahgal *This Time* 110-111)

I see Nita's search for a job as a means of delaying marriage by giving the excuse that she has just started working. In fact she does not have any passion for any career. I would like to disagree with Alladi Uma when she says: "Sahgal, who tries to break away from the traditional concept of women, does not view her women characters as 'wage-earners or career women but mainly as married women—as wives, daughters and mothers—and it is in these roles that they wish to experience freedom and to become aware of themselves as individuals to be accepted as equals' (Jain 1978: 44)" (9). Here in the case of Nita it is clear that she is not interested in becoming just a wife, especially to a man of her parents' choice. In fact, as of now, she is not interested in marriage. She wants to work and earn money. If not a "career" woman, she wants at least to be a "wage earner." She would like to take some time to marry. In other words she has chosen her job out of force. I use the word force because she does not want to marry at present. She has also sought the help of Rakesh, a family friend, to tell her parents that she is not interested in marriage at present but wants to work. She also uses Rakesh to get the job. In Nita's case it is clear that she is not interested in any career. She is willing to do "[a]ny work" as she tells Kalyan. Career is something one chooses and it does not depend on someone's mercy or influence. Kalyan asks a valid question—whether her parents would have any "objection." Many parents would not like their daughters to work. If Rakesh recommends, her parents will not object. A positive quality in Kalyan is that he identifies Nita as "an intelligent educated young woman" and so giving her a job is not at all a problem.

Like Maya in Desai's *Cry, the Peacock*, Uma in Nayantara Sahgal's *This Time of Morning* (1965) has an arranged marriage with Sir Arjun Mitra. Mitra has a western background but still he prefers to have an arranged marriage:

> It was not unusual that despite this background of westernization his marriage should still be arranged for him, but for years Arjun resisted the idea of marriage. He was absorbed by his work and his books and there would be time enough to marry later. His family did not press the point. A man could, in fact, marry at any age. Arjun would always be eligible. When he decided to marry there would be no difficulty in finding a suitable girl for him. Parents would fall over each other in their eagerness to offer their daughters to the grandson of the renowned Sarat Mitra. And they did. The Mitra family had no dearth of offers. The one Arjun chose when the time came was the nineteen-year old daughter of a judge of the High court. It had hardly been a choice on his part. Uma of the round young face, the feline brown eyes uplifted at the corners, and the magnolia skin had jolted him to earth from his books, and pitched him into the realization that he had not even begun to savour life's offerings. He was thirty-three years old, still the dreamy-eyed ex-student. (Sahgal *This Time* 25-26).

It is an arranged marriage and Mitra "chose" Uma to be his wife. He does not bother to find out from Uma whether she likes him or not. Perhaps his stature and family background have made him take Uma for granted. Moreover, he may have felt he was an "eligible" bachelor. He has had several offers of marriage. He assumes that since it is an arranged marriage, she will obey the man chosen for her. That is the mistake committed by Mitra. How could he, a man of thirty-three choose a girl of nineteen as his wife? Is he conscious of their ages?

The huge age gap and lack of intimacy, tenderness, communication and companionship between Arjun Mitra and Uma are the main reasons why Uma has an extra-marital relationship with Neil Berensen. Arjun Mitra should have been broad-minded to understand that Uma is not mature enough to understand married life. Instead, he fails to understand her and concentrates only on his files and office work:

> He had been a dutiful son, a brilliant student and he filled his office with distinction. Life as a district officer suited him. It brought him into contact with small towns and villages, yet kept him in touch with the central authority. [...] He played tennis, enjoyed the company of a small social group that drank moderately and entertained in a friendly, informal way. The smooth course of this idyllic existence was interrupted by the arrival of Uma—Uma who hated the dull districts after life in Calcutta, Uma in whom marriage had released a torrent of hungry seriousness that brought to startling focus her exotic feline beauty.
>
> The childlike petulance that had so entranced him began to upset him. He could not understand her boredom. He himself had never been bored. Other women occupied themselves. Why couldn't she? He gradually abandoned his attempts to interest her in his library or the neighbourhood and he began to feel helpless to cope with her. [...] She was only twenty, a mere child, or twenty two or twenty-four, as the years went by and they moved from one district to another. [...] He began to retire to his study after dinner. The smoke of his pipe and his favourite books in their shelves insulated him against the discord in his house. (Sahgal *This Time* 26-27)

Arjun "fails to understand" her "boredom" at home. A.V. Krishna Rao also opines that, "Uma feels extremely bored with her fruitless marriage and continually seeks to escape into the fakery of sexual freedom" (144). Arjun only compares her with other women who are occupied with household work. He wonders why Uma cannot do the same thing. He seems to be a "bookworm" for as soon as he finishes his "dinner" he goes back to his "study". He cannot understand the desires of a young bride and a passionate woman. He has grown up physically but his mind has not grown up enough to understand a young woman's feelings and aspirations. At one of the parties, Uma happens to see an oil painting of the Rani of Mirpur illuminated by a band of light beneath the frame. Neil says:

> "It is exquisite, is it not?" a foreign voice behind her spoke. "Yes." She [Uma] did not know the man, but decided he must be from one of the embassies. Black hair, swarthy skin, silky voice. A South American perhaps.
>
> "If I may say so", he bowed slightly, "not as exquisite as Madame." [...] "May I get you some champagne? That is, if you will not disappear while I go to fetch some for you."
>
> [...] The stranger returned.
>
> "I drink to your eyes, Madame."
>
> She neither encouraged nor discouraged him. She let his hand take hers, slide up her arm, go round her waist. Her headache receded slightly and she felt a relief in his skill and deftness. He got up again to lock the door. She wondered afterwards what it had to do with love. [...] It was complete in itself and needed no explanation. When he left she lay on the sofa a little while, soothed by the darkness. (Sahgal *This Time* 109)

From the above lines, we can see how a married woman allows a stranger to make "love" to her. Why does she allow him to take advantage of her? Is there lack of love between Arjun and Uma? She does not even feel guilty about the action. Another interesting question one can ask is as to why Uma does not protest against a proposal where there is an age gap? She could have avoided all these problems had she protested against the proposal. Both Uma and Arjun are at fault in entering into marriage when there is such a wide age difference.

Rashmi in the same novel must have had an arranged marriage. Rashmi too is involved in an extra-marital relationship with Neil. The break-up of Rashmi and Dalip leads to the close relationship between Rakesh and Rashmi. Rashmi seeks divorce from Dalip. She is not happy with Dalip. She does not "hate" him and does not want to "harm" him. Moreover, she cannot think of the two of them any longer as "we" as the differences between herself and Dalip are too much. Nayantara Sahgal herself opines: "Rashmi leaves her husband when her incompatible marriage becomes intolerable" (84). She uses the phrases, "prolonged starvation", "wrong marriage", "defeating courage" and "will" to show why the marriage cannot last. Rashmi has to say this about her break up with Dalip:

> The thought of a break burdened her with the guilt that her best had been enough, and that there was so frighteningly little truth or permanence in even what one most wanted. Only one thing seemed clear at this moment, that love, if love is the terrible desire for one person, had left her, never to return. (Sahgal *This Time* 13)

The thought of a "break" is burdensome to Rashmi. Any marriage breaking up is always painful. There will be guilt in divorce. In fact, both Rashmi and Dalip do not want the "frightening truth" of separation, yet they do separate. The separation takes place as there is no "love" between them. There is a difference between separation and divorce. Separation can bring two people together even after a long gap but not so divorce.

We only know through Rashmi that they are separated. We don't come across Dalip's views but are told about him and his relation with Rashmi:

> "Does your husband come to Delhi often?"
>
> "Fairly often on business. We are ...separated."
>
> [...] "Marriage" remarked Neil conversationally, "does not really make for happiness. I think there is something wrong with people who stay happily married."

> [...] "A lot of people are happily married", she protested.
>
> "But they don't continue to be. That shows their intelligence."
>
> She laughed again and he went on, "Discontent is the medium of our age." (Sahgal *This Time* 140)

Rashmi declares that she and her husband Dalip are "separated." She wants to clarify to Neil that she is "single." Neil takes advantage of this situation and comments that marriage does not really provide "happiness." If there are couples with a "happily married life," then, "there is something wrong with them" he says. This view is not acceptable and Rashmi immediately replies that most of them are "happily married." She wants to tell him that just because she and her husband are separated, it does not mean that all married people are unhappy. Perhaps Neil is trying to please Rashmi for his own selfish needs and desires. Although she does not agree with him, she continues to converse with him because she needs to talk to him.

Rashmi's mother has not been happy with her daughter's decision to get separated from Dalip. She says:

> Rashmi's announcement was worse than bad news. It was a mortal blow to all she held sacred. What had brought Rashmi to this pass? What reason under heaven could sever the marriage bond? Women stayed married, had since time immemorial stayed married, under every conceivable circumstance, to brutal insensitive husbands, to lunatics and lepers. And Dalip, God forbid, was none of these things. Fulfilment had lain in service and sacrifice. If there was suffering, too, it was a part of life. Her despair went far beyond Rashmi's decision to unknown dangers she could not comprehend. Much of the distress she saw about her she put down to the tasteless parody of a transplanted modernity. And now it had invaded her own home.
>
> "We've known for a long time that she has been unhappy," said Kailas slowly. (Sahgal *This Time* 146)

Mira wonders as to what made Rashmi sever her "marriage bond" with Dalip. She seems to expect her daughter to continue with her married life. She falls back on the Indian tradition with its emphasis on marriage in a woman's life. She does not find fault with Dalip but with her own daughter. Dalip is a sincere worker who is ready to sacrifice his personal life for the sake of service. It is his work that feeds him and his family. At least "educated" women should understand this dedication of their husbands rather than blaming them and taking extreme steps to separate from their husbands. I too agree with Dalip and Mira as far as service and sacrifice are concerned. That leads us to Rashmi who has been narrow-minded. She has unnecessarily spoiled her married life and has an affair with Neil, an outsider. Mira also considers Rashmi a victim of modernity. Kailas, Rashmi's father, has no special feeling and concern for his daughter's life except to say that she has been unhappy with Dalip for a long time. Rashmi decides to separate from Dalip because she finds his spending time at work unacceptable. At the same time he too should have considered her feelings and could have looked for alternatives. She is not justified in her act of separation, as we can see from her mother's reaction too.

Like Maya, Uma and Rashmi, Monisha too in Anita Desai's *Voices in the City* (1965) has an arranged marriage with Jiban and has no career or job. Perhaps Monisha does not want to say no to her father's choice of a bridegroom. This is wrong especially as far as "educated" women are concerned. However, her sister Amla is not happy with the proposal. She thinks to herself:

> Why had [her] father chosen him from amongst other young men surely known to him, or to his friends and relations, whose names must have been proposed when word was sent around that the eldest daughter was to marry? Was it merely because Jiban was so unquestionably safe, sound and secure, so utterly predictable? Or was it because fathers did, unconsciously, spite their daughters who were unavailable to them? And why did Monisha,

> with that powerful silent stubbornness of hers, never rebelled? (198)

Amla tries to question her father's "proposal" and her sister's "powerful silent" acceptance of the match without any signs of rebellion. Further, she enquires from her aunt who has also played a role in this marriage proposal:

> "Aunt," Amla asked, "why did they marry?"
>
> Her aunt shook her long hands at the ends of stiff wrists in an awkward gesture that denoted bafflement.
>
> "Did you meet him before they were married?"
>
> "Yes. Your father asked me to visit his family and report, so I did. I met Jiban and his family before your parents did."
>
> "And what did you report?"
>
> "That they were a respectable, middle-class Congress family, completely unsuitable to Monisha's tastes and inclinations. So your father decided he was the right man, that it was the right family." (Desai *Voices* 198-199)

So, after the visit, her aunt did report that Jiban and his family are from a "respectable" family. They belong to a "middle-class Congress" family. However, Jiban and his family are "completely unsuitable" to Monisha's "tastes and inclinations." In spite of all this, her father has Monisha marry Jiban, whom he considers the "right man" for Monisha. Harveen Sachdeva Mann opines that:

> Intelligent, well-read, and self-aware, Monisha is, however, given no voice in determining her spouse and hence the course of her life after leaving her parents' home. Her marriage with Jiban appears, at first, to have been arranged for the sake of social expedience [...] [S]he [Monisha] saw herself as a sacrifice to her parents' floundering marriage; because she felt compelled to play the part of a dutiful daughter conforming to the patriarchal practice of arranged marriage; or because she

> was overwhelmed by a sense of fatalism at the lot of Indian women. (162-163)

Amla in the same novel does not marry because she has seen the problems of her sister at her in-law's place. Ruth K. Rosenwasser observes: "As a modern woman, Amla has freedom of choice, and with choice comes the anxiety and stress of role conflict in deciding which direction her life will take. Though employed outside the home with career opportunities open to her, Amla hears Monisha's warning against marriage, to 'go in the opposite direction', meaning not to follow the path that she, Monisha, had taken" (95-96). In other words, Amla has followed her sister's suggestion and has remained unmarried. However, she has chosen a career of a commercial artist in an advertising firm. Amla's choice of career has been appreciated by her Aunt Lila who wants her to enjoy her new job and independence. Aunt Lila says:

> "Of course I'm glad you've come, Amla, it was inevitable, and perhaps you will not let it oppress you but will enjoy your new job and independence."
>
> "Of course I will!" Amla insisted with laughing relief. "And Calcutta doesn't oppress me in the least—you can't imagine how exciting it is to arrive, to drive through Dalhousie Square with all its red gingerbread houses, their domes and cupolas and pigeons. When I drove into Ballygunge and saw its weather beaten old mansions and palm trees, I kept thinking of John Company and Sir Thomas Roe at Jehangir's court. It *excites* me, aunt"[...] "Good"[...] "That's the spirit in which to start your career, my girl. That's what I like to see in young people—spirit. There's not too much of it around," she added darkly. (142)

Amla is very confident about her career even at its starting stage. Amla shares her excitement of arriving at Calcutta. She is excited at the sights that interest her: "red gingerbread houses," "domes and cupolas," "weather beaten old mansions and palm trees." Her aunt is happy about her initial reaction and would like to see this spirit continue throughout her career. Amla meets her brother Nirode and informs him about her taking up a job at Calcutta:

> "I've come because I've got a job here, in an advertising firm, as a commercial artist. I start work next week. I thought it was going to be exciting and wonderful but—" she saved her hand at the clumsy, formless traffic on the curdy river, "this city, this city of yours, it conspires against all who wish to enjoy it, doesn't it?" (Desai *Voices* 153)

Amla seems to express her unhappiness regarding the crowd in Calcutta to her brother. She comes to Calcutta with a lot of enthusiasm. However, she is not able to adjust to the "formless traffic on the curly river." She had expected that it will be "exciting and wonderful" to work in Calcutta. But she shares her feelings with her brother about the lack of enjoyment in her career in Calcutta. When Amla tries to find out whether he has any friends, he mocks at her and says she will make dozens of friends. She gives a befitting reply:

> "I have come here to work," she said, made defensive by that laughter. "I have played enough in Bombay. And I've heaps of ideas—I wonder if I'll get the chance to use them, as a commercial artist." (Desai *Voices* 154)

She firmly says to her brother that she wants to have a flourishing career. Moreover, she has come to Calcutta with heaps of ideas and given a chance she would like to implement them. The above lines clearly indicate how strong her conviction is in wanting to use her ideas. When Amla expresses her ambition of being a commercial artist again, Nirode looks down on it. He says: "Commercial artist. Sounds too bloody awful for words. Poor old Amla, do you really expect anything from a career stamped commercial?" (154)

He does not seem to like Amla's career. That is the difference between Nirode and Amla. She has chosen her own career. Her career has not been suggested to her by anyone. She wants to try out and do what she can. She does not want to be upset about his comments on her career. In fact, she comments on his career: "'Ah, I heard you had lost your faith in commercial writing,' her hurt pride gave her the nerve to say" (154).

After meeting her Aunt and her brother she goes to meet Monisha, her elder sister. Monisha's mother-in-law overwhelms Amla with non-stop questions. In fact Monisha wants to ask Amla several things but her mother-in-law does not give her any chance:

> While Monisha sat silently on the divan beside her sister, the mother chattered and chirrupped avidly as a sparrow at a social gathering. She had so many questions to ask of Amla, concerning her career and her education in Bombay. "Is it true that the Parsis there throw their dead to the vultures? They do—ah, so I had heard [...] Is it true that young girls there wear frocks? [...] Were there any men students in your college with you? [...] Do you draw these pictures we see in the newspapers? They are getting more and more improper. There is one of a girl coming out of her bath, it is an advertisement for hair oil—do you know who drew it? [...] How do you go to work everyday? (Desai *Voices* 159)

Apart from people trying to know about her career or to appreciate her career, there are those who discourage her career. Amla herself has assessed her career prospects. Monisha asks Amla whether she has heard anything from their mother. Amla says that she has been busy and has no time to reply to her mother's letters:

> "Do you come home very late from the office?" Monisha asked, without the faintest curiosity, standing still to study a spider enthroned on the exact heart of its sagging, sticky web between two twigs of the magnolia tree. "No, I get away from there as early as I can. I don't think I'm really made for a job in an advertising firm—" she pushed and pushed at the Tibetan turquoise ring on her finger—"it doesn't seem to be the right career at all." [...] "For me. I don't think I should have gone straight from art school into advertising, it is too violent a let-down." (Desai *Voices* 195)

Amla says that as far as possible she would like to go back "home" "early." She expresses that she has made a mistake by choosing to work in an advertising firm. In other words, she seems to tell that she should have worked as an art teacher rather than in an advertising firm. S. K. Tikoo opines: "Amla, a commercial artist with an advertising firm, has also romantic dreams of rising high in her job. But soon she finds that people around her are interested not in her art but in herself." (118)

Like Maya, Monisha and Uma, Gauri in Nayantara Sahgal's *Storm in Chandigarh* (1969) too has an arranged marriage with Nikhil. She has studied up to high school and she has no college degree. Vishal Dubey wants to know about Gauri's marriage:

> "Yours was arranged?" asked Dubey.
>
> "I never expected anything else. And I had no college degree either. I went to a convent in Calcutta and then sat around for a couple of years until Nikhil was found for me and then I married him." (160-161)

Perhaps, this arranged marriage has made her go for an extra-marital relationship with Dubey. Obviously, her opinion was not sought before her marriage to Nikhil. However, she has no complaints against Nikhil in any matter. She seems to be happy with her industrialist husband; yet she develops an extra-marital relationship with Vishal without any guilt:

> After dinner they drove with Nikhil to the airport and then back to the house. During the four years since Dubey had known her, the urgency between him and Gauri had evaporated and they had settled into a friendly familiarity. But he had not been able to bring to an end the affair so mindlessly begun. As she undressed in the half light of her bedroom and came, warm and pliant, into his arms, he realized he could have done without making love to her for some time now and enjoyed just the sight of her. (Sahgal *Storm* 18-19)

Gauri just feels like having an affair with Vishal and she does it. Gauri seems to be unfaithful to her husband Nikhil by getting involved in an extra-marital relationship with Dubey.

Her husband has neither troubled her nor has he ignored her. Why then does she develop an intimacy with Vishal that leads to a sexual relationship?

In the same novel Saroj is married to Inder Mehra. Saroj is candid with her husband and reveals her pre-marital relationship with her boyfriend. This is a blow to Inder. Jasbir Jain says: "[T]he concerted effort of Inder is to make Saroj feel guilty for a pre-marital relationship" (15). He starts hating his wife. How can he start hating his wife who is trying to be frank with him? What would he have done if she had not revealed the fact? Would he have any evidence about the relationship? Perhaps his ego is badly hurt. We will see in a short while how he reacts to Saroj's frankness.

Inder, in order to show that he too like Saroj can have an extra-marital relationship develops one with Tamara. However, Tamara is married to Jit who is a businessman. She herself has a career of running a school. The novelist does not provide many details about how she looks after the school but we gather that she is successful in running the school. According to T.R. Dash[2], "Mara [...] blissfully runs a kindergarten school all by herself. She symbolises the boldness and freedom of woman with her westernized outlook, and her occupation provides her with the opportunity for energy release"(99). There is only one place where we see her in her office. Inder comes to her office to see her on the pretext of taking the children home:

> There were days when it soothed Mara just to arrive at the school and look at her own handiwork. This was not one of them. Her batteries needed recharging. She was in her office. Smoking her midmorning cigarette, piano music and sunlight from the schoolroom just beginning to weave a pattern of peace, when Inder arrived, filling the doorway with his restless brooding energy.
>
> "I left office early," he [Inder] said unnecessarily.
>
> "Have you come for the children? It's not nearly time, but I'll call them if you like."

> "No," he said quickly. "I'll wait"[...]
>
> "Can't you leave the school for half an hour?" he said suddenly. "I've got a painting just arrived from Delhi for the office. Gauri sent it—along with a vanful of things from kitchen utensils to heaters. And I have no idea where to hang it."
>
> She considered this a minute. "I suppose I could. The children have singing from now till the end of the hour." (Sahgal *Storm* 168-170)

From the above lines Mara seems to be dedicated to her school. Inder was there neither to see his children nor to take them with him but he wanted Mara to go with him. She politely "considers" his request and decides to go with him so long as it does not affect her work in school. She does not compromise on her career. For her everything is after "school hours." That is the commitment she has towards work.

Mara has a relationship with Inder. Inder, in order to show his manliness, has an extra-marital relationship with Mara. B. D. Sharma and S. K. Sharma opine: "Inder [...] believes in two codes of morality, one for himself and another for his wife as even though he himself is not faithful to his wife Saroj, he resents her having lost her virginity before her marriage" (75). If Inder had forgiven and understood the pre-marital relationship, he would have been a great man. Instead he starts developing two codes of morality. At least he could have maintained his faithfulness to his wife. Sahgal seems to suggest that men can never tolerate if their wives have pre-marital or extra-marital relationships. Men also expect their women to be virgins and faithful wives. However, Mara comes out of the relationship with Inder after a talk with her husband Jit: "Jit is fond of Mara and of the school she runs on modern lines for children. Jit helped Mara out of the emotional jungle by talking to her of an unhappy experience of his own. Jit made communication possible with Mara on all fronts" (Rajendra 182).

Ultimately, Inder becomes lonely and loses his wife too. His wife has a relationship with Vishal Dubey. Saroj and

Vishal go for evening walks. Gradually Saroj cannot live without Vishal. Once Inder tries to order Saroj not to go for evening walks with Vishal. Saroj says she cannot spend a day without going for a walk with Vishal. She openly declares this fact. Ultimately Saroj leaves Inder and goes away with Vishal Dubey and lives with him. In the novel there is no indication that Inder and Saroj obtain a divorce. But it is clear that Saroj wants to lead her life with Vishal. One has to carefully understand Saroj's stand. When Inder can have an extra-marital relationship with Tamara, why can't Saroj leave Inder? In other words, why should she not divorce him and marry Vishal? In fact Saroj is open in revealing the fact that she had pre-marital sex with her boyfriend. Saroj thinks:

> Marriage is meant to provide comfort and strength through love and communication, and not through material possessions. It should be devoid of all secrets and firmly rooted in honesty and truth. Then only can the marriage bond strengthen itself and no incidents of the past destroy the future. Marriage does not allow either partner to be selective. (Sinha 106-7)

Thus, she does not want to maintain any "secrets" with her husband. She wants to be "rooted in honesty and truth." Though he takes it as an offence, he commits the same mistake. Perhaps he wanted to show Saroj that if she had a pre-marital relationship, he too could have an extra-marital relationship with Tamara. However, he becomes a victim of his own ego. At the end, he has neither his wife nor his lover.

Vishal Dubey is a widower and has relationships with more than two women. Even before his affairs with Gauri and Saroj, his wife Leela had an extra-marital relationship with Hari. She lives a "life of pretence and hypocrisy" (Rajendra 180). Unfortunately she dies in the hands of an incompetent abortionist. Leela's relationship with Hari has led Vishal to convert his friendships into relationships. Gauri and Saroj seemed to be happy with their husbands. But when they meet Vishal, they enter into a relationship with him. The result of the affair is that Saroj's marriage with Inder breaks up. There was a danger of Tamara and Jit's relationship breaking up too.

However, it is saved because of open discussions between them.

On the other hand, Nikhil does not know that Gauri has an affair with Vishal. Otherwise their relationship would have been in trouble. What I am trying to point out here is that women are drawn into extra-marital relationships. If Tamara and Inder had continued their affair, Tamara would have spoiled her life. Perhaps it could have led to divorce.

Most of the marriages portrayed in the 1960s' novels are arranged like that of Maya, Monisha, Uma, Rashmi, Saroj, Leela, Gauri, Tamara. There is one love marriage of Leila portrayed in these novels. Compared to the 1950s, there are two educated women, Amla and Leila, who have careers and Nita, who has a job so as to postpone her forced marriage. The first ever case of divorce is that of Nila and one that follows is that of Rashmi. Saroj leaves her husband, with an intention to divorce.

Extra-marital relationships may be one of many reasons leading to divorce. But divorce as we have seen does not imply the rejection of the institution of marriage. While the women in these novels who get divorced or decide to go in for divorce have had arranged marriages, we cannot conclude from this that love marriages do not end up in divorce. Let us see how this issue is dealt with in the following decades.

WORKS CITED

Chaudhary, J.N. *Divorce in Indian Society (A Sociological Study of Marriage, Disruption, and Role Adjustment)*. Jaipur: Printwell, 1988.

Cherlin, Andrew J. "The Consequences." *Marriage Divorce Remarriage*. Cambridge: HUP, 1981. 69-92.

Dash, T.R. "Nayantara Sahgal and Feminism." *Feminism and Indian English Fiction*. Ed. P.M. Nayak and S.P. Swain. Bareilley: PBD, 1996. 97-100.

Desai, Anita. *Cry, the Peacock*. Delhi: Orient, 1963.

Desai, Anita. *Voices in the City*. Delhi: Orient, 1965.

Devi, Shakuntala. *Women's Status and Social Change*. Jaipur: Pointer, 1999.

Jain, Jasbir. "Towards the 21st Century: The Writing of the 1990s." *Indian writing in English: The Last Decade*. Ed. Rajul Bhargava. Jaipur: Rawat, 2002. 11-25.

Mann, Harveen Sachdeva. "'Going in the Opposite Direction': Feminine Recusancy in Anita Desai's *Voices in the City*." *Post-colonial Literatures: Achebe, Ngugi, Desai, Walcott*. Ed. Michael Parker and Roger Starkey. London: Macmillan, 1995. 155-175.

Meitei, M. Mani. "Feminism and Anita Desai's *Cry, the Peacock* and *Where Shall We Go This Summer?*" *Feminism and Indian English Fiction*. Ed. P.M. Naik and S.P. Swain. Bareilly: PBD, 1996. 43-55.

Pandeya, Prabhat Kumar. "The Poly-timbred Voice: Women in *Cry, the Peacock*." *Indian Women Novelists Set I: Vol. III*. Ed. R.K. Dhawan. New Delhi: Prestige, 1991. 36-46.

Rajendra, Susheela P. "Individual Freedom as the Central Motif in *Storm in Chandigarh*." *Indian Women Novelists Set II: Vol. IV*. Ed. R.K. Dhawan. New Delhi: Prestige, 1993. 173-184.

Rajeshwar, M. "Anita Desai's *Cry, the Peacock*: The Father's Unconscious." *Indian English Literature Since Independence*. Ed. Ayyappa Paniker. New Delhi: IAES, 1991. 44-48.

Rani, T. Ashoka. "Women In Marriage: Novels of Nayantara Sahgal and Shashi Deshpande." *Critical Studies in Indian Fiction in English*. Ed. R.A. Singh and V.L.V.N. Narendra Kumar. New Delhi: Atlantic, 1999. 124-130.

Rao, A.V. Krishna. "*This Time of Morning*: A Critical Assessment." *Indian Women Novelists Set II: Vol. IV*. Ed. R.K. Dhawan. New Delhi: Prestige, 1993. 138-156.

Rosenwasser, Ruth K. "Voices of Dissent: Heroines in the novels of Anita Desai." *Journal of South Asian Literature* 24.2 (1989). 83-116.

Sahgal, Nayantara. *This Time of Morning*. Delhi: Orient, 1965.

——. *Storm in Chandigarh*. Delhi: Orient, 1969.

——. "Passion for India." *Indian Literature* 32.1 (1989). 78-88.

Sharma, B.D and S.K. Sharma. "The Contribution of Women to the Development of the Indian English Novel." *Contemporary Indian English Novel*. New Delhi: Anamika, 2001. 74-81.

Sinha, Lakshmi. "Nayantara Sahgal's *Storm in Chandigarh*: A Search for Values." *Studies in Indian Fiction in English*. Ed. G.S. Balarama Gupta. Gulbarga: JIWE, 1987. 104-112.

Tikoo, Prithvi Nath. "Pro-feminine Reforms." *Indian Women: A Brief Socio-Cultural Survey*. New Delhi: B.R., 1985. 104-124.

Tikoo. S.K. "Heroism and Pathos in *Voices in the City*: A Thematic Analysis." *Indian Women Novelists Set. I: Vol. III*. Ed. R.K. Dhawan. New Delhi: Prestige, 1991. 111-121.

Uma, Alladi. *Woman and Her Family: Indian and Afro-American—A Literary Perspective*. New Delhi: Sterling, 1989.

NOTES

1. Nayantara Sahgal writes in her article entitled "Passion for India" [*Indian Literature* 32.l (1989): 77-88]: "When *This Time of Morning* was published, a lady here in Delhi called me a very naughty girl. She wanted to know why I had let Nita, a young unmarried girl, have an affair with the Minister, Kalyan Sinha? This lady didn't realize that characters can't be told what to do. Once they are on the page they have a life of their own. They speak and act as they want to. The writer is literally a witness" (85).
2. In his article entitled "Nayantara Sahgal and Feminism" [*Feminism in Indian English Fiction*. Eds. P.M. Nayak and S.P. Swain. (Bareilley: PBD, 1996), 97-100.] T.R. Dash mentions the character's name as "Mira." That is not correct. The correct name is "Tamara" but in the novel she is always addressed by the shortened name, "Mara."

"Rebellious Spirit": The 1970s

4

The educated women characters I am going to deal with in this chapter are: Simrit from Nayatara Sahgal's *The Day in Shadow* (1971), Lalitha from Kamala Markandaya's *Two Virgins* (1973), Sita from Anita Desai's *Where Shall We Go This Summer?* (1975), Manasi from Kamala Das's *Alphabet of Lust* (1976), Devi from Nayantara Sahgal's *A Situation in New Delhi* (1977), Geeta from Rama Mehta's *Inside the Haveli* (1977) and Shree from Raji Narasimhan's *Forever Free* (1979) will be looked at in terms of the issue of marriage; Simrit from Nayantara Sahgal's *The Day in Shadow* (1971), Lalitha from Kamala Markandaya's *Two Virgins* (1973), Manasi from Kamala Das's *Alphabet of Lust* (1976), Ila Das from Anita Desai's *Fire on the Mountain* (1977), Devi from Nayantara Sahgal's *A Situation in New Delhi* (1977) and Shree from Raji Narasimhan's *Forever Free* (1979) will be discussed keeping in mind the issue of career; and Simrit from Nayantara Sahgal's *The Day in Shadow* (1971) and Shree from Raji Narasimhan's *Forever Free* (1979) will be dealt with to discuss the issue of divorce.

Simrit in Nayantara Sahgal's *The Day in Shadow*[1] (1971) falls in love with Som and marries him without her parents' consent. This earliest novel in the 1970s discusses love marriage. In Shruti Vaidya's words: "[…] Simrit shows some rebellious spirit when she decides to marry Som much against the wishes of her family" (75). When a girl marries against her parents' wishes as a rebel, she expects her husband to be everything. She cannot expect any support from her parents even if her marriage fails. Sahgal is making her protagonist take a bold step and breaking the traditional concept of an arranged marriage. Simrit has resisted her parents' wishes of getting her married to a man from a decent family. Simrit has married Som with a lot of pride but all in vain. The reason is that he is a male chauvinist. Simrit has not studied Som's mind properly. Asha Choubey opines that Simrit falling in love with Som may "be described as infatuation" (79). Some love marriages take place just out of infatuation. Also, "[h]er Brahmin parents with their instinctive withdrawal from anything outside the fold had been frankly upset at her choice of a businessman husband, but her friends had not liked him either" (Sahgal *The Day* 3). The above lines clearly indicate that both her "friends" and "Brahmin parents" have not approved the match. Perhaps the Brahmin parents may not like the business profession. She realizes later that she has made a poor choice. She chooses love marriage, but it turns out to be unsuccessful.

Simrit has undertaken writing as a career. However, she does not write for commercial purposes but for her own personal satisfaction. She is an occasional freelance writer for the newspapers. In her conversation with Joshi and Mr. Shah, Simrit reveals this information:

> "Then you must be working," said her companion. They had fixed her with a twin Joshi look. It made her feel she had broken out in spots and scales.
>
> "I am a writer."
>
> It sounded so terse and self-advertising.
>
> "Which newspaper do you write for?"
>
> "I freelance. But I don't write much for the newspapers. Only the occasional article."[...]
>
> "Simrit Raman?" the first woman placed her. "I've seen a book by you. It was about a place—a valley, wasn't it, or a stream?"
>
> "A river," said Simrit, tormented.
>
> "A river?"
>
> "Yes," said Simrit [...]

> "Mrs Raman, you have written a book about a river," stated Mr Shah. "I have read it." (Sahgal *The Day* 6-7)

Simrit has chosen her career as a "writer" out of interest. She has in fact written a book.

Though she had married Som for love, the marriage has now lost its meaning to her as there is no warmth or understanding between them. Som also should have the responsibility of taking care of his wife's needs. A couple marrying out of love look forward to being happy throughout their life. So it is unfortunate that such a couple wants a divorce. The reason for the divorce, according to T. Aṣhoka Rani is as follows: "Simrit and Som's relationship is marked by lack of tenderness and warmth, communication and compatibility" (74). I agree with Rani that in love marriages, tenderness, warmth, communication and compatibility are of prime importance. If these qualities are not shared between the couple, then there is no meaning to a love marriage. One may find it difficult to find these qualities in arranged marriages. Thus Sahgal takes a stand that if the husband does not have these qualities, then it is better to divorce him rather than lead a life of compromise. Susheela P. Rajendra too expresses her view in a similar way: "[...] lack of proper companionship, communication and equality between man and woman [could] wreck [a] marital relationship resulting in divorce" (233). Rajendra adds two additional qualities of companionship and equality between man and woman in a love marriage.

There is no warmth and tenderness between Som and Simrit. Their relationship is only business-like: "Simrit respects certain values of life more than material prosperity. But there is no end to Som's ambitions. For him the end is more important than the means. He does not hesitate to drop out a friend or his own wife if he feels he or she no longer serves him any purpose. He fails to comprehend the sensibilities of Simrit" (Bai 169). It is only a materialistic life that they lead. I always have a feeling that business people have no warmth and tenderness towards their family members as the case of Som suggests. People like Som think that they are doing the most for the family. But they forget that they spend very little time with family members, especially with the wife. Som says:

> You have everything in the world any woman could want. [...] "Stop crying, Simrit. What on earth is there to cry about? I'm a damned good husband to you, aren't I? What have you got to complain about? We're having a wonderful life and it's going to get better and better." [...] "Think of it, we can go abroad any time we want, any bloody time, buy anything we want. We can air condition this whole place, furnish it all over again, and Rudy's right. You ought to have something to mark the occasion. What would you like? You didn't say." [...] She began, "Som, the world is so full of violence." "Yes of course it is. It always has been. Don't tell me that's what you're crying about." [...] I don't mean war—that's far away. I mean people with each other. And look at the arid way we live, without friends." (Sahgal *The Day* 88-89)

Som believes that he is providing and can provide all that Simrit wants. He says that Simrit has "everything" in the world any woman could want. Som is only talking about the materialistic things that a businessman can provide. He claims himself to be "a damned good husband." For him a wonderful life is one where a person has all the comforts money can buy. Simrit does not subscribe to this view for she sees violence all around her. Though Som thinks that she is talking about the outside world, she is in fact describing her family world. She does not talk about "war" between people or between countries but with "each other," between Som and herself. She is here pointing out the lack of affection and communication.

If Simrit feels cheated in her marriage because her husband has no affection for her and is not able to communicate with her, Lalitha in Kamala Markandaya's *Two Virgins* (1973) has been cheated and exploited by a film Director who has made her pregnant and does not marry her and who has not offered her a role in the films. Avadhesh Kumar Singh observes: "Lalitha appears more as a rebel against traditions and social taboos than as a violator of moral code" (123). Whether

Lalitha "appears as a rebel against traditions and social taboos" or "as a violator of moral code," it is Lalitha who has to suffer humiliation as she has to abort the foetus and she finds it difficult to show her face to people. There is no marriage for her. She has chosen to act in films on her own though she has been advised to choose teaching as her career by her teacher Miss Mendoza:

> There are a number of careers open to girls like her, Miss Mendoza was saying. Have you thought of a career? She wanted to know, fixing her eyes which were beady but brilliant on Appa and Amma in turn. [...] Appa cleared his throat. He said young women these days did go in for careers, and he brought out that, yes, his daughter might have one too. What had she in mind? he asked Miss Mendoza, and nothing was more clear than that his was quite blank.
>
> Teaching, said Miss Mendoza, which made Amma stiffen. Or nursing, she said, which turned Amma to stone, some kind of glittering rock which you felt would draw blood if you so much as touched it. (61-62)

Miss Mendoza comes to Lalitha's place to find out what Amma and Appa have in their minds with regard to their daughter's career. Though Appa pretends to be open it is clear that he had not really given a thought to it as his expression "was quite blank." Amma too does not like Miss Mendoza's suggestions as is evident from the way her body stiffens and turns into a rock. But Lalitha is very particular about acting in films:

> Lalitha told Appa and Amma. She had to, to get their cooperation, without it she could not have seized her opportunity. No one was clear what that was, not even Lalitha. A film star, she said, a film actress, a chance to be in a film: she whittled it down to fit the reality which would eventually have to be conceded. Appa said We must see. He said One must have the full facts of the matter to enable one to come to the right decision. Not in this world, said Amma, in this world it is not possible

> to have the full truths on any subject. It was clear they were talking for the sake of it, to save face in front of their children by refusing to admit the subject was wholly outside their scope and experience. Appa said the Indian film industry was the second biggest in the world. He said it gave employment to two million people. (Markandaya *Two Virgins* 81)

Appa saying, "we must see" is not totally dismissive. However, Amma straight-away disagrees. Both of them are unwilling to admit that "the subject was wholly outside their scope and experience." Later on Miss Mendoza also encourages Lalitha and hands her over to Mr. Gupta so he can help her act in a documentary film and later on in a film:

> Miss Mendoza simpered, she took it as a compliment. We like to give our girls total opportunity, total experience, she said. Some are able to take advantage, she said in a vibrant voice; they are, shall we say, gifted. Her brilliant gaze was beamed straight on Lalitha. One of our most promising pupils, she cried, that is why, Mr. Gupta, I have not hesitated to bring her to your attention! Her hand was laid on his sleeve, Mr. Gupta looked at Lalitha, who was doing her eye act. Delighted, delighted, he murmured abstractedly, then suddenly became brisk, said crisply what he could use was some good folk dancing, or a spirited Indian solo. (Markandaya *Two Virgins* 90)

However, it is a futile attempt for Lalitha. Mr. Gupta, a director of documentary film exploits Lalitha. She becomes pregnant and aborts the foetus, as he does not want to marry her. Markandaya seems to suggest that the film profession is dangerous for people like Lalitha who have dreams of becoming film stars. In order to impress the directors, the girls have to give in to their desires. Moreover, there is no guarantee that the directors would fulfil the girls' dreams of becoming film stars. P. Geetha observes: "With her illegal relationship with Gupta, she is crippled morally. She has no place in her society. Her parents try to hush up the whole affair, getting the abortion done in secret. But Lalitha does not have the moral courage to face her fellow beings" (176). Geetha is very right. How could a girl who has had an illicit relationship, face society and fellow beings? The blame is on her teacher and her father. Appa's sister has cautioned her brother not to push her into acting in films. However, he ignores her suggestions and pays the price for it. Alice Drum also expresses a similar view:

> When the village becomes the subject of a documentary film, Lalitha's dreams of a career and an escape [from the village] become a reality. Having been given a role in the film, she quickly begins a flirtation with the director and is invited by him to come to the city after the film is completed. There she is seduced by, or seduces, him—depending on who tells the story, Appa the father or Gupta the lover. In time, Lalitha's pregnancy and abortion bring the family, with the exception of Aunt Alamelu, to the city, where their problems are intensified by the pressure of urban existence. (324-325)

What happens to an urbanized woman like Sita in Anita Desai's *Where Shall We Go This Summer?* (1975). Unlike Simrit, Sita has an arranged marriage with Raman. Raman is an industrialist. He is the son of Sita's father's friend. That is the reason why Sita is married to Raman. It is like Maya and Gautama in *Cry, the Peacock*, marrying each other as a result of Gautama and her father being friends. It is a common belief that if parents are friends, their children too will have the same kind of relationship and understanding. Friendship is different from married life. There is a problem in Raman and Sita's marriage. Sita delivers four children. Again she is pregnant. At this point Sita is prepared neither to deliver the child nor to abort the foetus. She thinks that it is her choice whether to deliver the baby or not. Maithreyi Krishnaraj also supports Sita and says: "A woman's role in the reproduction of human beings far weighs that of a man. It is invariably a woman who mothers. Motherhood and mothering are usually perceived as naturally related" (34). For this reason Sita goes back to her native place. She does not want to be with her husband Raman. Look at the connotations of the name, Sita. See how she does not adhere to the values that Sita of the Hindu epic

Ramayana stands for. Sita in the novel never objected to deliver her earlier children. However, she does object to deliver the fifth child. Sita seems to prove that it is ultimately the mother's choice to deliver the baby or not.

Like Sita and unlike Simrit, Manasi in Kamala Das's *Alphabet of Lust* (1976) has an arranged marriage with Amol Mitra. Manasi is not happy with her marriage. She has high ambitions. Her husband belongs to an aristocratic family. But, later on, after his father's sudden demise due to liver disease, he is content with his job and looks after his family. However, Manasi is not content with her life with her husband and daughter. Look how Amol has come to his present status:

> [...] Amol managed to graduate on a scholarship and joined the Government service as a clerk.
>
> It was his flamboyant background that fetched for him a marriage proposal from the father of Manasi. Who had not heard of Barrister Mitra? And one of the palatial mansions where he had lived and entertained? True, he died prematurely of a liver disease. But why blame the son for his father's excesses? Manasi's father was a true Bengali snob and liked the idea of his daughter marrying the son of an aristocrat. Amol was modest and unassuming. He did not ever talk of his father or of his glorious childhood [...]. (110)

Amol Mitra is a "modest and unassuming" person. That is why Manasi's father likes him. At the same time Manasi's father overlooks the age gap between them. Manasi is not happy with this marriage because of the age gap. We have already seen this problem in the case of Arjun Mitra and Uma in Nayantara Sahgal's *This Time of Morning*. Amol Mitra "looked old enough to be her father" (9). In an arranged marriage there could be a lot of age gap between the couple. There is a reason for this deliberate choice. If the wife is much younger, then the wife can look after the husband in his old age. She will have more energy than the husband and so can look after her husband, which is a part of her duty in married life. But I do not agree with this view. It is because of this age gap that a woman looks for a relationship outside marriage like Manasi with Vijay Raje and Uma with Neil in Sahgal's *This Time of Morning*. Vijay is "a womaniser, a young and depraved politician, now a Minister, and a rising sun in politics. She [Manasi] wishfully feels that theirs would have been an ideal pair: 'We would have made an excellent pair. Poetess and politician'" (Srivastava 119).

However, Manasi goes to the extent of having an extra-marital relationship with Vijaya Raje, the confidant of Mr. Desai, the Prime Minister, only in order to get political advantage and become a minister. She does not feel guilty, like Gauri in *Storm in Chandigarh*. She has gained from the relationship. She is a Bengali poet. She gets the Padmashree award just because of her extra-marital relationship with Vijaya Raje. He takes Manasi to Shimla for a week. Manasi can go to any extent for her selfish motives and even surrender sexually to Vijaya Raje.

Manasi initially has chosen writing poetry as her career and later on enters politics. Manasi is a good example of someone winning the highest literary award from the central government with the help of political links: "Manasi won the highest literary award for her latest book of poems in Bengali, and was invited to Delhi to receive the long citation and the money" (Das *Alphabet* 19).

This is a politically obtained award rather than an award achieved through one's own effort. However, once it is declared, it is considered an authentic award. Once she gets this politically obtained award, she does not stop there. She moves on to politics. She has been given a minister's post in the central cabinet. She has sexual affairs to get this ministerial position. There are two people involved in Manasi getting the award. First, it is Vijay Raje who introduces Manasi to the Prime Minister. Manasi expresses her desire:

> I do not want to be only a poetess, she [Manasi] said. I want to be a woman who can be admired and loved. How like a child you speak, exclaimed Vijay. Today I am going to introduce to you to the Prime Minister,

> who wished to meet you. We are dining with the Minister for Information and Broadcasting who has also invited the P.M. (Das *Alphabet* 31)

One could ask why Vijay shows interest in Manasi. It is because she has no problem in having an affair with him. Moreover, he is her childhood friend and is in love with her. Manasi agrees to go to Shimla with Vijay to spend a week with him. So he shows an interest in Manasi. Apart from that, Manasi does not want just to be a "poetess" but also wants to "be admired and loved." Vijay understands her feelings regarding her aspiring for some political power through her body. Therefore, he wants to "introduce" her "to the Prime Minister" and recommends her for some ministerial position. After her meeting with the P.M., the P.M. is impressed with Manasi and intends to give her the portfolio of "Minister for Information and Broadcasting" provided she fulfils what the P.M. wants, that is to sleep with him:

> The P.M. has fallen for you, and wants you to join his cabinet as the Minister for Information and Broadcasting. [...] Manasi straightened up all of a sudden. "But"? she asked him. Why do you say "but"? The Prime Minister is a womaniser, said Vijay. He will not leave you alone. Your name will soon be mud in the country. [...] Vijay, I am willing to do whatever the P.M. wants me to do. It is not as if I am a chaste woman now. A *pativrata*. You saw to it that I became a mere tart. I rented out my body for a pair of diamond earrings. And hereafter for power I shall rent it out to the influential tenant I can hope to get. (Das *Alphabet* 40-41)

She tells Vijay that she is willing to do anything that the P.M. wants for the sake of her career. She is no longer a "chaste woman." She has lost the confidence of her husband after having an affair with Vijay for the sake of getting "a pair of diamond rings." Therefore, why would she hesitate to sleep with the P.M. if she were going to get the post of a minister? However, she is in a dilemma:

> The Prime Minister was above fifty. But he had a boyish appeal which women found difficult to resist. Manasi

> frowned for a moment, debating within, whether she ought to be unfaithful to Vijay, her lover of a mere year, and be the P. M.'s mistress. It was obvious that the man wanted to make love to her. She smiled once again. (Das *Alphabet* 59)

The dilemma is that of being "unfaithful" to her lover Vijay. Where is the question of "faithful" and "unfaithful" as far as Manasi is concerned? She is already "unfaithful" to her husband. For the sake of enhancing her career she does not hesitate to go to any extent. She need not be in a dilemma of being "unfaithful to" her lover "Vijay." She should think about her husband not her lover. Strangely she does not think about her husband at all. After the affair with the P.M., the P.M. discusses the matter of the cabinet reshuffle with his "principal adviser" (135) Vijay:

> Vijay, we can have a reshuffle, said the Prime Minister. We can give Singh, Defence.
>
> Ha, that will be another blunder, said Raje. He dislikes war. You must give Defence to a militant person. Manasi, for instance. Manasi? asked the Prime Minister, Why do you call her militant? She was a Naxalite once upon a time, said Raje. I used to read her articles in a journal devoted to the Naxalite movement. Set a thief to catch a thief. Perhaps I could give her Home, said the Prime Minister. It is entirely up to you, said Raje. (Das *Alphabet* 130)

From the above conversation it is clear that Vijay wants the Prime Minister to give Manasi the Defence portfolio. But the Prime Minister wants to give her Home Ministry. Thus Manasi is able to shift from being a poet to that of a Home Minister. There is something negative about the way she comes up in her career. But it happens with some people. Kamala Das seems to suggest that politics is dirty. No longer do political leaders work for the sake of people but for the sake of their own selfish desires, either for earning money or for sexual pleasures.

Unlike Simrit and like Sita and Manasi, Geeta in Rama Mehta's *Inside the Haveli* (1977) has an arranged marriage with Ajay, a lecturer in a degree college. Ajay is a member of a joint family. Geeta is from an orthodox family but she is given freedom to mingle with "men and women." Malashri Lal opines: "[M]arriage brought Geeta from the outer world of modernity to the enclosures of the threshold. She had grown up in the bustling metropolis of Bombay. At a co-educational college, she was accustomed to a 'free mingling of men and women' (13) and had known of a different conservative society" (88). However, Geeta's opinion is sought about her future husband:

> Two years ago when she left her parents' home in Bombay, she did not know that she was leaving behind a way of life in which there was a free mingling of men and women. Geeta had met her future husband Ajay in the company of her brothers' friends. She was not quite sure which of the young men had come to see her. When her parents asked if she liked the man in the grey suit, she had said, "Yes." Her parents seemed sure that she would. Her mother had told her that Ajay came from an old aristocratic family of Udaipur but he, unlike many in such families, was highly educated. He was a science professor. He was not interested in entering a more prestigious service much to the disappointment of his parents. Geeta's parents' only doubt seemed to concern Ajay's family. The women of the upper class in Udaipur, among them his mother, remained in purdah. Geeta had been differently brought up. She had gone to college and studied with boys. How would such a girl learn to live in the constricted atmosphere for a world of women, to give her elders the traditional deference? [...] Her parents' anxiety was not really so much about Geeta's adjustment, but about whether a girl like her would be approved by Ajay's parents. The more orthodox relatives might be afraid of an educated girl and caution them against her, particularly one who was not from Udaipur. Geeta knew that her mother had worried that she would spoil everything by talking too much on the day Ajay came to see her. (Mehta *Inside* 15-16)

In an arranged marriage, it is quite common for at least some of the family to go and see the girl to find out if she is suitable for the boy or not. In fact, they have to be satisfied. Only later is it the choice of the boy and girl. In the same way Ajay comes with some "young men" and Geeta does not know who Ajay is. In the meanwhile, she has been asked her opinion as to whether she likes the boy. This is the first instance in a novel where an "educated" woman's opinion has been sought when the marriage is an arranged one. She gives a positive reply to her parents. In addition to seeking her opinion about Ajay, she has been briefed about Ajay's family background, that he comes from an "old aristocratic family." In other words she has been advised to behave in an "orthodox" manner. Ajay is well-educated as he is "a science professor." He does not want to hold any other higher post as it would embarrass his family members. He gives importance to his family members. Geeta has also been told that her mother-in-law is still in "purdah." Naturally she expects her daughter-in-law to be in "purdah." Geeta's mother is also apprehensive about consenting to the match as Geeta has been "brought up" in a different environment where she mingles freely with "boys and girls" due to her higher education. Orthodox families generally avoid highly educated girls. After the marriage, Geeta has been advised by her mother to "[k]eep your head covered; never argue with your elders; respect your mother-in-law and do as she tells you. Don't talk too much" (Mehta *Inside* 16). It looks like Geeta is ready to face any kind of challenge to win her in-laws' favour and acceptance. She has been listening to every advice and does not react. It shows that she has been digesting all the suggestions given to her. If the girl is happy with the choice then everything will be all right. The only thing is that the bride should be happy with the kind of match parents bring. Moreover, Geeta's opinion has been sought. This is an appropriate action taken by her parents.

Geeta as an "educated" mother does not accept for her thirteen year-old daughter Vijay, the marriage proposal from Daulat Singhji of his son Vir Singh. Vir Singh is an arts graduate but would like to go abroad for higher studies. Geeta refuses to accept this marriage proposal: "'My daughter's marriage is my concern. I will never agree to Vijay's engagement like this, no matter what happens. Even if it were the son of Maharana of Udaipur, I wouldn't agree,' replied Geeta as if she had thrown all restraint aside" (Mehta 215). If a mother like Geeta exists in the generations to come, one can be assured that child marriages will not take place. One has to appreciate the kind of boldness she has shown in a traditional and joint family set-up. She is firm and blunt in her disagreement. For Geeta, Vijay is her daughter and it is her "concern." She bluntly replies that she will not agree to the marriage proposal and to the "engagement." She is ready to face any kind of consequence. Even Geeta's father-in-law Bhagwat Singhji is in support of her and tells Geeta that the proposal is not acceptable on his deathbed: "'I have told Daulat Singhji that under no circumstances would I permit Vijay to be taken out of school. I am against early marriages. Girls must study; they cannot be kept ignorant.' As if the exertion were too much for him, he fell back on the couch and closed his eyes" (Mehta 248). If the initiative is taken by the mother, then the elders of the joint family members too may support her. Bhagwath Singhji endorses that "girls must study" and "they cannot be kept ignorant." After revealing his conversation with Daulat Singhji, Bhagwat Singhji passes away. In support of Geeta, Kamal Bhasin says: "Personally, as a mother she would have the right to decide about her daughter's future. For her, women's education is a first essential step towards self-reliance" (120). This step of Geeta as an "educated" mother is a welcome step and an eye-opener to all the "educated" women and mothers.

Geeta's work can be called a real and voluntary "career" of teaching the haveli maids and their children. Initially, she teaches a boy called Ravi. Later on, she teaches the other boys and girls of the servants' quarters of the haveli. Can we call Geeta's teaching social work? Is social work a career? Yes, we can consider it so. It is a career with a difference. It is one of the greatest careers I would say. Generally people want to earn money, name and fame. But a career-oriented person is not just after money. Getting a name also brings in money. However, Geeta has chosen a career out of her own free will. She is teaching the boys and girls of a haveli without any charge nor is she offered any amount. It is a kind of social work. She has not been employed. As an "educated" woman she wants to help uneducated boys and girls of the servants' quarters. The following encounter with a boy, Ravi, motivates Geeta to undertake teaching:

> "What did you do in the village?" asked Geeta. She was touched by the boys's sad, vacant eyes.
>
> "In the morning, I helped my mother to collect cow dung, milk the cows, and in the afternoon I took the cows out grazing. My mother was going to send me to school, but then she got fever and now she is dead," said the boy acceptingly as if there was no point challenging fate.
>
> "If you want to learn, come home in the morning," said Geeta, not knowing what else to say to the boy who stared at her big diamond ring. The next day after breakfast the boy stood outside Geeta's room and so from that day she started teaching him. After two days other boys and girls from the servants' quarters came up to Geeta's room with Ravi. The children sat quietly while Geeta first told them stories and then wrote out the alphabet and asked them to copy it. No one made a noise and after Geeta had finished with the lessons, instead of going home, they sat on practising the letters of the alphabet. (Mehta *Inside* 160)

Geeta initially has no intention of teaching the children in the haveli. However, she is moved by Ravi's sad story. As a result she thinks of teaching him only. But it does not stop there. Rather, she becomes so popular that there is a rush to her house to learn from her as she has been showing interest and kindness towards them. Gradually it becomes a kind of a school or tuition centre without any fees. Malashri Lal opines: "Mehta points out that upper class educated women must provide the leadership to those born in less privileged conditions.

For this they may need to sacrifice some of the modern principles of liberation that they could have grabbed for themselves" (101). I agree with Malashri Lal about the upper class educated women providing the leadership to the girls who are born in less privileged conditions. It is not just the upper class women enjoying the fruits of liberation but the need to share. Therefore, Geeta has initially started telling them "stories" and later on she teaches them the "alphabet." Even after finishing the "lessons" they don't go home; rather they go on "practicing the alphabet." The satisfaction that the career woman gets in this kind of situation is immense. Later on:

> News of the classes spread like monsoon floods and the young maids from the havelis came and joined the children. At first they just listened to the stories; they did not dare to take pencil in their hands for they were afraid the children would laugh at them. But gradually they started to print the letters and to their surprise found the alphabets were after all not so difficult to learn. Soon the maids began to recognize words, the meaning of which they understood. (Mehta *Inside* 160)

So the maids also show interest in learning the alphabet. It has been a great success. The simile of "spread like monsoon floods" very beautifully conveys the success of the "classes" of both "children and young maids." As usual the elders are hesitant to learn along with "children" as they might laugh at them. Geeta is very happy that being an "educated" woman she is doing something for the children and the young maids. Malashri Lal's observation of Geeta's initiative in establishing a school in the haveli is worth quoting here:

> The school in the haveli is the outcome of Geeta's complex emotions about tradition, modernity, poverty and affluence. Her agenda to introduce subtle change is nothing short of revolutionary. Education will pull down the barricade between the haveli and the outer world. The poor children will find employment beyond the haveli because the old system can no longer offer patronage. For the servant-maids too, Geeta has her

> own proposal for vocational instruction in sewing and needle-work if they find book learning difficult. As for the high-born women, they are welcome to the classes should they wish to use their time more profitably than in gossip. (95)

Unlike Simrit, Sita, Manasi and Geeta, Pinky in Nayantara Sahgal's *A Situation in New Delhi* (1977) has a love-cum-arranged marriage. Pinky has fallen in love with Arvind and has taken the consent of her parents. From the following conversation, we know how the love-cum-arranged marriage has taken place:

> "Veena, how much does Pinky know about sex?"
>
> "There you go being modern. What do you want her to know? Her in-laws are very conservative. They don't want one of these smart newfangled girls."
>
> "Still—" began Devi doubtfully."You and I did all right," interrupted Veena, "It's rubbish, this modern business about knowing everything before you marry." Parents had chosen one's husband, but then, as sometimes happened, as had happened to Devi, one fell tenderly, distractedly in love with him. But the Pinky-Arvind combine didn't strike her that way. Veena said with a ring of triumph in her voice, "Pinky couldn't have done better, Devi. How do you like the boy?" "Did she choose him herself?"
>
> "Yes, of course. As soon as we heard about him we arranged a meeting. And then we asked Pinky how she liked him. We put it to her frankly like that. And she gave her consent."
>
> "I hope it's going to be all right." (41)

The above conversation also reveals that Devi's marriage with Ishwar was a love marriage. But their married life does not last long as Ishwar dies very early in his life, leaving his son Rishad behind with Devi. Coming back to Pinky and her parents, this is one of the best marriages among all the marriages we have seen so far. I appreciate both Pinky and her parents—the way they have "arranged the meeting" with Pinky and Arvind and have asked their opinion before arranging the marriage. The parents are very liberal and broad-minded and are friendly with their daughter. The parents respect the choice of their daughter. Veena, the mother, is very confident and proud of her daughter's choice when Devi asks suspiciously about the love affair between Pinky and Arvind.

Devi in the same novel has a love marriage with her husband Ishwar and is a widow after her husband's death. She has a career in politics and is the Education Minister. Unlike Manasi who uses her body to become the Home Minister, Devi becomes an Education Minister on her own merit. She lives alone after resigning from her ministership and the deaths of her husband Ishwar and her son Rishad. She has a career of a cabinet minister but resigns as there is a rape case in the University Registrar's office and there is a strike and rustication of three students from the university. As an aftermath of this incident, she has had to resign her post on moral grounds. Devi is thus very different from Manasi.

Ila Das in Anita Desai's *Fire on the Mountain* (1977) remains single and has a series of jobs before she becomes a Welfare Officer. She starts her career as a lecturer in Home Science. She says to Nanda Kaul:

> You know, it wasn't easy at that time. To start teaching at the age of forty, Nanda dear, really wasn't so easy. I couldn't seem to control the girls. The teachers seemed—ooh, you know, of a different *class*, Nanda, do you understand me? And my eyes were giving way. (120)

Ila Das has started her "teaching" career very late. If you start a career "at the age of forty" it will be difficult to understand the psychology of the students. That is why Ila Das faces problems with students. She "could not control" the girl students. Even her colleagues are from a "different class." Moreover, her eyesight troubles her. She is given this job due to the influence and recommendation of Mr. Kaul, the husband of Nanda Kaul, her schoolmate:

> As for Ila, there was nothing for it but for Nanda Kaul to suggest to her husband, the Vice-Chancellor, that he

> create a job for her in the Home Science College. He had been gracious and kindly about it, and it was to this comparatively blessed period of her life, secure for a while as a lecturer, sure of her meals and a bed in the hostel, that Ila Das's jolly talk of badminton doubles and lawn parties belonged. (Desai *Fire* 124)

So the post of lecturer has been "created" in the Home Science College for her sake. She has "secured" a job "as a lecturer", is assured "meals", "bed", a game of "badminton" and "lawn parties." However, she is unable to continue the job. As she is unmarried, she has done a course in social work hoping to get a job:

> For a while her sister had kept her, literally dividing each piece of bread in two between them—fortunately the mother died before she starved—and then Nanda Kaul had heard of the course in social service which, if Ila was willing to take it, would definitely lead to a Government job and with it would go the usual emoluments of pension, provident fund and medical aid that now seemed like pieces of gold to her. She had taken the course, triumphantly collected the rubber-stamped document qualifying her to be a social worker, and arrived in the Himalayan foothills to do her duty amongst the peasants, wood-cutters, road labour and goatherds. (Desai *Fire* 125)

Ila Das has proved that one can become or try to become whatever one wants to do at any age. At the age of forty doing a course in social work and getting a job as a Welfare Officer are eye openers to girls and women who aspire to become something. Ruth K. Rosenwasser enlightens us further on the achievement of Ila Das:

> Ila Das is an example of woman's courage and strength when confronted by male dominance in terms of inheritance and education which perpetuate dependency. From her own experience, Ila Das realizes the importance of an education that will prepare women for the world outside of the home and the need for women to look

> after their own well-being. By challenging male authority, Ila Das espouses the feminist cause through her conscious need to empower women. Rather than becoming angry and destructive, she, as a social work (sic), tries to restructure the lives of the poor and oppressed village women. Ila Das feels that it is necessary to "shoulder our responsibilities and do what we can." As a heroine and a feminist, Ila Das combines energy, determination, and courage to protest male dominance which relegates women to positions of subservience and submission. (102)

Apart from this, Ila Das has been writing for magazines and journals about Home Science:

> Ila Das began to bounce again, as she piped optimistically, "I've been writing around to magazines and journals. I thought if one of them were interested in a column on home science, I could write one every month—or every week—and perhaps earn twenty rupees above my salary. Thirty rupees—" her eyes boggled behind the bifocal lenses—"thirty rupees would cover the cost of feeding me. It would be a *fortune*!" she exploded in a spray of happy spit, and swung her little legs back and forth. (Desai *Fire* 127)

Though she is working as a Welfare Officer, she has not forgotten her earlier career of teaching Home Science in the university. So she has found time to write in "magazines and journals" about "home science" in the "columns." She does this not just to be in touch with her subject but also to earn "twenty rupees" or "thirty rupees" "above [her] salary."

As a Welfare Officer, Ila Das also compares herself with the poor people, the kind of struggle she has undergone before she became a Welfare Officer. She says:

> "Oh, I *do* feel ashamed of myself," shrieked Ila Das. "Ooh, I do, when I think how much better off I am than the poor, poor people around me. Why, you wouldn't believe the things I see, Nanda. It isn't just that I have this little bit of security, this tiny bit of

> status—" she gave a shout of laughter at herself—"you know, as a welfare officer employed by the Government, while they simply starve if their cow dries up or the weevils destroy their potato crop—but the horrible, horrible degradation in which they live—ooh, Nanda," her voice plunged down, down into the deepest gloom, "why then, I *do* see the worth of our kind of upbringing after all. At least one is saved *that* degradation. (Desai *Fire* 127-128)

It is very rare that one finds welfare officers being compassionate towards the poor. She even "feels ashamed" of being their officer. She shares her experience with Nanda but Nanda cannot understand what she sees in the "poor" families. She gives examples of "cow drying up" or "the potato crop getting destroyed" or the "starvation" they face. They have such degrading lives.

Like Sita, Manasi, and Geeta who have an arranged marriage and unlike Simrit and Devi who go in for a love marriage, Shree in Raji Narasimhan's *Forever Free* (1979) has an arranged marriage. She has a B.A. degree. She shows the certificate to her father and mother. Perhaps to please Shree, her mother Dhanalakshmi shows "eighteen sovereigns of gold" (6) to her daughter. This is perhaps to indicate that now that she has got her B.A. degree, she can get prepared for her marriage. After passing B.A., Shree wants to take up dancing. Shree's mother is traditional:

> She showed me the jewellery again that night.
>
> "I want none of all this, mother."
>
> "What do you want, then?"
>
> "I just want to go dancing."[...]
>
> "Don't let anyone hear you say such things," she snapped shut a casket.
>
> "Mother."
>
> "What?"
>
> "You wanted to go away."
>
> "I did."

> "Mother, make it so for me that I don't have to go away."
>
> "You have your B.A. degree, by the grace of God."
>
> "Blast my B.A. degree! I want my freedom!" (9)

Shree does not seem to be impressed by the "jewellery" Dhanalakshmi has shown her. She openly declares that she does not want "all" that gold. Dhanalakshmi asks what does a woman who is to be married very soon want if not attractive "gold." Shree indicates that she "wants" to learn "dancing." Look at the reaction of a traditional mother. Dhanalakshmi asks her daughter "let" not any one "hear" "such things." A member of a Brahmin family going to learn dance is a kind of sin, according to Dhanalakshmi. Shree is not satisfied with Dhanalakshmi's response to her desire and reminds her mother that it was she who wanted to leave her husband. For Shree's mother, the B.A. degree is something special. Look at Shree's reaction to it. She asks her mother to "blast" her "B.A. degree." What Shree wants is not just the degree but also her "freedom" to do what she wants to. For Dhanalakshmi education is the "best weapon" that she has gifted to her daughter. She says:

> "It's the best weapon I'm giving you! What I never had. Know its value? Sillyhead?"
>
> "We look a lot alike, mother, did you know that? For all my college-going, you and I look alike, do you know?"
>
> "We are not alike! Don't say that!"
>
> "Make me some other compensation, mother!"
>
> "If you mean dancing, save your breath."
>
> "You wanted to leave your husband!"
>
> "And I'm making sure that you live with honour with yours!" (Narasimhan *Forever* 10)

One has to appreciate Dhanalakshmi providing her daughter the "weapon" of education. She also reminds her daughter of the value of "education." It is true that only people who have missed education know the real value of education but people who have enjoyed the fruits of education do not realize its true value.

Shree has no permission to take up "dancing." Meanwhile, she has a marriage proposal from Swami. Shree's parents talk about the boy's visit to see Shree. Shree demands that she should be taken into consideration with regard to her marriage:

> In the evening my mother spoke straight without fuss to my father.
>
> "The boy's coming to see her in the vacation?"
>
> I put down the food I was carrying to my mouth.
>
> "Don't you 'hear' me! Speak to me! Speak to me! Am I dead?"
>
> She kept her gaze fixed on him.
>
> "This vacation?"
>
> "Look at me and speak! I exist!"
>
> "Shree, you can exist without being spoken to, Shree," my father smiled.
>
> "But I want to exist by being spoken to! Speak to me!" (Narasimhan *Forever* 16)

Shree's parents talk about the boy's visit "to see" Shree and settle the marriage proposal. As they talk Shree overhears and speaks out. She wants to be noticed. Meanwhile her mother wants to know whether Swami is going to visit in the coming "vacation." Shree constantly makes a point that she "exists." She is not a passive or dead woman. I am sure Shree is telling her parents that she is educated and she will have certain preferences and choices in marriage. She is indeed making her point that she too should be spoken to about her marriage. She also vehemently expresses her dislike of marrying Swami. The reason she gives for refusing to marry Swami is presented as follows:

> When they left, the play-acting went. The three of us looked at each other.
>
> My mother tackled me without ado.
>
> "You're not saying no."

> "Why?"
>
> "Are you?"
>
> "I might. I have every right to!"
>
> "Burn your right! Burn yourself! And then burn us both, your father and mother." [...]
>
> "Father!"
>
> "Yes?"
>
> "I can't marry him, father."
>
> "Can't you, Shree? Is it that final?"
>
> "Father, he didn't look at me right even once."
>
> "I'll search another boy for you, Shree" (Narasimhan *Forever* 19).

Swami has come to see Shree along with his family members and returns. Shree and her parents have to decide. Therefore, the three of them "look at each other." Dhanalakshmi insists that Shree "not" say "no" to the proposal. Shree questions her mother's attitude of taking her for granted. Shree feels she "has every right" to say "no" if he is not up to her expectations. Look at Dhanalakshmi's reaction to her daughter's response to her question. She asks her daughter to "burn" herself first, "and then burn both," her "father and mother." Most of the parents put forth this exploitative argument before the woman who is then compelled to marry despite her dislike. After hearing her mother's reaction to her saying no she now addresses her father and tells him that she "can't marry him." In order to confirm her opinion her father asks once again whether that is her "final" decision. At this juncture, Shree gives her reasons as to why she does not want to marry him. She says that the man did not even look at her once. Perhaps this has hurt her. She feels that Swami who has come to see the girl he is to marry has no individuality even to look at her once. He seems to be obliging his parents, rather than making his own decision. The father seems understanding enough to agree to look for someone else. However, Shree seems to understand her retired father's tension at having his daughter not married even after his retirement. Though she is not keen on marrying a man like Swami, she agrees to marry him, taking her father's tensions into consideration. Look at her innermost thoughts:

> No, you can't father, you can't. You don't ask the right way. You are tired. You never make it sound important enough. You make it sound so sad, father, gloomy, like the way you handed me over to Swami's father just now, both palms stretched out to him in such complete surrender. (Narasimhan *Forever* 20)

Having read her father's feelings, she gives her consent to her mother. So she is marrying Swami not out of complete willingness but to make her parents happy.

At the marriage ceremony Swami realises that Shree is not marrying him of her own accord. When either the bride or the bridegroom is not interested in marriage, she or he is reluctant about everything. She or he does not enjoy all the rituals of the marriage ceremony. So Swami asks Shree: "You are not marrying me of your own will" (Narasimhan *Forever* 27). She immediately asks him: "Are you?" (Narasimhan *Forever* 27). These are incidents that will lead to an unhappy married life. Furthermore, Swami is completely under the control of his mother. He also has a low opinion of women. He feels that they are nothing but sexual objects and ought to just listen to what the husband says. He seems to be a male chauvinist. He cannot bear certain things in Shree and uses his mother to ill-treat her. The first shock for Swami is Shree calling him by his name, while they are talking about the clothes women wear:

> He placed his palm on my body. "All this clothing. What things do ladies wear?"
>
> "Many things."
>
> "I am very innocent about these matters."
>
> "Are you? O it does not matter, Swami. See, I'm calling you by name. I know you don't like it. One day will you show me Arundhati? I never saw Arundhati. Did you?" (Narasimhan *Forever* 30)

Shree knows that he does not like his wife calling him by his name. Many of the husbands don't like their wives calling them by their names including educated men. Look at another of Shree's comments that irritates him—not having seen the star, "Arundhati" on her wedding day. She asks him whether he can show her the star. She asks him whether he has seen it.

Having seen Shree's attitude towards him Swami starts harassing her:

> "You have a mole here on this side of your neck. It's big. What does it mean? You must tell me what it means."
>
> "It does not mean cancer."
>
> "How can you tell now? Do you have any more? Let me examine you properly. Let me see the lines on your hand. The fate line and life-line must never meet in a woman's hand. They do, in your hand. Clearly." (Narasimhan *Forever* 30)

Swami seems to be trying to make Shree feel guilty about her "mole" and "long toes." He asks her for an explanation. In other words he is trying to trace all negative things in her. He goes on to say:

> "Look at your feet. The second toe is longer than the big."
>
> "What does that mean Swamy?"
>
> "It means adultery, they say." (Narasimhan *Forever* 30)

K. Meera Bai in her article, "Feminism as an Extension of Existentialism: Woman in Indian English Fiction" says: "She feels crushed when Swami reads adultery in her second toe which is bigger than the first. She is disillusioned about her relationship with Swami the very first day and is left with a feeling that her self is insulted and her body handled without care" (29). One is puzzled as to why Swami is pointing out all these negative things in her. This goes further:

> His hand swept down my body. "You have not enough fat? Why is that?"[...]
>
> "And your toes, the second longer than the first. I am afraid of that. I am very much afraid." (Narasimhan *Forever* 31)

In the above lines he is commenting on her lean "body." He is perhaps hinting that she has some disease. Also when he points to the "adultery" sign in her feet, he is perhaps deliberately criticizing and making her feel low about the shortcomings in her body. All this criticism is only because she has called him by his name. He has already started taking revenge on her.

One more reason why Shree takes divorce from Swami is that he is a pet of his mother as has already been mentioned. He does not have any individuality. He takes his mother's side rather than his wife's. Most of the wives would like their husbands to be on their side. Here is an example of Swami being on his mother's side:

> "And so the daughter-in-law has shown her paces!" Swami squatted on the kitchen doorstep. "She doesn't yet look the part, does she, mother? All that fluffy hair. Lovelocks they are called, do you know mother? Pull her lovelocks back and make her a tight, respectable plait, mother."
>
> "By and by, son, by and by. It's just launched, she is."
>
> "I want that ego of hers scorched and buried." (Narasimhan *Forever* 53-54)

Swami wants his wife to adjust and adapt herself to his family. He does not like her hairstyle. He does not express his feelings to his wife. Rather he asks his mother to bring necessary changes in her. What more does a mother-in-law want than this type of a son giving her this kind of a freedom to harass the daughter-in-law? Swami wants his wife's "ego" to be "scorched" and "buried."

In order to bury her daughter-in-law's "ego," Shree's mother-in-law deliberately makes her daughter-in-law serve food to all the family members:

> "Serve all those men you see sitting there. You know who they are? Yes, you know. The menfolk of the family. Each your superior in station! Don't like me saying this? But it's only a fact of life."
>
> She firmed the platter in my hand.

> "Serve them. Bend low. Serve them with humility." (Narasimhan *Forever* 50)

The way Shree's mother-in-law asks her to "serve" the men in the family is to intimidate her. She stresses on the "men" sitting there. She proudly mentions them as the "menfolk of the family." Moreover, they are "superior in station." In what way they are superior one does not know. Perhaps she means in terms of gender and age. However, what they are doing is not known. At the same time the mother-in-law reminds her that it is a "fact of life" and that she has to respect the menfolk. Furthermore, she asks Shree to "bend" low to serve food, as a mark of respect and "humility." How can an "educated" wife bear all this humiliation, making her feel that she has been brought to their home out of pity?

Shree's mother-in-law continues to harass Shree and kill her ego. One day she takes Shree to a temple and asks her whether she has prayed to god to give her a son:

> "Did you pray to Devi to give you a son?" Swami's mother asked me when we came out.
>
> "Yes," I said with good conscience. For I had been prayerful even if not praying.
>
> "How glad I am. You must deliver more. One every year, year after year. Are you afraid? Are you afraid you'll be ripped to death?"
>
> "That's not my fear," I tipped forward my braid and felt its thick, artful weave with false hair.
>
> "What is your fear?"
>
> "Nothing physical." My hands halted on the knob of the false hair they had set into my real hair.
>
> "Nothing physical? Then what's the delay? Do you want to be like your mother? Producing one child and sealing up your tubes afterwards?"[...]
>
> "Let me think it over," I said calmly, but laughing.
>
> "No thinking over," she caught my hand.
>
> [...] "And you have him on leash for the rest of your life! Understand? Give him full run of your body, then.

> Easy thing. Just let him tire himself out. And see him droop and sway to you afterwards." (Narasimhan *Forever* 56)

Shree informs her mother-in-law that she has done so. But her mother-in-law wonders if Shree is "afraid" of delivering the children until she is ripped to death. She warns her that she should not "think" on the lines of her "mother producing one child" and planning on a small family. Swami's mother is dictating terms to Shree about producing more and more male children. She asks Shree to "give him [Swami] full run of [her] body" until he "tires himself." She says this as though Shree has no part to play in this.

Shree finds the situation she is in with Swami unbearable. She decides to divorce him. There is a cousin of Swami called Vasu who has interest in literature and philosophy and loves to discuss books with Shree. Swami suspects she has had an extra-marital relationship with Vasu and wants to perform *shudhdhi* on her in order to continue having her as his wife, Swami says:

> "You are in need of cleansing."[...]
>
> "Witchcraft? Sorcery?"
>
> "Priescraft. Prayer. The priest comes at dawn tomorrow. He will perform the *Shudhdhi* ceremony on you. He will call upon the earth to draw you down into her jaws, lick away the impurities and spit you out wiped clean."
>
> "A clean wife to you. Yes? Swami?"
>
> "A clean wife to me, yes."
>
> "But not a clean woman. I want to be a clean woman, Swami. Will the priest clean me as a woman and not as your wife? You can't answer that, can you? You can't believe that I feel soiled a thousand times over, a million times over what you describe? It's my personal curse, my personal defilement, all my own. And I want a personal purification, my very own. Can you understand that?" (Narasimhan *Forever* 69-70)

Shree very diplomatically asks her husband to recommend to the priest to make her "a clean woman" not a "clean wife." She does want to be a cleansed woman, breaking clear of the ties of marriage. She also feels upset for being "soiled a thousand times over and a million times over." She wants to have a personal "purification" on her own.

Moreover, Swami asks his wife to abort the foetus as he feels that she has conceived because of her affair with Vasu. He says:

> "Can you choke this child of yours, Shree? Can you pretend he was never born? Can you swallow your ego, wretched woman? Be my wife, Shree! Forget all else. Walk round the fire with me again. Be woman by being my wife."
>
> "I am that yet, Swami. Woman by being your wife. You unwive me by wanting me re-wived. But I feel unwomaned. Shouldn't I be woman again to be wife, Swami?"
>
> "There's no help for you. The devil take you." He went back down the steps.
>
> I knew that a divorce had been pronounced. The room was absolutely quiet. So was the staircase. (Narasimhan *Forever* 70)

His obsession with chastity and his desire for a wife can be seen in his asking her to abort the foetus, in having a purificatory ritual and in performing the marriage rites once again after the purificatory process. She would rather be a "woman," an individual.

Raji Narasimhan seems to suggest that as long as the traditional kind of mother-in-law like Shree's and a husband like Swami exist, women who marry traditionally will suffer. They try to have control over a person like Shree. This may lead to divorce. In every possible manner, Swami and his mother try to have a hold on her. Shree would not have married him but does so only to oblige her father.

After leaving her husband she comes back home. Her father does not have anything against her but her mother cannot tolerate her leaving her husband and coming to her parents. She is not going to allow her daughter to stay with them. Her mother says:

> "What am I to do with you, luckless, ill-starred one? Cut loose?"
>
> "You wanted to be a cut-loose too, mother."
>
> She released me.
>
> "Go. Rent a flat. That's what you have to do. Pay rent every month and buy shelter for yourself."
>
> "How? You'll pay my rent, mother?"
>
> "I pay you nothing. I owe you nothing. You will get yourself a job."
>
> "I am trained for nothing, mother."
>
> "You are smart. You speak English."
>
> "And I am a B.A. Don't forget that."
>
> "You will find yourself a job. You have that luck granted to you." (Narasimhan *Forever* 77).

The mother, caught up in the traditional patriarchal set-up, is unable to accept her daughter's decision. Shree is, in a sense, forced to lead her own life in a "rented" flat. Her education comes in handy in finding a job.

She takes up "journalism" and looks after herself. I feel that her education up to B.A. gives her this confidence. She need not depend on her mother. In fact she wanted to depend on her mother. But her mother has forced her to become independent. There is no career as such for Shree. She works for a newspaper named "The National Scenery." Shree should be appreciated considering the circumstances under which she is forced to take up a job and to withstand the situation.

As a divorced woman she becomes very close to Rao. They enjoy life together. They booze and attend parties. They also have an affair. Then she is introduced to Carruthers, an Englishman. The association with Carruthers also results in an affair. He sees her as a goddess. In both these cases, the men have viewed her only as an object to satisfy their desires. Her father dies and she goes back to her mother and lives with her. After uniting with her mother she feels that she is forever free from men. She has a company of a woman, none other than her own mother. She is a divorcee and her mother is a widow. Both of them being single women thus feel forever free from men.

In the 1970s, we have seen how women react to various kinds of marriages and to the careers they opt. Sita raises an important question about a woman's choice to become a mother. Simrit opts out of an unfulfilled marriage to write; Lalitha opts to act in a documentary film but fails in the attempt; Geeta takes the right path in educating the underprivileged not caring for financial gains; Manasi and Devi enter politics for the first time in women's fiction and go up to the level of ministers. While one uses her body to do it, the other fights her way up the ladder. Ila Das changes different jobs to settle down as a Welfare Officer stressing that age is no bar. Shree after leaving her husband and mother becomes a journalist, and finally re-unites with her mother and remains forever free. Women like Simrit and Shree take divorce to emphasize their individuality. Between the two, one finds another man she wants to marry while the other remains a divorcee. Thus, in this decade we find at least some women protesting openly against stereotyped roles and trying to assert their individuality.

WORKS CITED

Bai, K. Meera. "Feminism as an Extension of Existentialism: Women in Indian English Fiction." *Indian Women Novelists Set III: Vol. I.* Ed. R.K. Dhawan. New Delhi: Prestige, 1995. 26-32.

——. "Husband-Wife Alienation in the Novels of Nayantara Sahgal and Anita Desai." *Indian Women Novelists Set I: Vol. I.* Ed. R.K. Dhawan. New Delhi: Prestige, 1995. 167-176.

Bhasin, Kamal. "From Modernity to 'Purdah': Geeta's Acculturation in Rama Mehta's *Inside the Haveli.*" *Women in Indo-Anglian Fiction: Tradition and Modernity.* Ed. Naresh K. Jain. New Delhi: Manohar, 1998. 114-127.

Choubey, Asha. "*The Day in Shadow*: A Study in Inertia and Submission." *Post-Independence Indian English Fiction*. Ed. Rajeshwar Mittapalli and Alessandro Monti. New Delhi: Atlantic, 2001. 77-87.

Das, Kamala. *Alphabet of Lust*. 1976. New Delhi: Orient, 1978.

Desai, Anita. *Where Shall We Go This Summer?* 1975. Delhi: Orient, 1994.

——. *Fire on the Mountain*. 1977. Delhi: Allied, 1990.

Drum, Alice. "Kamala Markandaya's Modern Quest Tale." *World Literature Written in English*. 22.2 (1983): 323-332.

Geetha, P. "Images and Archetypes in Kamala Markandaya's Novels: A Study in Cultural Ambivalence." *Journal of Commonwealth Literature* 26.1 (1991): 169-178.

Krishnaraj, Maithreyi. "Motherhood: Power and Powerlessness." *Indian Women: Myth and Reality*. Ed. Jasodhara Bagchi. Calcutta: Sangam, 1995. 34-43.

Lal, Malashri. "Rama Mehta's *Inside the Haveli*: A Discourse on Gender and Class." *The Law of the Threshold: Women Writers in Indian English*. Shimla: IIAS, 1995. 81-103.

Markandaya, Kamala. *Two Virgins*. 1973. London: Chatto & Windus, 1974.

Mehta, Rama. *Inside the Haveli*. 1977. New Delhi: Penguin, 1996.

Narsimhan, Raji. *Forever Free*. Delhi: Hind, 1979.

Rajendra, Susheela P. "A Journey towards Freedom, from Fear: A Study of the Feminine Sensibility in Nayantara Sahgal's *The Day in Shadow*." *Indian Women Novelists: Set III: Vol. 5*. Ed. R.K. Dhawan. New Delhi: Prestige, 1995. 230-235.

Rani, T. Ashoka. "Nayantara Sahgal's *The Day in Shadow*: A Feminist Perspective." *New Perspectives on Indian Writing*. Ed. V.L.V.N. Narendra Kumar. New Delhi: Prestige, 1997. 68-75.

Rosenwasser, Ruth K. "Voices of Dissent: Heroines in the Novels of Anita Desai." *Journal of South-Asian Literature* 24.2 (1989): 83-116.

Sahgal, Nayantara. *The Day in Shadow*. 1971. New Delhi: Penguin, 1991.

——. *A Situation in Delhi*. New Delhi: Himalaya, 1977.

Singh, Avadhesh Kumar. "The Element of Protest in Kamala Markandaya." *Contemporary Indian Fiction in English*. Ed. Avadhesh Kumar Singh. New Delhi: Creative, 1993. 117-124.

Srivastava, K.C. "The Novels of Kamala Das: Quest for Identity." *The Indian Novel in English: Essays in Criticism*. Ed. Ravi Nandan Sinha and R.K. Singh. Ranchi: Ankit, 1987. 117-122.

Vaidya, Shruti. "The Rejoicing Victim—A Sudy of Nayantara Sahgal's Simrit." *Victim Consciousness in Indian English Novel*. Ed. Usha Bande. Jalandhar: ABS, 1997. 74-80.

NOTES

1. In an interview by Atma Ram entitled "Interview with Nayantara Sahgal" published in a book edited by him, *Interviews with Indian English Writers* (Calcutta: Writers' Workshop, 1983), Nayantara Sahgal says: "Of the five novels I have written, only *The Day in Shadow* was autobiographical, i.e., based on my own life's experience. Otherwise bits of my heroines and of other characters have been drawn from my own personal experience, but *The Day in Shadow* took its main theme, that of a disastrous financial settlement made at divorce, from my own situation" (46). I quote this here to indicate that even the writer herself found the issue of "divorce" problematic.

"Self Determination and Assertiveness": The 1980s

5

In this chapter, I will deal with the following "educated" women characters to discuss the issue of marriage: Tara, Bim, Jaya and Sarla from Anita Desai's *Clear Light of Day* (1980), Saru from Shashi Deshpande's *The Dark Holds No Terrors* (1980), Indu from Shashi Deshpande's *Roots and Shadows* (1983), Paro and Priya from Namita Gokhale's *Paro: Dreams of Passion* (1984), Sonali from Nayantara Sahgal's *Rich Like Us* (1985), Jaya from Shashi Deshpande's *That Long Silence* (1988), Karuna and Anjali from Shobha De's *Socialite Evenings* (1988). Bim, Jaya and Sarla from Anita Desai's *Clear Light of Day* (1980), Saru from Shashi Deshpande's *The Dark Holds No Terrors* (1980), Priya from Namita Gokhale's *Paro: Dreams of Passion* (1984), Sonali from Nayantara Sahgal's *Rich Like Us* (1985), Jaya from Shashi Deshpande's *That Long Silence* (1988), Karuna and Anjali from Shobha De's *Socialite Evenings* (1988) will be taken up to see how the question of career is discussed in the novels. Jaya and Sarla from Anita Desai's *Clear Light of Day* (1980), Paro and Priya from Namita Gokhale's *Paro: Dreams of Passion* (1984), Karuna and Anjali from Shobha De's *Socialite Evenings* (1988) will be looked at keeping in mind the theme of divorce.

Tara in Anita Desai's *Clear Light of Day* (1980) falls in love with Bakul. Tara makes Bakul request her elder sister Bim to arrange a marriage between them. Here is a love-cum-arranged marriage. Unlike in the previous decade where the first novel dealt with love marriage, the first novel of this decade deals with a love-cum-arranged marriage. Bim's consent is necessary because she will have to take care of Baba, a handicapped brother if Tara marries Bakul for their brother Raja had already left them after marrying Hyder Ali's daughter. Bakul talks to Bim:

> "Bim," he [Bakul] said again with unusual suddenness, "would it add to your own worries or would it lessen them if Tara marries me?" "What?" She was startled. [...] "Oh. Oh, I see. You want to marry Tara. Yes, I thought you did. I think she wants to marry you too."
>
> "Yes, she says she does but wanted me to speak to you first." "Oh, did she?" laughed Bim. "I'm head of the family now, am I? You think so, so I must be." She shrugged, looking plain again. "I don't think you need to ask anyone—except Tara. Modern Times. Modern India. Independent India." [...]
>
> "I [Bakul] can speak to Raja, of course, if you think I should." "No, don't worry him," she said sharply.
>
> "I don't like you having all the worries of the family."
>
> "You are lessening them, aren't you, by taking Tara off my hands?" "Will I? Or is she a help to you? In that case, I won't press her now—not till later when Raja is well and Baba settled and your aunt—" [...] "There is no need to wait. Do marry—quickly. But what about your parents?"
>
> "They know Tara. They love her. And since I am to go to Ceylon shortly, they will agree to an early marriage."
>
> "An early marriage—that is exactly what I'd like for Tara," Bim said. "It will suit her. And she will suit you. Blessings, blessings," she called lightly, and began to laugh again as she saw Tara, half-hidden behind the bamboo screen at her door, listening, waiting. (Desai *Clear Light* 81)

Tara is clever in seeing to it that her choice of marrying Bakul is accepted. She makes Bakul talk about their marriage to her sister Bim. She knows that in the present scenario she cannot wait for her sister to get married. Therefore, she sends Bakul to convince Bim about their marriage. They have no parents. It is

Bim who has to accept their marriage. If she accepts, then there is no problem. Bakul is the Indian Ambassador to Sri Lanka. She wants to escape from the responsibility of their mentally retarded brother like her elder brother Raja. Tara is also clever enough to escape from a joint family system to a nuclear family. As Renu Juneja observes: "For Tara, marriage also provides escape from a strange, unhappy household. We may note Desai's care in avoiding all hints of self-sacrificing womanhood in Tara by making her escape into marriage during a time of immense crisis for the family—when, after the death of the parents, Bim must cope with Raja's illness and Aunt Mira's alcoholism" (83). Bim does not protest against both of them. She knows their intentions. She is a History lecturer in a college. She never tries to escape from her responsibilities. She too had an opportunity of getting married to Dr. Biswas who was very much interested in marrying her. I feel many academics would not like to escape from their responsibilities, as many of them are conscientious people. Thus Bim is not tempted to escape from the responsibility towards Baba. Dr. Biswas himself makes a statement as to why Bim does not want to marry him. She is not selfish. She has a moral responsibility. Tara's basic idea is to be in a nuclear family. She does not want to live in a joint family. It is inevitable that the nuclear family has its own advantages like less work, less expenditure, luxurious life, small family, enough privacy etc.

Unlike Tara, Bim remains unmarried out of both compulsion and choice. There is a compulsion because both her younger brother Raja and younger sister Tara escape from the responsibility of looking after their mentally retarded brother Baba. According to P. Bhatnagar, Bim "[...] opts out of marriage so that she could devote herself to the care of her mentally-retarded brother Baba, her old Mira-*Masi* and her younger brother Raja who she was very fond of" (151). When Bim and Tara discuss the Misra boys getting married without completing any degree, Bim says:

> "But they're not *educated* yet," Bim said sharply. "They haven't any degrees.

> They should go to college," she insisted.
>
> "Why?" said Tara [...]
>
> "Why?" repeated Bim indignantly. "Why, because they might find marriage isn't enough to last them the whole of their lives," she said darkly, mysteriously.
>
> "What else could there be?" countered Tara. "I mean," she fumbled, "for them."
>
> "What *else*?" asked Bim. "Can't you think? I can think of hundreds of things to do instead. *I* won't marry," she added, very firmly. (Desai *Clear Light* 140)

The above quotation shows how Bim is committed to education. Bim does not view marriage as the most significant thing in a person's life. Rosenwasser claims, "Bim's remaining unmarried is voluntary, a choice, based on the negative images of her mother, her sister and her aunt. Her admirer, Dr. Biswas, misunderstands Bim's refusal to marry, assuming that her family responsibilities cause her to sacrifice her own future" (105). I do agree with Rosenwasser's view that Bim remaining unmarried is "voluntary" and "a choice" based on the negative images of the women members of her family. However, I do not agree with Rosenwasser's view that Dr. Biswas misunderstands Bim's "refusal to marry" him due to her "family responsibilities." It is true that Bim has refused to marry Dr. Biswas, as there is no one to look after her mentally retarded brother Baba. A. Clement reinforces my argument: "Bimla, the enlightened and emancipated heroine [...] chooses to stay single to take care of her retarded younger brother, spurning the offer of help of the others including the offer of marriage of their young family doctor [Dr. Biswas]" (238). Both Raja and Tara have left for Hyderabad and Sri Lanka respectively, leaving Bim alone. Otherwise Bim has no reason to refuse to marry Dr. Biswas. So both her brother and sister are escapists, leaving the responsibilities to Bim. Ultimately Bim has to sacrifice any thought of marriage. An opportunity to marry Dr. Biswas who was interested in her slips away from her. But she makes it appear as if it is her choice of remaining unmarried. She dedicates her life to teaching.

As far as career is concerned, "[...] Bim takes up a teaching job after finishing her education and also takes care of Raja, Baba and Aunt Mira" (Gupta 239). Teaching is her own choice and is not forced upon her by anyone. Bim tells Tara: "I shall work—I shall *do* things," she went on, "I shall earn my own living—and look after Mira-*masi* and Baba and be independent" (Desai 40). Bim is very keen on making her students too become aware of this idea of "independence" and "independent thought." Rosenwasser says: "Bimla's determination to instil independent thought and self-sufficiency in her students results from her anger at the deficiencies of her own education: 'I'm always trying to teach them, train them to be different from what we were at their age—to be a new kind of woman from you or me—and if they knew how badly handicapped I still am'" (104).

Bim is very determined to work as she says that she "shall" "earn" her "own living" not just for her own sake, but in order to look after "Mira-*masi* and Baba" who are her dependents. Moreover, she wants to be independent. This word "independent" is very crucial for Bim. In other words she wants to say that an "educated" woman has to earn and be "independent." Her use of the modal "shall" suggests her determination in choosing a career.

In the same novel it is not clear as to what kind of marriage the neighbours of Tara and Bim, Jaya and Sarla have. But we know that Jaya and Sarla who are also called "the Misra sisters" are married but have been abandoned by their husbands. Under forced circumstances, they run a school after their husbands abandon them. Since it is their own school, they are able to show to the society that they too have some work. Though they look after the school, they teach without loving the children. It is not a career for them. It is only to cover up their lost prestige. They behave that way. In fact, they need not feel bad that they are abandoned. They can even declare that they have been abandoned. Because they teach without love for teaching, Bim expresses her hatred for them. Bim says:

> "Least is the right word—the very least," said Bim with asperity. "I think they hate it really—they hate children, they hate teaching."
>
> "Do they?" said Tara, shocked. Hate was a word that always shocked her. The image of a dead dog immediately rose before her, bleeding. "Then they shouldn't teach."
>
> "Oh they don't say they do—perhaps they don't even know they do—but you can see it by the way they look, so haggard and eaten up." (Desai *Clear Light* 151)

Bim's comment is very crucial here for those who "teach." A teacher should have love for her "children" and for "teaching." Otherwise he/she should not teach. Tara is shocked to know that Jaya and Sarla do not "love children" and "teaching."

Coming to the issue of divorce, Jaya and Sarla have not been legally divorced but they can be considered under the "divorce category." As P.F. Patil rightly says: "[T]he Misra daughters, Jaya and Sarla, belong to the 'once married' category, used and thrown away like old pieces of comfortless furniture" (141). The husbands of Jaya and Sarla do not give them divorce in legal terms but they have abandoned them for reasons stated below:

> "And Jaya and Sarla," Tara said sympathetically, almost tearfully, feeling for them as well as for herself, feeling for all women, helpless and abandoned.
>
> "Poor things."
>
> "Yes, abandoned by their husbands. Isn't it odd how they were married together and abandoned together?"
>
> "Abandoned? Are they actually divorced?"
>
> "I think they are—but it's not a word that's used in their family, you know. In their case, it was the husbands who were too modern, too smart. They played golf and they danced and gave cocktail parties. Imagine poor Jaya and Sarla who only ever wanted to knit them sweaters and make them pickles. They soon came home to Papa and Mama—were *sent* home, actually. For years they used to talk of going back to their husbands and

> make up reasons for not joining them where they were—they were in the army and the navy, I think, which was convenient. Now I notice they no longer do. Now all they talk about is their school."
>
> "At least they have that."
>
> "Least is the right word—the very least" said Bim with asperity. "I think they hate it really—they hate children, they hate teaching." (Desai *Clear Light* 151)

Jaya and Sarla have been shown sympathy for their abandoned condition. Tara seems to be very sensitive in "feeling" pity for Jaya and Sarla and for such women generally. She feels particularly odd that they were "married together and abandoned together." From the above conversation it is clear that they are not legally divorced but are separated or "abandoned." Jaya and Sarla's parents are very secretive. They do not reveal whether their daughters are divorced or abandoned. However, they are separated and not on talking terms. The husbands of Jaya and Sarla seem to be smarter than the Misra girls. They enjoy playing "golf" and "giving cocktail parties." On the other hand, Jaya and Sarla seem to be interested only in "knitting sweaters" and "making pickles" for the husbands. The couples seem to be incompatible. They were "*sent*" back to their "homes" very early after their marriage. When anyone asks them about their going back to their "husbands," they make up false reasons. Finally, they stop talking about their husbands; rather they talk of their school which is owned by their parents.

On the other hand, Saru in Shashi Deshpande's *The Dark Holds No Terrors* (1980) has a love marriage with her collegemate Manohar who is a lecturer in a degree college. As Barche remarks, "Against her parents' wishes, Saru married a boy from a lower caste. Her marriage to Manu is a sign of her turning away from the traditional ways and values her orthodox mother adhered to. She married to attain autonomy of the self and to secure the love lost in her parental home" (86-87). If the parents do not provide "love" to their daughter, it is obvious that she will seek love from outsiders, like Saru seeking Manohar's love. However, after marriage there are problems between the couple. The main reason for Saru going in for a love marriage is that her mother hates her. She does not allow her to do whatever she wants to do. Her mother discourages her in every respect. Barche further says: "Saru receives education in spite of her mother. Her education makes her see the difference in the treatment of a son and a daughter by the same parents" (86). Why do parents, especially mothers, not permit their daughters to go in for higher studies? Vijaya Lakshmi Pandit gives the answer in the following lines:

> Even in middle class urban families sending girls to higher studies is considered to be a wastage of money because, they have to go for a bridegroom with high educational qualification. An employed bachelor with higher qualification means more amount of dowry. Increasing cost of education, i.e, admission fees, transportation, textbooks etc. prevent some parents from sending their daughters to higher studies. (29-30)

Moreover, Saru's mother pampers her son and neglects her in every respect. For example, look at her attitude towards her daughter:

> Don't you go out in the sun. You'll get even darker.
>
> Who cares?
>
> We have to care if you don't. We have to get you married.
>
> I don't want to get married.
>
> Will you live with us all your life?
>
> Why not?
>
> You can't.
>
> And Dhruva?
>
> He's different. He's a boy. (Deshpande *The Dark* 45)

Kamala, Saru's mother, feels a burden about her responsibility. Her attitude makes Saru react that she does not intend to marry. Saru wants to continue to be a burden on her mother. Saru feels that she has been neglected. Later on, when she wants to marry Manu, her mother reacts: "I know all these 'love marriages.' It's love for a few days, then quarrels all the time. Don't come crying to us then. To you? God, that's the one thing I'll do. Never!"(69)

Saru's mother Kamala is of the strong opinion that "love marriage" means quarrelling, as if there are no quarrels in arranged marriages. She feels that the effect of "love" will last only "for a few days." Her mother is very confident that Saru will come to her crying but she will have no time or sympathy if such a thing happens.

Saru has married into a nuclear family. She marries Manohar against her parents' wishes. It is an escape from her mother's clutches. Saru's mother would have found her a match in a joint family. Saru's mother tries to curb Saru's interests and likings so much that she is aware she will never be happy with her mother's choice. Perhaps that is the reason why Saru chooses Manohar as her husband and marries him. The fact that Saru's mother discourages Saru's interest to pursue medicine reveals how narrow minded her mother is. Can any mother curb her daughter's interest, questioning the use of education for girls after a certain age? This is the biggest reason for Saru choosing Manohar as her husband. In fact, Saru has eased her parents' burden regarding her marriage. Saru opts for a nuclear family. However, she is not happy with her choice. The reason is that Manohar does not understand her fully. He develops a complex as he earns less than her. The society is also responsible for their problems. But her mother is not willing to forgive her even on her deathbed.

Saru flirts with Boozie, as there is a misunderstanding between her and Manohar. It is quite natural that if there are misunderstandings between a couple, either of them starts flirting with the opposite sex as Saru does with Boozie here. However, later she discovers that Boozie is gay. This relationship does not affect her marriage drastically; nor does it lead to any divorce. In other words, Saru has respect for the institution of marriage.

Saru has chosen the career on her own. In Sarabjit Sandhu's words: "She is brought up in a traditional atmosphere but the education she receives makes her a changed person with a rebellious attitude towards tradition. As an educated young woman, she does not accept anything without reason. Her mother almost forces her to stay within the four-walls of the house. She does not give her permission to take admission in the medical college, but Saru does not listen to her [...]" (88). However, it is not an easy choice for her, as she has to convince her father. Baba asks Saru:

> "What subject do you want to take up for your B.Sc., Saru?"
>
> "I'm not going on for a B.Sc." [...]
>
> "I want to do medicine," I [Saru] said. [...]
>
> "You mean you want to become a doctor?" [...]
>
> "Are you sure you want to do it? Have you thought it over?"
>
> "Yes, Baba."
>
> "You can't change your mind later. This isn't something like taking singing lessons."
>
> I flushed. Why remind me of that?
>
> "I am eighteen now. Not a child."
>
> "It isn't easy. You'll have to work enormously hard."
>
> "I know that. I can work." (Deshpande *The Dark* 141-143)

Saru is very determined to do "medicine." She expresses her desire to do medicine but not "B.Sc." Baba is testing Saru by reminding her that doing medicine is not a joke and it is not like opting for "singing lessons" and abandoning the singing lessons when one is not interested. She asserts and tells Baba that she is old enough and is aware of the "work" involved in studying medicine. It is very rare that an "educated" woman chooses her career with so much of confidence. She is able to convince her father and he has no other doubt about her choice.

Some years later, Saru starts practising as a doctor and earns more than her husband Manohar. As Meenakshi Shivram rightly says: "She [Saru] is a doctor; financially independent, and runs her family of husband and two children with her earnings. Her husband, Manohar (Manu), does not belong to her privileged caste. He also finds it increasingly difficult not to depend upon his wife's earnings which is substantially much more than his" (180). Here the caste issue has been raised. Even in love marriages the caste issues become prominent, especially when the wife earns more than the husband. The husband will have guilty feeling about it. Premila Paul also feels that "the career becomes an indispensable crutch as it gives her so much importance and power over the others" (63). It may appear as if Saru has obtained some power over Manu in terms of the income she earns. There is no doubt that Saru has obtained power over Manu in terms of the income she earns.

Like Saru,[1] Indu in Shashi Deshpande's *Roots and Shadows* (1983) goes in for a love marriage with Jayant and unlike Geeta in *Inside the Haveli* who goes from a nuclear family to a joint family after her marriage with Ajay. As T. Ashoka Rani says, "Indu [...] views marriage as a gateway to freedom and marries Jayant, a man of her choice defying her authoritarian family" (127). Although there are no direct references to love marriage, we do get some sense of Indu and Jayant's marriage from the following conversation:

> "Can I massage your head, Atya? I've become an expert now. Jayant has headaches like you. Then I have to sit and massage his head like this until he goes off to sleep." I felt her hand on my wrist for a second. "Are you happy with him, Indu?"
>
> "Happy? Who can say that? But I know I can't be without him."
>
> "How glad I am, Indu, it's all right. I can remember Akka saying, 'Such marriages never work. Different castes, different languages [...] it's all right for a while. Then they realise [...]'" (Deshpande *Roots* 67-68)

Akka is the eldest and the guardian of the family. She does not approve of Indu's marriage with Jayant. Nor do any of the family members dare approve and invite them. Akka believes that "love marriages" do not work. Love marriage could involve "different castes" and perhaps "different languages." Falling in love might not last a life-time. It is almost like Saru's mother's belief in *The Dark Holds No Terrors*. Akka is an important person in the family. Kaka is also afraid of Akka and does not invite Indu with her husband after their marriage. He says:

> "How does it feel to be back, Indu?" Kaka asked me. "You don't know how happy I feel to see you home. I felt guilty we never asked you to come home with your husband. The first Divali [...] I did think of it. But Akka [...]"
>
> "Really, Kaka! The way you talk! Why were you so terrified of Akka? What did you imagine she would do to you if you disobeyed?"
>
> "It's not that, Indu. You people will never understand. For our generation, elders were to be feared, respected, obeyed. We used to sit up when they entered the room, and touch their feet when we went out; yet there was affection too." [...]
>
> "You youngsters now...you're a different breed altogether." (Deshpande *Roots* 46).

Akka has made Indu her legal heir and also the head of the family. Therefore, Kaka asks Indu how she feels returning to the family which did not even invite her with her husband for the first "Divali" after their marriage.

Indu marries Jayant who comes from a joint family but decides to live in a nuclear family after marriage. She marries him without her parents' consent. However, she later on moves from a nuclear family to a joint family again as she has been made an heir to Akka's family. Financial power in a joint family system is very crucial. Even "educated" women are willing to run a joint family provided they are given financial power as we see from two examples, one of Geeta in *Inside the Haveli* and the other of Indu in this novel. Why does Indu accept the responsibility? Did she not protest against the system when she was part of it? Was she not against the system when she married Jayant? Why this dual view? Why this opportunism?

Moreover, Indu has a guiltless extra-marital relationship with Naren, like Gauri with Vishal in *Storm in Chandigarh* and Manasi with Vijaya Raje in *Alphabet of Lust*. I call it a guiltless relationship because nowhere does Indu feel that she is wrong in having an affair with Naren. There is a reason why she is involved in an affair with Naren. Jayant is like any other male figure having a typical patriarchal attitude. He tries to control Indu in every aspect. Indu surrenders totally to Jayant. When she is feeling unhappy with her conjugal life she is made heiress to the whole property. Thus she gets an opportunity to be away from Jayant. She accepts the responsibility and stays there. As she is alone in Akka's house, she develops an intimate relationship with Naren. Initially, when Naren tries to make some advances, Indu resists saying, "[F]or me, it's one man and one man alone" but later on she offers herself to Naren. She feels that it is the body's requirement of which she does not have any control. I am surprised at Indu's behaviour. According to Jasbir Jain, Indu's "[...] adulterous relationship does not lead to a sense of guilt, instead it liberates the psyche from false restrictions" (15-16). I do not agree with Jain's theory of "liberating the psyche from false restrictions." In another context, Jain in her article "Positioning the 'Post' in Post-Feminist: Reworking of Strategies" says: "When Indu has a physical relationship with Narendra, it is not infidelity to her husband, nor is it an involvement with him; it is merely the use of something she owns, in order to show that she cares for him as a human being"(88). How can anyone bring in the "physical relationship" with someone other than the husband and defend the woman's sexual act as "something she owns" and call it "car[ing] for him as a human being?" Whether a woman has a physical relationship once or more than once, she is definitely called "infidel." I also disagree with Anita Singh when she says: "She [Indu] suffers no guilt in her extra-marital relationship with Naren and decides not to tell Jayant about it [...]" (125). No guilt in Indu is something that I cannot digest in a married woman. The same argument applies to married men too. One can fight against "false restrictions" but not a guiltless affair. What happens if men also think in Indu's manner? Will there be any respect to the institution of marriage? Look at the total surrender of her body to Naren:

> I lay down impelled by his thrusting body, feeling at first a passive languor. Oh, blessed, blessed hardness. An ecstasy filled my body and I could not be still any more. There was a joyous sense of release, of passion I could experience and show and participate in. I clung to him convulsively, marveling that I did not have to hold myself back. And when it was over, we lay back, both of us, exhausted and shuddering. I said, "Thank you, Naren." And languidly he lifted a hand to my hair and smiled at me. Later, he lay floppily, untidily, as men always do, in a kind of supine bonelessness. While I felt in myself an intense desire for activity. I got up and began to tidy myself. Naren, who lay watching me through half closed, drowsy eyes, said, "You look like a bird smoothing its ruffled feathers."
>
> "I wish I could say the same for you," I retorted. (Deshpande *Roots* 151-152)

Indu participates in this affair with so much of passion. As a result of this affair she is "filled" with "ecstasy in her "body." She calls it "a joyous sense of release" and she could "experience" "passion" and "participate" in it without any guilt. She even "thanks" Naren for the affair, indicating that she has no feeling of guilt. She finds in herself "an intense desire for activity." Naren even compares her happiness "to a bird smoothing its ruffled feathers." Naren happens to be her childhood friend. That does not mean she can use this opportunity of living apart from her husband due to the compulsion of protecting the property of her ancestors and safeguarding it to have an affair. She does not feel any kind of guilt whatsoever.

Indu does have a job before she becomes the heir to Akka's property. Indu has had to choose her career out of force and compulsion. She marries Jayant without her parents' consent.

In order to support her family expenditure she has undertaken to write stories for a magazine. She is a creative writer unlike Simrit who is a freelance writer and who authors a book on the river. There is a difference between Simrit and Indu in the sense that the former writes for self-satisfaction and the latter writes for money. Indu expresses her view on writing thus:

> I no longer have any desire to mould people, to change them, to reform society. There is only one thing I know I can do [...] I can write. And I am writing the book that has been in me these past few years. Whether any publisher will accept it, whether it will win acclaim, appreciation accolades... I school myself not to dream of such things. Rave reviews and worldwide fame, a best-seller that will stun the world and generations—these exist only in the fantasies of immature minds and publishers' blurbs. (Deshpande *Roots* 15)

Indu asserts that she has no "desire" in "reforming the society" through her "writings." While writing she also feels tired and goes to the extent of wanting to abandon her writing:

> The other day, I came away from my writing, tired, dishevelled, almost in tears. "And after all," I cried out despairingly to Jayant, "it may be still born. If no publisher accepts it [...]" "I'll publish it for you," Jayant said, putting his arms comfortingly around me. [...] Yet, when I had first told Jayant about my plans [...] that I would give up my job and give myself to writing, he had been unbelieving. Then, confident of his influence over me, he had been sure I would change. (Deshpande *Roots* 13-14)

Indu is trying to suggest that any sort of "writing" is not easy. Look at the words Indu uses—"tired", "dishevelled" and "tears." Any writer will have the fear as to whether any "publisher" "will publish" the work. This is so with Indu too. However, her husband says he will "publish" it for her. That is not a happy thing for Indu. There will be a negative impact if her husband publishes for her. Hence she wants to give up her "job" as well as her "writing." A writer should write out of a need or for commercial purposes.

Paro in Namita Gokhale's *Paro*: *Dreams of Passion* (1984) marries Bubu, her collegemate. In fact, it is Bubu who is interested in Paro. He sends his father to Paro's house to ask for her hand in marriage. Perhaps Bubu is infatuated with her and sends his father. Perhaps because it is only an infatuation, that the marriage terminates. The details as to why the marriage breaks up are not mentioned in the novel. Paro says:

> "Then, in college, I met Bubu [...] Man, did he fall for me like a tonne of bricks! His father sent a proposal. Apparently, they hadn't heard about my rape-scene. Funny thing is that I wasn't raped, I loved every moment of it. Anyway, Daddyji was so glad to get Bubu off his hands that he didn't bother to scrutinize the police record too carefully. Maybe if I had a Ma-in-law she would have been more careful. And so there it was. Marriage." She paused. "I always knew it sounded too good to last. And it didn't." (Gokhale *Paro* 31-32)

Paro then marries B.R., a businessman who runs the Sita Sewing Machine Company. It is believed that B.R. marries Paro out of infatuation. This is a verdict given by Priya who has been involved in a sexual relation with him even after her marriage with Suresh, a lawyer. The narrator of the novel Priya says, "A month later, he was married to Paro. It took all of us at the office completely by surprise. I have never forgotten, nor forgiven, a hurt" (Gokhale *Paro* 3). And again, "The day after, the girls at the office were all agog with tales of her beauty and B.R.'s obvious infatuation with her" (Gokhale *Paro* 6).

Even after this marriage, Paro's life is not stable and she has an extra-marital relationship with "Bucky" Bhandapur. This extra-marital relationship is known in public because Bucky is a test cricketer. He is a public figure. That is why everybody talks about Paro and Bucky's relationship. Bucky is also like B.R. Both of them have the name, "A known Romeo."

B.R. divorces Paro because she is involved in an extra-marital relationship. But how is he any less to blame for he has affairs with several women. She gets an alimony and lives with "Bucky" Bhandapur. The narrator says:

> She had left B.R. only six months before. Everybody was talking about it. She was living in open adulterous sin with "Bucky" Bhandapur, test cricketer and scion of a princely family. The "Bucky," I gathered, was in commemoration of his faintly protruding front teeth, which lent a strange charm to his lean face. He was, like B.R., what the boys in the office used to call "A known Romeo." He was also a little younger than her. (Gokhale *Paro* 27)

Perhaps Paro's attraction towards Bucky is because he belongs to a "princely family." In addition to his family background, Bucky is "a little younger" than Paro.

In the same novel Priya, the narrtor of the novel goes in for an arranged marriage with a lawyer. She has been working in B.R.'s company before she gets married to Suresh. She resigns as secretary to B.R. once her marriage is arranged. In an arranged marriage the prospects of the bridegroom are considered. Suresh is a good match for Priya. He is "a lawyer in Delhi" (Gokhale *Paro* 20). As soon as this proposal comes for Priya, her photograph is sent to Suresh and "he [finds] no fault with neither, and within a week" Priya is married to Suresh. But in her office she has been asked whether it has been an arranged marriage or a love marriage. Priya replies that it is an arranged one. Her colleagues are disappointed. Even Priya is not happy with this proposal. Even after her marriage with Suresh she "sometimes think[s] of B.R. and [she] would sigh. But my head told [her] that [she] had not got such a bad deal after all" (Gokhale *Paro* 21).

Priya does not have a career. However, she had taken up jobs such as that of a typist and of a sales girl in a bookshop. Initially, she was a typist and later she was promoted to the post of secretary to B.R. She was working as a typist so that she could find a suitable job. She does get a marriage proposal from a lawyer from Delhi. As her marriage has been fixed with the lawyer she has to resign the job:

> B.R. elected me from the typists' pool to become his secretary. [...] When I told them at the office, they all asked excitedly, 'Is it Arranged or Love?' When I told them it was arranged they all looked a little disappointed. My marriage was a middle-class one, much as any other. We did not have many relatives, and so it was uneventful, even a little boring. My husband was a virgin, and did not seem to notice that I was not. B.R. accepted my resignation with equanimity. (Gokhale *Paro* 15-20)

Priya's colleagues are "disappointed" when she says that she is going to have an "arranged marriage." The problem with Priya is that she does not find out whether she could continue with the same job or find one elsewhere as she is used to working. In "middle-class" families "educated" women have no independent role to play. Priya considers herself a "non-virgin" whereas her husband is a "virgin." They have to abide by what their parents dictate to them. This is what happens in women such as Anita and Priya. However, after marriage Priya does take up a job as a sales girl in a bookshop owned by her friend on a part-time basis:

> A friend of mine had a small bookshop in the Oberoi Hotel. She asked me if I wanted a part-time job, and I agreed eagerly. It was a quiet, peaceful place, and I would spend hours, curled up in a corner, leafing through books and magazines. Occasionally a customer would stroll in, and I would rise, show him around, and settle down to my private thoughts again. (Gokhale *Paro* 100)

I think Priya has done the right thing by taking up "a part-time job" as a salesgirl in "a small bookshop." She has broken her silence as Alka Saxena says: "One can not ignore the fact that women have taken up jobs only after having obtained the consent of the male members of their family. Hence, under prevailing situation, women must realize that they have to save themselves. Unity, firmness of purpose,

...ness have to be
...Without taking
...p the "job"
...at will she
...quiet" and
...her time. She
...gh the books and
...private thoughts."
...pset at my taking up a
...society. Why, people will
...enough for her to take up
...100). Why should Suresh be
...part-time job" in a "bookshop"?
...as she has already worked at Sita
...n an opportunity has been given to her
...ut taking her husband's permission. Why
...rmission from her husband? She is "educated"
...eady worked. As Priya says:

> ...was unmoved, for that job represented escape ...m my empty home. Of course, it wasn't my first job either, for I had put in three years of service with Sita Sewing Machines. It was pleasant to earn some money again, however little it might be. I worked from nine-thirty in the mornings, when Suresh left for court, until four in the afternoons, at which time he normally returned. I was paid a thousand rupees a month. I never spent any of the money on myself, since personal maintenance and so on I took to be my legal due from Suresh; instead it accumulated in my personal account, a little nest-egg of my own. I think I deserved it, even if I do say so myself, for I was very conscientious about the cash box, and even put an end to all the pilfering that had been rampant earlier. (Gokhale *Paro* 100-101)

Although Suresh was upset with her taking up a "job," she is "unmoved." She feels working is important for her. She justifies her act because of her past experience. She feels happy earning some money so as to avoid depending on her husband. She has been paid a "thousand rupees" for her "job." It is not

a small amount for her. Moreover, she has
that amount. For her "personal maintena
taking from her husband. She calls it a "leg
husband for having married her. She feels it is
to pay for her "personal maintenance." I do
Priya on this point. She has been earning. W
demand a "personal maintenance" from her husb
been "accumulating" all her salary in her "person
Why should she bring a "legal" point here? She
allowed to work, though unwillingly, by her husband
be a small or meagre amount for her husband. But for
all. She also justifies her timings for her job. She work
her husband is away from home and she is back by th
Suresh is also back. Then what is the problem for Suresh
problem for him is her working in "a bookshop." He ar
that he has a prestige in the "society" as a lawyer and she
spoiled his status. I think Suresh should not have any proble
about her working in a bookshop. I agree with Priya and
justify her choice of the "job."

Priya is asked to take a divorce for having an extra-marital relationship with B.R. and loving someone other than her husband and confessing this to her husband. Priya has worked as secretary to B.R. who is the Proprietor of Sita Sewing Machine Company and has resigned the post as soon as she gets married to Suresh, a lawyer. However, Priya has fascination for B.R. and continues to have an affair with him even after her marriage with Suresh. Suresh asks Priya:

> "Have you really had a liaison with B.R.?" he asked.
>
> "No, of course not," I shuffled.
>
> "Do you have any intention of trying to get that thing published?" he asked next. […]
>
> "And do you love B.R.?" he hammered unremittingly.
>
> "Yes, Yes," I continued, still lost in my private rhapsody.
>
> "In that case I think we would be best advised to live apart, at least for a while," he said, and his voice had the ring of finality. […]

> "It is the only home I know," I said stubbornly.
>
> "But a separation cannot do us any harm," he said, "just to think matters over."
>
> "But where can I live? Even my mother's dead," I said in desperation. "There is always your brother's house," he said. "Or you can continue to live here, but then I shall have to shift out. And I do, after all, have to continue to live in Delhi to earn a living. My chambers and library are here. I have commitments to my clients." (Gokhale *Paro* 128-130)

Look at Priya's confession to her husband—that she loves B.R., that she has an extra-marital relationship with B.R. A natural response to her confession is that it is better to live "apart" from each other. J.N. Chaudhary, in his field study on "Illicit relations," finds the following: "The premium on illicit sex conduct is secrecy, and if it is proved or discovered, it may become for a married man or a woman, a sure ground for filing a suit for seeking divorce under adultery. Illicit relations as the cause of strained relations between the spouses in our study, were discovered among 30 cases" (55). Any husband who comes to know about his wife's involvement in an illicit relationship would ask for a separation. No husband would ask his wife to continue with her married life when she loves someone other than her husband and has an affair with him. Priya has no regrets about her affairs rather she asks for alimony for her maintenance. She says: "'What about maintenance, alimony?' I asked. The question of money was, after all, pressing and all-prevailing. Panic flew in waves around my head at the prospect of becoming Dolly's drudge, the object of pity, a poor relative." (Gokhale *Paro* 130)

The fact that Priya asks for maintenance and "alimony" indicates that she has been preparing the ground for the divorce. Suresh reacts thus:

> "My dear Mrs Priya Kaushal," he said grandiloquently, "one thing you cannot, I repeat, cannot, accuse me of is ever even attempting, I repeat, even attempting, to shirk or evade my responsibilities. I may be fat, I may even—

> in your eyes—be a buffoon, my love-making may leave you cold, but I do certainly abide by my duties. Even the fevered phantoms of your imagination cannot distort that irrefutable fact." (Gokhale *Paro* 130)

Suresh is generous enough to assure her that he will not "evade" his "responsibilities." Thus Suresh and Priya get divorced with mutual consent.

Like Bim, Sonali too in Nayantara Sahgal's *Rich Like Us* (1985) remains unmarried. She has been interested in marrying Ravi Kachru who has been her childhood friend and classmate. However, she has stopped thinking on the lines of marriage, as he has become corrupt in his office. Unfortunately, Ravi has become a corrupt officer and this is opposed to Sonali's ideology and principle. She can not compromise on her ideology and principle. Sonali remains unmarried[2] having loved him and intended to marry him. She is the epitome of true love. She does not want to marry any other person. She concentrates only on her career.

Sonali has been asked to choose a particular career by her father. Sonali has been asked to write the I.C.S. She does take help from her parents and they are very cooperative. As Sonali says about her father:

> Papa, a member of the I.C.S. himself, had said with a pride I was used to hearing in his voice, "Sonali, people like you, especially women like you, are going to Indianize India." It was the day my name had topped the list in the competitive examination for the civil service. He was an emotional man and that day, fifteen years ago, there had been tears in his eyes with the achievement—his as much as mine—of having passed on to me, and only to me of his two daughters, a precious responsibility he had carried, and his firm faith that huge historical change could be peaceful. (Sahgal *Rich* 24)

Sonali's pride has been boosted when her father encourages her to become an I.C.S. officer. The expectation also forces an "educated" woman to work harder than her capacity. If there is support, then it leads not just to success but to topping the list. We can also argue from this that it is possible for an "educated" woman to occupy any position, not just men.

Thus she has chosen her career as an I.C.S. officer out of her Papa's interest. Just because her Papa was an I.C.S. officer he wanted his daughter too to become an I.C.S. officer. However, it is not easy to pass the I.C.S. exam without great effort. Everyone can dream of becoming of an I.C.S. officer but in reality only a few people can succeed. Sonali is one of them.

After becoming an I.C.S. officer, she really shows her dedication in her career. She is willing to accept any kind of demotion for her principles. As I have stated elsewhere:

> [...] Sonali, an ICS officer[...] has shown that principles are more important than promotion or demotion in discharging her duties as a sincere, honest, dedicated and patriotic officer [...] She has stuck to her principles. Dev in collaboration with Mr. Neuman wants to establish a fizzy drink factory, which is not the sole purpose, but "is really a cover up for the import and storage for car-parts required for the manufacturing of an indigenous car by the Prime Minister's son." Having realized the reason, Sonali as per her principles, doesn't recommend the file writing a negative remark and raising her voice: "I wrote a brief rejection in the wide margin of the proposal on my desk." Sincere officers are not afraid of any higher authority. They don't even care for transfer or demotion. Here is a person who "rejects" the proposal without any hesitation. It is the power of the pen. Since officers always go according to the rules, she even tells the visiting representation about her stand. They don't have to oblige anyone. She is not corrupt. The result of rejecting the proposal is obvious that she is demoted to a lower cadre and transferred to her own state. Surprisingly, the replacing officer is none other than her own childhood friend, classmate, batchmate in "service" and the deserted lover. (Manohar 34)

All in all what I feel about Sonali is that she is very serious about her career and is dedicated to it. She does not bother about her losses in her attempt to follow her "principles" and her stand: "[...] Sonali refuses to submit to the will of those who try to force her into toeing the line of "Madam"[...]. This results in her losing her post as Joint Secretary" (Varalakshmi 368). She does not care about losing the post of "Joint Secretary."

Like Paro and Priya and unlike Tara, Saru and Indu, Jaya in Shashi Deshpande's *That Long Silence* (1988) too has an arranged marriage. It is interesting to see that Jaya's husband Mohan has certain conditions about marrying a girl. Jaya's brother Dada says: "I believe what he wants is an educated, cultured wife. He says he isn't bothered about dowry, money and all that. An educated, cultured wife [...]" (90).

I strongly agree with Mohan when he says that he wants to marry an "educated" and "cultured" wife. We might ask why only an "educated" and "cultured" wife. The reason is that an "educated" wife will be "cultured" and have a broad understanding of issues so as to lead a happy and peaceful life. She will know how to behave with both the "educated" and the "uneducated." It is not just that an educated wife will find a job and bring extra money to the family. But it is to have an understanding and a good mannered wife. She can even correct the husband if he goes wrong or is tempted to go wrong. Moreover, Mohan does not "bother about dowry, money and all that." He only wants an "educated" and "cultured wife." Nothing more.

Although Jaya does not like this proposal, here is what she says about her brother and his responsibility:

> Only later had I come upon them with a painful awareness. Dada had wanted me off his hands; he had wanted to be free of his responsibility for an unmarried younger sister, so that he could go ahead with his own plans. After Appa's death, the *Kakas* had never let Dada forget his role as the man of the house. And so Dada had cleverly manoeuvred me into a position from which

> not marrying Mohan would have been childish, irresponsible and unfair to Dada. ("I know I'm only your brother, I know I have no real right to tell you what to do, if only Appa had been here...") And, if there had been no reason why I should have married Mohan, there had been no reason not to marry him either. (Deshpande *That Long* 93)

It is not whether the woman is happy or not in "marrying" a person. There is the "responsibility" of marrying "off" his sister, as he is the man of the house. Obviously he wants to be free from his responsibility. Unless he completes his responsibility he cannot make any plans for himself. Moreover, Dada has been forced to bring in proposals for Jaya. Though she feels Dada has "manoeuvred" her she feels she has "no reason why" she "should" not "have married Mohan" as he could provide a safe and secure life.

Much discussion goes on in the house of Jaya as to whether Mohan ought to be Jaya's husband. Jaya at last says:

> By the time they had finished wrangling and Dada had restored Ai's good humour, as I had known he would, I had made up my mind. I would marry Mohan. The decision would be mine, not Ramukaka's, not Dada's, not Ai's. [...] But all this is actually a futile exercise, trying to figure out why I married Mohan; the truth is that he had decided to marry me, I had only to acquiesce. (Deshpande *That Long* 94)

Perhaps Jaya may have felt irritated with the prolonged discussion. Therefore, she makes up her mind that she "would marry Mohan." Deepakshi Kotwal opines: "Jaya ha[s] married Mohan to defy her mother. Curiously Deshpande's women not only rebel against male domination but ferociously satirise their mothers and grandmothers who had not taught them to articulate their desires and needs. Jaya represents a naïve young girl who sees marriage as a passport to freedom from the oppressive control of the parental home" (42). She feels that "trying to" find out why she has decided to marry Mohan is a "futile exercise." The fact is that it is Mohan who has made the decision as he likes her "educated and cultured" background. She has only agreed to Mohan's proposal. Thus hers is an arranged marriage. On the whole, she has no role in her marriage.

Jaya chooses a career of creative writing. She writes for a magazine to come out of the boring situation of a housewife. She has been encouraged by her husband and her friend Kamat to make use of her writing ability. First of all her husband says:

> [...] "Why don't you take up a job?"
>
> "A job? Me?"
>
> "Yes, I thought [...]"
>
> "But you never wanted me to. That time when I wanted to try my hand at teaching [...]"
>
> "Oh, that was different. Circumstances were different then. But now, may be you should try."
>
> "What can I do? And who'll give me a job?"
>
> "A magazine. One of the weeklies. Surely you should be able to get something?"
>
> "I don't know. You can't get any job just like that. And at my age [...] I've no experience, either." (Deshpande *That Long* 98-99)

Is this the reason why Mohan wanted to marry an "educated" wife? He is asking her to "take up a job." Jaya is surprised. At the same time Jaya reminds him that he was not in favour of her trying for a teaching position in a school. He tells her that the situation then "was different." The main reason is that he is about to lose his job in a corruption case. She feels that she is too old for the job. Moreover, she has "no experience." But her friend Kamat has suggested: "Take yourself seriously, woman" (Deshpande *That Long* 99). Mohan continues:

> "But you have been writing [...]"
>
> "It's not the same."

> "You can try. You don't lose anything by trying. Suppose, by some chance, I lose my job?" [...]
>
> "Thank God you have your column. And your "Seetha" fortnightly. And your stories. That's something. Not much money in it, but [...]" (Deshpande *That Long* 99)

Mohan is preoccupied with the idea of Jaya taking up a job. He is apprehensive about losing his "job." So he wonders what will happen to the family if he loses his job. Therefore, he puts pressure on Jaya to take up the job. According to Rose Laub Coser: "Whenever women are gainfully employed, they gain power in the family (Coser, 1987), and men lose power. As Sorenson and McLanahan have shown (1987), if women work at home they are completely dependent on husbands. They decrease their dependency in the measure in which they are gainfully employed" (206). She further says: "In 1940, white married women, on average, relied on their husbands to provide 86 per cent of their economic support. By 1980, their dependency had been reduced to 58 per cent (Sorenson and McLanahan 1987, p. 670)" (206). I extend this to the Indian situation also. Jaya too is going to "gain power" though she has been asked to take up a job by her husband. Mohan is making her independent and providing her the "power." Mohan however feels thankful to god that she has her "column" to publish her stories. As a result of publishing the stories they would get some money. That money may not be much. However, something is better than nothing. Mohan had once discouraged Jaya when she wrote a story, in the story-writing contest, about a couple having published and winning a prize for it. She did point out that she was unhappy that he had tried to identify himself with the male character and had thought that people would think that the story was about Mohan and Jaya. Except for this discouragement, she has no obstacles in her career. But this episode has created a storm in Jaya's mind. That is why she does not show any interest in writing stories. When he has needed some income from her writing he has encouraged her to write. He has shown his shrewd attitude in arguing according to his convenience.

Through her career, Jaya develops a close relationship with Kamat and gets inspiration from him in order to write more and more short stories. He is a kind of a guide to her. She even discusses things with him that she does not discuss with her husband Mohan. This reveals how intimate she becomes with Kamat. Kamat becomes Jaya's confidant. He even permits her to use his address for her correspondence. Kamat says: "You want to use my address for your mail? Sure, go ahead. You can use my typewriter too if you want to" (Deshpande *That Long* 146). It leads from just a close contact to a physical relationship:

> And then he has said "Jaya" once again, and this time he held my face lightly within his palms, so light a touch that I had scarcely felt his hands. "Your name is like your face," he had said to me once, and passed his fingers lightly over my face. And the touch had meant nothing. But this time...His eyes had looked steadily, almost dispassionately at me. And my body had responded to that look, that voice, that touch. I had almost felt his body on mine, becoming a part of mine, I had felt his mouth on mine, I had almost been able to smell and taste his lips. [...] There had been no anger in me when I had done that; there had been no outrage, either. There had been nothing but an overwhelming urge to respond to him with my body, the equally overwhelming certainty of mind that I could not do so. Later there had been confusion. "Jaya" he had said and I had become only Jaya. It had annihilated Mohan entirely; it had frightened me the way it had annihilated Mohan entirely. (Deshpande *That Long* 157)

If Mohan had looked after Jaya, she would not have allowed Kamat to "touch" her this way. She has developed a liking for him. The effect of his calling her name has made her "annihilate" Mohan entirely. At the same time how can she justify her actions with Kamat? On the other hand, how can Kamat justify his physical intimacy in the name of helping and sharing?

Karuna in Shobha De's *Socialite Evenings* (1988) too has an arranged marriage, although she had a boyfriend. She marries her husband because her parents force her. She is not happy with her marriage. Karuna has this to say:

> And even though I had married well in my parents' eyes [...] I was stuck in an increasingly meaningless marriage. [...] What was wrong with my marriage? What had gone wrong? [...] My marriage went sore because I married the wrong man for the wrong reasons at the wrong time. My husband was not a villain. He was just an average Indian husband—unexciting, uninspiring, untutored. Why he did marry me, I shall never know. I asked him often enough and he always laughed it off. (De *Socialite Evenings* 64-65)

Karuna marries her husband for the sake of her parents. In "her parents' eyes" she is a happy wife. However, for Karuna it is a "meaningless marriage."

Karuna has an extra-marital relationship with Krish, a friend of her husband. The reason why she has a relationship with Krish is because she is bored with her husband, Bunty, a rich businessman. Another interesting fact is that she tells her husband that she has an affair with his friend. This conversation between Krish and Karuna reveals the fact:

> Krish phoned the next morning when the husband was in the bath. I promptly interpreted it as a good omen. I spoke to him on the kitchen phone and turned the TV up to muffle my voice.
>
> "Guess who's here?" I croaked.
>
> "Who?"
>
> "Your friend."
>
> "Which one?"
>
> "Black Label." (We had nicknamed him that in memory of the first night.) "You're kidding! What's he doing there?"
>
> "He has found out about us."

> "Oh hell! What a bore. So what does he want to do? Kill me?" "No—he wants to take me to Venice." (De *Socialite Evenings* 188-189)

Extra-marital affairs make persons become secretive and cheats. Look at the use of a nickname to maintain secrecy. She also tells Krish that Bunty has come to know about their affair. Once an affair starts, it will go on, whatever may be the hurdles.

Karuna chooses a career of modelling and she has been exploited in the name of a career. She does not allow her photograph to be published in a newspaper for an advertisement. She is interested in modelling. Charlie, Karuna's collegemate, has an uncle who runs an ad agency. Charlie goes along with him to take her photograph. Mr. Chopra and Charlie discuss Karuna and ask her to pose as a trial. Charlie's uncle says:

> "Mr. Chopra would like some photographs of you." I looked quickly at Charlie who winked and mouthed, "Say 'yes'!" I was totally confused. I suppose the client thought I would be flattered, but uppermost in my mind was Father's reaction. "I haven't asked my parent's permission." I stuttered.
>
> "They will get angry."
>
> "Don't worry we will not print these pictures without your permission. These are just trial shots for our files. Your parents will never find out." Uncleji said.
>
> "I don't know [...]," I said weakly.
>
> As it turned out, the client liked my photographs and they got used—without my permission and without any payment. (De *Socialite Evenings* 23-24)

Actually Karuna is not interested in modelling for the "ad agency." One fine morning Karuna's father finds his daughter's photo in the newspaper, recognizes his daughter, asks his wife and summons Karuna:

> One morning I heard father calling out to Mother "Isn't this Karuna?" Mother replied nervously, "Must be some mistake [...] let us ask her." I was summoned. Father

> flashed the newspaper in front of me. "When did you do this? How dare you? Do you want to disgrace us completely? This is not something girls from respectable families do. How did this photograph get here?" I just stared and stared at the ad. Actually it looked pretty good, and I looked pretty good too. A smile must have appeared on my face, because suddenly I felt Father's palm hitting me sharply across the face. "Disgraceful! Cheap! Filthy! No Brahmin girl has ever stooped so low. Tell me— how did this photograph get here?" (De *Socialite Evenings* 24)

Karuna's "father's" angry questioning and chastisement come from the feeling that such an act is disgraceful to a good Brahmin family. But Karuna is not apologetic; in fact, she smiles.

After going through a number of experiences, as Urbashi Barat says, Karuna finally turns to a career as a writer for ad-film scripts and is able to return to her parents: "Karuna is now secure enough to return to her parents and come to terms with her past—an important phase in the progress towards identity. This sparks off her creative spirit, and she begins writing scripts for ad-films almost as though inspired" (127). Subhash Chandra has this to say about Karuna's career:

> Even though she is not precisely gifted or trained for any profession, she is made to fight her way up, getting recognition in advertising and television productions. She becomes financially self-dependent, carves out her own niche in the professionally competitive world of advertising and acquires all the resources to flirt *ad infinitum*, which she is shown doing with a married journalist, Ranbir Roy. (147)

Karuna gets divorced from her husband because of her extra-marital relationship with his friend Krish and because she conceives Krish's child. Karuna is surprised when her husband proposes to divorce her. He points out that the child Karuna is carrying is his friend's:

> "How would I know? These days you are up to all sorts of tricks. You might call your activities 'theatre-related.' But I don't trust you. If you could screw around with my friend Krish, right under my nose, you could be screwing the whole town. Adultery is an addiction—it's only the first time that's difficult. After that, it's only a matter of one fuck here or there—isn't that right?" (De *Socialite Evenings* 215)

Karuna has been having a relationship with Krish secretly. Whenever she is asked, she tells her husband that she has been busy with "theatre-related" activities. However, her husband does not "trust" Karuna. Krish has cheated his friend and has sex with his friend's wife. Karuna's husband tries to moralize saying that "adultery" is "an addiction." Once you start you don't know where you are and what you are. Adultery is worse than cigarette smoking. Karuna asks:

> "What are you trying to tell me?"
>
> "I think you are clever enough to know. I don't think there's any point in continuing this farce. I've been thinking about it. We'd better call it off."
>
> "Call it off?"
>
> "Our marriage."
>
> "Are you serious?"
>
> "Of course I'm serious. I've discussed it with my mother."
> "Before even talking to me?"
>
> "Why should I consult you, my dear? Did you expect me to seek your permission? You didn't 'consult' me when you jumped into bed with Krish. Fair and square." [...]
>
> "I don't owe you any explanations. I mean, look, did you really believe you could have your little tryst in Venice and come back like nothing had happened? Do you know what I did the moment I reached Bombay? I saw a lawyer. I wanted to check on the legal position. Let me tell you a few things—you don't stand a chance in hell. I'd suggest you go along with my plan. Let's file

> for divorce by mutual consent. That way we'll save a lot of time, money and headaches. My lawyer has briefed me on this. I'm not interested in prolonging the proceedings and going through a bitter court battle. In any case, there's nothing to contest." (De *Socialite Evenings* 215-216)

Karuna does not seem to think a divorce is warranted. She is also appalled that an important decision has been taken without even consulting her. But her husband feels it is inevitable and the charge of adultery cannot be contested. Thus they are divorced and Karuna wants to go to her parents. I think what Karuna's husband did is right. No husband would live with his wife if she has not only an extra-marital relationship but also conceives a child outside marriage. It is justifiable from her husband's point of view. Even her parents do not support Karuna and refuse to entertain her when she calls her parents:

> I called my parents. My misfortune hadn't stopped—Father picked up the phone. I asked for Mother but was told she was having a bath. I should have put the phone down then, but I wasn't thinking, I just told him the whole story—expecting what—sympathy, I guess. All he said was: "What you've done is unacceptable, totally unacceptable. Nobody in our family has done it before, nobody will do it in the future. You've made the mistake, now you pay the price. We're old people and we cannot help you. You were the one who wanted to marry your husband, it was your decision. Now we don't want to get involved. We have only a few years left to us, let us live them as peacefully as we can." Having said that he put the phone down. (De *Socialite Evenings* 218-219)

Her father is angry and finds the entire thing unacceptable. Had her mother picked up the phone, perhaps her reaction may have been different.

Karuna is responsible for her divorce. Karuna's husband Bunty is innocent. She feels lonely as her parents refuse to justify her act. No husband can tolerate it if his wife has an affair with another man. It is traumatic for any husband. It could be the other way too. Extra-marital relationships cannot always be kept a secret. They will surface one day or the other. Especially, after a few years of married life a husband and wife can easily understand the mind of each other. Moreover, Karuna is carrying Krish's child. If Karuna has felt she has not been able to conceive due to a problem with her husband, they should have expressed their anxiety to a doctor. As we have already seen, Karuna is not happy with her husband. She has been feeling bored with him. If a wife is not happy with her husband she should be bold enough to say that she does not want to continue living with him. There are also opportunists who want to have extra-marital relationships. As a prey to Krish's opportunism, she is left alone, away from her husband, from her parents and also from her lover Krish.

In the same novel, we have, Anjali, a friend of Karuna, who has a love marriage with Abe without her parents' consent. We are told about the Anjali-Abe marriage through Karuna:

> Anjali had married Abbas "Abe" Tyabjee when she was just nineteen. [...] Anjali and Abe had met on flight. She'd joined Air India as an air hostess like other attractive girls of her generation. She later explained, "Basically I wanted to get out of the closed, boring, middle class environment of my family. I wasn't interested in studies. I wanted to be on my own, independent. To see the world, meet people, buy lovely clothes and perfumes. What else does a pretty girl at that age want anyway?" (De *Socialite Evenings* 11-12)

Anjali is an ambitious girl at the age of nineteen. She wants to "get away" from a "middle class" "family." She wants to earn on her "own" and be "independent." I appreciate her desire for an independent life and an independent income.

Anjali has an extra-marital relationship and feels that she has fulfilled her desire that has long been due. When Karuna asks Anjali about her affair with Pierre she says:

> "You're awful. You don't have any romance in you. You just want to spoil everything by asking crude questions [...] But to answer your nosiness—yes, I have slept with him. It was wonderful. I felt the earth move. Just like in those books. For the first time, I felt something." (De *Socialite Evenings* 74)

Anjali does not want to share her experience with Karuna but she shares her feelings with her. She even calls this affair, "the experience [she] has been waiting for" (De *Socialite Evenings* 78).

Anjali has chosen her career on her own. She is from a middle class family. She is tired of this middle class life. Anjali has initially become an air-hostess not to make a career but to earn money and to get out of the "boring life." Moreover, she is "not interested in studies." I think what she feels is that education up to a certain level is enough to earn and be "independent." She seems to be quite practical. She seems to suggest that she has had enough education to get a job and earn her own "money." When she says she is not "interested" in "studies" what she means is that she is not interested in further studies. That does not mean education is not necessary for her or for anyone. Nor does she mean that education is not interesting. After earning and becoming independent, she wants "to see the world", "meet people" and "buy lovely clothes and perfumes."

Anjali has divorced her husband Abe, a Muslim. Theirs has been a love marriage. Anjali has a problem with Abe:

> [...] "I have lost all my girl-friends to Abe. The minute he meets them, he starts his seduction plans. It doesn't take very long. One lunch, two drinks—and boom–they're in bed. I don't want to lost (sic) you." "But do you find him sexually attractive?" she asked anxiously. "No!" I almost yelled back.
>
> "I know Abe finds you attractive. He has told me so. He even asked me, 'Would you mind very much if I went to bed with her?' I didn't say anything. But he

> could tell from my expression that I was upset." (De *Socialite Evenings* 43)

What more reason can a wife need to divorce her husband than his having affairs with or trying to have affairs with her "girl-friends." He may be talented in seducing his wife's girl friends. But he is not talented enough to save his married life. Therefore, Anjali cautions Karuna and expresses to her that she does not want to lose her friend.

The reasons why Anjali divorces her husband are evident from the following lines:

> Anjali's divorce (yes, it finally happened) wasn't easy. While Abe wasn't bothered one way or the other, Anjali suffered in style: she wept into expensive Swiss hankies or into whisky-sours in various five star bars. There were suddenly a whole host of sympathizers—mainly male—willing to listen to her tales of neglect, abuse and torture. "What a bastard that man is," would run their refrain, as they counted the minutes to when their sympathetic shoulder could be switched for an even more sympathetic bed. (De *Socialite Evenings* 64)

In the novels of this decade, there are two unmarried women Bim and Sonali, one woman Tara who has a love-cum-arranged marriage, three women Saru, Indu and Anjali who marry for love and four women Priya, Paro, Jaya and Karuna who have arranged marriages. There are varied careers that "educated" women opt for. Bim teaches in a college; Jaya and Sarla run a school; Saru practices medicine; Priya becomes a P.A. to a businessman and a salesgirl in a bookshop; Sonali holds the high designation of an I.C.S. officer; Jaya becomes a creative writer; Karuna becomes a model and Anjali becomes an air-hostess. This decade seems to be opening up several careers for the "educated" women as the range of careers of these "educated" women demonstrates. As far as the issue of divorce is concerned we find Jaya and Sarla being abandoned, Paro, Priya and Karuna being divorced for having extra-marital relationships, and Anjali divorcing her husband for being involved in an extra-marital relationship.

WORKS CITED

Barat, Urbashi. "From Victim to Non-Victim: *Socialite Evenings* as a Version of Kunstlerroman." *The Fiction of Shobha De*. Ed. Jaydipsinh Dodiya. New Delhi: Prestige, 2000. 119-128.

Barche, G.D. "*The Dark Holds No Terrors*: Assertion of the Feminine Psyche." *Feminism and Indian English Fiction*. Ed. P.M. Naik and S.P. Swain. Bareilley: PBD, 1996. 84-90.

Bhatnagar, P. "The Theme of Man-Woman Relationship in the Novels of Shashi Deshpande." *Indian Women Novelists Set I: Vol. II*. Ed. R.K. Dhawan. New Delhi: Prestige, 1991. 143-154.

Chandra, Subhash. "Family and Marriage in *Socialite Evenings*." *The Fiction of Shobha De*. Ed. Jaydipsinh Dodiya. New Delhi: Prestige, 2000. 142-148.

Chaudhary, J. N. *Divorce in Indian Society* (*A. Sociological Study of Marriage Disruption and Role Adjustment*). Jaipur: Printwell, 1988.

Clement, A. "'The Centre Cannot Hold': The Vulnerable World of Anita Desai." *Indian Women Novelists Set III: Vol. I*. Ed. R.K. Dhawan. New Delhi: Prestige, 1995. 213-243.

Coser, Rose Laub. "Reflections on Feminist Theory." *Feminism and Sociological Theory*. Ed. Ruth A. Wallace. New Delhi: Sage, 1989. 200-207.

Desai, Anita. *Clear Light of Day*. New Delhi: Allied, 1980.

Deshpande, Shashi. *The Dark Holds No Terrors*. New Delhi: Penguin, 1980.

——. *Roots and Shadows*. 1983. New Delhi: Orient-Disha, 1996.

——. *That Long Silence*. 1988. New Delhi: Penguin, 1989.

De, Shobha. *Socialite Evenings*. 1988. New Delhi: Penguin, 1989.

Gokhale, Namita. *Paro: Dreams of Passion*. New Delhi: Penguin, 1984.

Gupta, Santosh. "Bridging the Polarities of Imagination and Reason in *Clear Light of Day*." *Indian Women Novelists Set I: Vol. III*. Ed. R.K. Dhawan. New Delhi: Prestige, 1991. 236-250.

Jain, Jasbir. "Positioning the 'Post' in Post-Feminist: Reworking of Strategies." *Indian Feminisms*. Ed. Jasbir Jain and Avadhesh Kumar Singh. New Delhi: Creative, 2001. 80-95.

——. "Towards the 21st Century: The Writing of the 1990s." *Indian Writing in English: The Last Decade*. Ed. Rajul Bhargava. Jaipur: Rawat, 2002. 11-25.

Juneja, Renu. "Identity and Femininity in Anita Desai's Fiction." *Journal of South Asian Literature* 22.2 (1987): 77-86.

Kotwal, Deepsheekha. "Gender and Sexual Identity in Shashi Deshpande's *That Long Silence*." *English Studies in India: A Journal of Literature and Language* 7 (1999): 38-44.

Manohar, D. Murali. "Women's Voices: Some Indian English Women Novelists of 1980s." *POETCRIT* 25.2 (2002): 31-39.

Pandit, P. Vijaya Lakshmi. "Obstacles for Women's Education." *Empowerment of Women Through Distance Education: A Case of Dr. B.R. Ambedkar Open University*. Hyderabad: Booklinks, 1997. 29-35.

Patil, P.F. "The Theme of Marital Disharmony in the Novels of Anita Desai." *Indian Women Novelists Set I: Vol. II*. Ed. R.K. Dhawan. New Delhi: Prestige, 1991. 127-142.

Paul, Premila. "*The Dark Holds No Terrors*: A Woman's Search for Refuge." *Indian Women Novelists Set I: Vol. V*. Ed. R.K. Dhawan. New Delhi: Prestige, 1991. 60-81.

Rani, T. Ashoka. "Women in Marriage: Novels of Nayantara Sahgal and Shashi Deshpande." *Critical Studies in Indian Fiction in English*. Ed. R.A. Singh and V.L.V.N. Narendra Kumar. New Delhi: Atlantic, 1999. 124-130.

Rosenwasser, Ruth K. "Voices of Dissent: Heroines in the Novels of Anita Desai." *Journal of South-Asian Literature* 24.2 (1989): 83-116.

Sahgal, Nayantara. *Rich Like Us*. London: Heinemann, 1985.

Sandhu, Sarabjit. "The Image of Woman in *The Dark Holds No Terrors*." *Indian Women Novelists Set I: Vol. V*. Ed. R.K. Dhawan. New Delhi: Prestige, 1991. 82-89.

Saxena, Alka. "Feminism: Time to Stop Suffering in Silence." *Indian Women Novelists Set III: Vol. I*. Ed. R. K. Dhawan. New Delhi: Prestige, 1995. 18-25.

Shivram, Meenakshi. "Locating the Woman in Post-colonial Discourse: A Reading of Shashi Deshpande's *The Dark Holds No Terrors*." *Post-Coloniality: Reading Literature*. Ed. C.T. Indra and Meenakshi Shivram. New Delhi: Vikas, 1999. 179-185.

Singh, Anita. "A Voice After the Long Silence: Shashi Deshpande's *Roots and Shadows* and *That Long Silence*." *Post-Independence Indian English Fiction*. Ed. Rajeshwar Mittapalli and Alessandro Monti. New Delhi: Atlantic, 2001. 124-128.

Varalakshmi, S. "Nothing to Lose but Our Chains: Nayantara Sahgal's Women in Their Social Context." *Mapping Cultural Spaces: Post-Colonial Indian Literature in English*. Ed. Nilufer E. Barucha and Vrinda Nabar. New Delhi: Vision, 1998. 359-372.

NOTES

1. In Shashi Deshpande's *Come Up and Be Dead* (1983) the two educated women characters, Devayani and Kshama who are cousins, remain unmarried and the third woman character in the same novel Mrs. Jyoti Raman remains a single parent with a daughter. There is no indication of their marriage and as such there is not much discussion of marriage in the novel. All the three characters have a job in a school. These three women characters are, however, not committed to their careers.
2. I agree with Nayantara Sahgal's view in her article "Passion for Indian" (*Indian Literature* 32.1 (1989) 79-88): "[...] Devi in *A Situation in New Delhi* and Sonali in *Rich Like Us* do without dependence on men, and are whole and complete without them. What I feel, I suppose, is that men are not yet ready for equal partners; for true everlasting love, for real give and take, a love that transcends misunderstandings" (84).

"Rejecting the Hegemony": The 1990s

6

In this chapter I will look at the following novels written by women in the 1990s with reference to the issues of marriage, career and divorce. In the previous chapter we have seen varied careers and a number of cases of divorce. Let us now consider "educated" women characters in the fiction of the 1990s. Malini from Shobha De's *Starry Nights* (1990), Devi from Githa Hariharan's *The Thousand Faces of Night* (1992), Amrita from Shobha De's *Strange Obsession* (1992), Mikki from Shobha De's *Sisters* (1992), Urmila, Kalpana and Vaana from Shashi Deshpande's *The Binding Vine* (1992), Gudiya from Namita Gokhale's *Gods, Graves and Grandmother* (1994), Nisha from Shobha De's *Sultry Days* (1994), Reema and Aparna from Shobha De's *Snapshots* (1995), Parvati from Namita Gokhale's *A Himalayan Love Story* (1996), Sumi from Shashi Deshpande's *A Matter of Time* (1996), Maya from Shobha De's *Second Thoughts* (1996), Ammu from Arundhati Roy's *The God of Small Things* (1997), Padma from Anjana Appachana's *Listening Now* (1998), Virmati and Ida from Manju Kapur's *Difficult Daughters* (1998) and Uma from Anita Desai's *Fasting, Feasting* will be dealt with in terms of the issue of marriage. Malini from Shobha De's *Starry Nights* (1990), Mikki from Shobha De's *Sisters* (1992), Amrita from Shobha De's *Strange Obsession* (1992), Urmila, Vaana and Kalpana from Shashi Deshpande's *The Binding Vine* (1992), Nisha and Pramila from Shobha De's *Sultry Days* (1994), Aparna from Shobha De's *Snapshots* (1995), Maya from Shobha De's *Second Thoughts* (1996), Virmati from Manju Kapur's *Difficult Daughters* (1998) and Padma from

Anjana Appachana's *Listening Now* (1998) will be discussed with regard to the question of career. Devi from Githa Hariharan's *The Thousand Faces of Night* (1992), Aparna from Shobha De's *Snapshots* (1995), Sumi from Shashi Deshpande's *A Matter of Time* (1996), Ammu from Arundhati Roy's *The God of Small Things* (1997), and Ida from Manju Kapur's *Difficult Daughters* (1998) will be looked at keeping in mind the issue of divorce.

In the 1990s, there is a change in the authors' perspective regarding their characters. However, there is a slight similarity between the 1980s and 1990s. Let us see what these similarities and differences are in this chapter.

I will begin the discussion with Malini Arora in Shobha De's *Starry Nights* (1991) who goes in for an arranged marriage based on mutual understanding with Akshay Arora. Malini has a career, in that she is a *ghazal* singer even before her marriage. But she has been asked to give up her career as a *ghazal* singer after her marriage. The reason why Akshay wants his wife to give up her career is that he wants his wife to be a home-maker and not a career woman. He says:

> [...] "I want a home-maker. Someone who will be a good mother to my children. I don't want to marry a painted doll; some cheap film girl who will flirt with all my friends. Malini is the right woman for me." Malini, in turn, had explained her decision to quit her career. She was a *ghazal* singer who was just beginning to get noticed, when Akshay proposed to her. "My husband means more to me than a career. I believe a wife's place is in the home, not in a recording studio. Akshay is an old-fashioned man. I will never displease him." A cheeky reporter has asked her, "But about his affairs? Will you tolerate them?" Malini was tight-lipped. "I trust my husband. He will never do anything to hurt me." (40)

What prompts Akshay to want his wife to be "a home-maker" is that children would be affected if both husband and wife have careers. He has seen personally how some women go to the extent of doing anything for a flourishing career. However, he cannot generalize that every film girl will flirt as he imagines. He is wrong because he has not been able to see the positive characteristics of a career woman which could have evoked respect for such women in him. But, at the same time, he flirts and is involved in an extra-marital relationship with Aasha Rani. He is a hypocrite and does not believe in providing freedom to let Malini have her own career. Therefore, he has chosen Malini to be his wife and lays down a condition that she has to "quit her career" of *ghazal* singing. Malini agrees to the condition. The question to ask is why she should "quit her career." Does she not have the desire to have a flourishing career? Malini is quite talented. Perhaps, she has not been successful in getting marriage proposals. Having a career is one of the biggest problems for "educated" career women who want to get married. Unless the husband is broad-minded and wants to encourage his wife, women will have a tough time getting married and continuing with their careers. Here is a case where Malini has been asked to "quit her career." This is very unfortunate. Why should she compromise and say that a wife's place is in the home but not outside home?

Like Malini, Amrita in Shobha De's *Strange Obsession* (1992) has an arranged marriage with Rakesh who is broad-minded enough to accept Amrita who was involved in a lesbian relationship. He knows that Minx (Meenakshi) has exploited Amrita. Minx haunts Amrita until she gets married. Minx has been obsessed with Amrita's beauty. She has a strange obsession of possessing Amrita and trying to do anything for the sake of holding on to Amrita. Amrita is in a state of turmoil and is guilty of her relationship with Minx. Rakesh in fact falls in love with Amrita as soon as he is asked to meet her at a hotel in Bombay. Amrita's mother Mrs. Aggarwal is very particular about Amrita's marriage with Rakesh. He too believes in an arranged marriage as he tells Amrita that he has taken his parents' "official permission" to marry her: "I'd gone to meet my parents and got their official permission to marry Amrita, that is, if she still wants to marry me. I'm an old fashioned man in that respect—I wanted my parents to give me their blessings" (156). It is interesting to note that people like Rakesh who believe in an arranged marriage are generally considered "old fashioned." On the other hand, Amrita has been helped and saved by a friend who loves her, Karan from the clutches of Minx. He books the flight ticket and makes sure that she reaches Bombay safely. He takes photographs and a video movie of Amrita's wedding. The wedding is described thus:

> As the flames from the sacred fire rose higher and smoke swirled around the decorated *mandap* Amrita looked up, squinting her eyes to keep them from watering. And there through the haze stood Karan at the edge of the small crowd, his eyes fixed on her face. Amrita was so glad to see him. [...] She could not wait to introduce the two of them to each other. She turned her face to stare at her husband-of-a-few-minutes. [...] "He is my best friend. He saved my life in more ways than one." (De *Strange* 167)

Before Amrita gets married to Rakesh, she wonders whether Rakesh would accept her or not. She is to be appreciated for discussing her previous lesbian relationship with Minx frankly and candidly with Rakesh. He understands her problem and does not show any anger about her past relationship with Minx.

On the other hand, Minx hates men and has a lesbian relationship with Amrita who aspires to become a model. In order to lure Amrita, Minx creates stories that have an element of hatred towards men. She goes to the extent of saying that her father raped her at a young age. In fact, it is a falsely created story so as to make Amrita develop hatred towards men. At the same time Minx tries to have a hold on her lesbian relationship with Amrita. She even murders Amrita's competitor in modelling in order to retain her relationship with Amrita. However, at the end of the novel Amrita is saved from Minx's clutches and a life of ruin. I am not suggesting that a lesbian relationship is wrong or immoral. I am only suggesting that any relationship be it lesbian or heterosexual should not be out of force. Until and unless both partners agree mutually, no relationship is acceptable. The point here is that an individual and his/her feelings must be respected.

Amrita has chosen a career on her own with her parents' full support. Amrita goes from Delhi to Bombay to be successful in her career, as there are more possibilities in Bombay. Amrita gives the reason as to why she wants to move to Bombay:

> "Mrs. Aggarwal, you are spoiling your daughter. What nonsense this is! How can you allow such a young girl to go to Bombay all by herself?" [...] "It's not as if there are no models in Delhi," Mrs. Sethia continued. Amrita overheard the remark and snapped, "Yes there are [...] third-rate models posing for Ludhiana Wollen Mills. That's not my style." (De *Strange* 1)

Many parents are afraid of sending their daughters to distant places, either for education or for a career. The reason is that the daughters are "young" and either they have to be accompanied or placed in relatives' house. How can a daughter be restricted from going to distant places if she gets an opportunity to do a course or to pursue a career? Opportunities do not come to one's doorstep or at one's own place. One has to go in search of opportunities; otherwise someone else is always there to take one's place. Amrita's parents have to be appreciated for sending their daughter with full confidence in her. Mrs. Aggarwal defends her daughter's choice of going to "Bombay" to establish herself as a model. Amrita does not want to be a "third-rate model" in Delhi for a small company product. She wants to bag a well-reputed company project.

Amrita has a problem with Minx who is a lesbian trying to possess her for life. Neelam Tikka argues:

> Amrita feels close to Minx since she fulfils most of her needs, so love is from within and not without. She also helps her in developing her career. Amrita has everything, a good house, somebody taking care of her finances. She is taken care of very well. The only thing she lacks is a child. If that need could be fulfilled, she would prefer this relationship to a heterosexist one. (225)

I disagree with Tikka's view that Amrita is not required to marry as every "need" including "her career" has been provided by Minx. Consider the following:

> Amrita continued in a low voice. "May be I should just forget about this whole modelling thing and go back to Delhi."
>
> Karan stared at her in surprise, "Are you crazy? You are going to be the most sensational discovery on the modelling scene after our new campaign gets released. You already have half a dozen prestigious contracts in hand. Tomorrow you might get flooded with movie offers. And you want to throw all that away because of some mad woman?"
>
> Amrita confessed, "I am scared to death of her, Karan. I feel she could harm me some day. I can't go anywhere without the creepy sensation that she is close by somewhere, watching me. It's a horrible position to be in." (De *Strange* 24)

Look how terrified Amrita is of Minx. But her friend Karan urges her to be brave and stay back. But Amrita is horrified at the prospect of continuing in Bombay.

In spite of being scared of Minx, Amrita has been successful as a model in Bombay. Yet she has a fear of not getting modelling chances and expresses doubts of her survival to Sheila, her model friend:

> Amrita continued to voice her doubts. "What if I don't get assignments for a month? How do I pay the rent and share expenses? With Mrs Pinto it was a fairly flexible arrangement. I don't want to ask my brothers or parents to subsidize me [...] my self-respect is at stake." (De *Srange* 50)

It is common in any competitive field like modelling or acting to experience a fear of not getting enough offers and opportunities. So Amrita has expressed her "doubts." She is very independent and wants to show that she can lead her own life without any family member's support. She has become a role model for any "educated" woman who wants to be independent. I like this kind of a woman who always thirsts for an independent life without depending on her family members. The work of parents ends when they give women enough support to get them educated. What more does one need than education and the confidence to start one's own career and establish oneself? Her friend Sheila says:

> [...] "Oh my! Such a propah little lady. Don't worry. I'm a real Shylock. I'll get the money out of you. Besides, stop being so bloody modest. You've put us all out of business after getting here. If you don't get assignments, what about the rest of us?" (De *Strange* 50)

Amrita, who has been successful, feels that way what about the "rest" of the models who are less popular than Amrita. As the narrator says:

> Amrita laughed. It was true. She had been hogging all the plum jobs and her rates had gone through the roof, upsetting the market. This had led to some hostility and jealousy, but she had been far too busy to bother about it. Some of the girls, like Sheila, had accepted her supremacy with grace and good humour. Others had not been as sporting. But Amrita was smart enough to realize that nobody did anybody a single favour in the cut-throat modelling business. You either delivered, or you were out. And right now Amrita was delivering—ad after sensational ad. (De *Strange* 50)

Like Malini and Amrita, Devi too in Githa Hariharan's *The Thousand Faces of Night* (1992) is highly educated and has an arranged marriage. She is doing her M.A. in U.S.A. when her mother reminds her that it is time to get married. Her mother is very particular about an arranged marriage. She finds the proposal from the Sreenivasans good enough for her daughter. The Sreenivasans would like to see the prospective bride and settle the marriage. The following lines reveal their expectations from their prospective daughter-in-law:

> So they were looking for an accomplished bride, a young woman who would talk intelligently to her scientist husband's friends, but who would also to be, as

> all the matrimonial ads in the Sunday papers demanded, fair, beautiful, home-loving and prepared to "adjust." (Hariharan *Thousand* 17)

What is interesting here is that the "bride" has been asked to prepare to "adjust." This adjustment can be anything, be it with regard to the hectic work at home, be it with the husband leaving the wife for days together in the name of official tour, be it with regard to an impotent husband, or one who does not encourage further studies etc. Moreover, she has to be "fair", "beautiful" and "home-loving." Though Devi rejects this particular proposal, she marries Mahesh with expectations similar to those of the Sreenivasans. No matter where she has studied and what she has studied, no matter if she is educated or uneducated, a woman goes through the same process. Even if a woman dislikes a particular man she has to suppress her dislike and pretend so as not to disobey her parents.

Mahesh, Devi's husband, is a regional manager in a multinational company that makes detergents and toothpastes. C. Vijayasree calls Mahesh "a diligent and serious minded business executive" (177). Mahesh is most of the time away on tours, like Dalip in *This Time of Morning* and Som in *The Day in Shadow*. He has no time to spend with his wife. Husbands who are in business might have problems such as this with their wives and their marriage may end in a divorce as in the cases of Dalip, Som and now Mahesh. After the marriage Devi is fed up with Mahesh. She says:

> I find I can barely suppress my increasing longing to say, yes, we have said enough about your work, your tours, your company. A marriage cannot be forced into suddenly being there, it must grow gradually, like a delicate but promising sapling. What about us? What kind of a life will we make together? It seems too foolish, too intense a question to ask of this reasonable stranger who has already carefully examined, experienced, dissected, and is now ready to file away as settled, something as fragile and newborn as our marriage. Can this acute businessman's eyes, with all their shrewd power, really

> be weak-sighted? Does he not see that it is too early for quietness? Too soon for the companionship of habit? (Hariharan *Thousand* 49)

According to Pradeep Trikha: "Devi has some expectations from her husband, Mahesh to support and understand her on emotional grounds but her expectations are never realized" (9). On the other hand, Mahesh expects his wife to become his companion as soon as he marries her. Devi has been examining her husband's mind to realize that he is taking her for granted.

Devi is interested in learning Sanskrit and goes to her Baba to converse with him. But she finds it very difficult to understand Sanskrit. So she expresses her desire to learn Sanskrit. Mahesh responds thus to this wish of Devi:

> "Why," Mahesh asked.
>
> "So I can understand Baba's quotations better," I said.
>
> "Don't be foolish," he said. "The English translations are good enough. And what will you do with all this highbrow knowledge?" (Hariharan *Thousand* 52)

Rather than understanding her desire, Mahesh cross-questions her and brushes it aside. It is for her to decide whether it is good to understand a Sanskrit quotation. It is not his concern. The reason is that he has never interacted with Baba. Moreover, Mahesh considers Sanskrit "highbrow knowledge" and wonders what use such knowledge is to her.

When Devi wants to apply for the position of a research assistant, he discourages her:

> "I must look for a job, I have so little to do," I said. My hands spread before me on the table, palms upward, empty.
>
> "What can you do?" Mahesh asked, like a ruthless interviewer stripping away the inessential. When he says the words, they become true. What *could* I do?
>
> "I saw a post for a research assistant advertised in the paper," I said. "You need at least one more degree for that," he said. "And what will you do when the baby comes?" (Hariharan *Thousand* 64-65)

Devi thinks that as there is not much to do at home, she would like to work to overcome her boredom. But Mahesh questions her capacity. Moreover, he sees her only as a home-maker, a mother.

In fact, there is no news of Devi becoming pregnant after their marriage. Look at what Mahesh tells Devi:

> "Let's have a baby," Mahesh said. "There's no reason to wait. I want you to have my baby," he said, and after a night of purposeful love-making, he left the next morning on a month-long tour.
>
> He is far too civilized to raise his hand and bring it down on my rebellious body. He snarls instead about women's neuroses and my faulty upbringing.
>
> Am I neurotic because I am a lazy woman who does not polish her floors every day? An aimless fool because I swallowed my hard-earned education, bitter and indigestible, when he tied the *thali* round my neck? A teasing bitch because I refuse him my body when his hand reaches out; and dream instead, in the spare room, of bodies tearing away their shadows and melting, like liquid wax burnt by moonlight? (Hariharan *Thousand* 74)

He wants Devi to have his baby, to have a control over her body and emphasizes the role of a mother. But having a baby is not like buying or selling a product.

Devi is then attracted towards Gopal, who is her neighbour and allows him to touch her:

> Gopal strolls into our garden every day, his raw-silk kurta strangely out of place among the coarse, weed-ridden bushes. His music is his life; he walks a straight and narrow path as purposeful as Mahesh's. But he misses nothing. He knows every muscle on my face, he sees the shadow before it falls across my eyes. We talk, he sings. When he takes my hand and brushes the fingertips with his moist mouth, the lush prison around me dissolves into a green blur. I sleep less and less every night. I ache for that drug, that blissful numbness. Waiting for him,

> even the trees outside do not stir in their breathless anticipation. (Hariharan *Thousand* 77-78)

Eventually Gopal writes a letter to Devi asking her to elope with him: "A letter from Gopal like a mirror. He sees himself, the artist, scaling dizzy heights with arrogance. Come with me, he says. You must decide for yourself, he says" (Hariharan *Thousand* 89). Gopal extends his hand to her asking her to accept him as her lover and elope with him. Mahesh writes a letter to Sita, the mother of Devi, saying that Devi has run away with Gopal:

> The promise made to her, the promise she had made to herself, was not fulfilled. After months of silence, Sita received a terse telegram from Bangalore, not from Devi, but from Mahesh. Devi has run away, he said. Letter follows. All necessary action being taken. (Hariharan *Thousand* 108)

Sita has never interfered in their married life. She receives "a terse telegram from Bangalore," not from Devi but from Mahesh, about Devi running "away" with Gopal. C. Vijayasree remarks that after running away with Gopal, Devi

> seeks [an] escape in the company of a musical celebrity Gopal, remains for some time on the fringes of the ambitious maestro's world of fans and fame, and finally returns to the arms of her mother not a defeated or dejected loner, but a fugitive sure of her survival, determined "to stay and fight, to make sense of it all," "to start from the beginning[139]." (177)

Devi runs away with Gopal thinking that her life now will be better than that with Mahesh. Unlike it was with Mahesh, who has been away from her most of the time, she can spend time with Gopal. So she makes her choice to go with Gopal. She finally realizes that Gopal too is self-centred and makes the decision of returning to her mother to start life anew.

There are some similarities between Shree in Raji Narasimhan's *Forever Free* and Devi. Both are "educated." Both leave their husbands, are attracted to other men but finally go back to their widowed mothers to live with them. In both the novels women's bonding is highlighted.

Unlike Malini, Amrita and Devi, Urmila in Shashi Deshpande's *The Binding Vine* (1992) opts for a love-cum-arranged marriage with Kishore who works in the Navy. Urmila is an English lecturer and marries a childhood friend. She falls in love with Kishore in her adolescence and gets the consent from both the families. As I have said earlier, this is the best type of marriage. The reason is that they are in love with each other and have the consent of their family members. There will be lack of family support if there is no consent either from Kishore's family or from Urmila's family or from both the sides. Urmila and Kishore have perfect understanding. They do not quarrel even on the first night when Urmila walks out on Kishore without having sex and the next day they continue with the daily routine as if nothing has happened the previous night. On the contrary, Akka who is Kishore's mother has a different story to tell. In fact, Kishore's father sees Mira in a marriage he attends and falls in love with her. Remember, he is already married to Akka who has a son Kishore and a daughter Vaana. Akka agrees to her husband marrying Mira as a second wife. She does not mind, as she is a traditional woman. She respects and obeys her husband's wishes. Thus, Mira, who is eighteen years old and doing her third year B. A. course, is married to Kishore's father. Later on, Mira's tragedy of her sexual abuse by her husband is revealed to us through her poetry. This has been discovered by Urmila, her daughter-in-law, who gets the poems published. Evageline Shanti Roy says: "Mira's poems are in Kannada, and as Urmi pieces their meanings together with difficulty, she is horrified to find that, running through all her writing, is a strong, clear thread of an intense physical revulsion for the man she married" (77-78). The above lines reveal how horrifying her sexual experiences with her husband have been. Although he has married her with a lot of passion, in reality he has been a failure and has abused her sexually. J. P. Tripathy has this to say about Mira's death: "Mira, the mother of Urmila's husband Kishore, who died in the second child birth and could not emotionally adjust with the possessive egoistical love of her husband" (151).

Urmila has chosen teaching as a career out of her own interest. She loves teaching and enjoys it. Urmi expresses her fascination for her career to her brother Amrut:

> "What are you planning to do?"
>
> "Go back to work, what else?"
>
> "Are you sure Didi? You want to go on with teaching?"
>
> "What do you mean? I always wanted to teach."
>
> "I know. Gives you a chance to be bossy, huh?"
>
> "I enjoy my classes."
>
> "Good enough for now, but I can't see you going on and on with undergraduate teaching. You've got to start on your doctorate work—last time you told me you'd start as soon as [...]"
>
> "Anu was older, yes, I'd planned that."
>
> "Then get going, Didi, don't postpone it."
>
> "Do you know, Ambu, you sound like Papa. He always felt teaching was something too lowly for his daughter." (Deshpande *Binding* 26-27)

Teaching is what Urmila enjoys. Enjoying a chosen career is very important. The above lines also reveal that Urmila has kept her "doctoral work" pending because her child was growing up. The conversation makes it also clear that her Papa is not happy with his daughter's choice of teaching. It is therefore crystal clear that the choice of a career is Urmila's own.

Vaana in the same novel tries to become a doctor and is unsuccessful, as she does not get enough marks to get a medical seat. However, she works as a medical social worker and chooses this career on her own. Later on, she works in a hospital as a nurse. Vaana has always had a passion for a career in medicine:

> When she was still in school, she made up her mind to be a doctor. She worked hard, adhering rigidly to her

> schedule, not letting anything distract her from it. And yet, in the crucial year, she fell short by a few marks of what was then needed, and couldn't get into any medical college. She collapsed. She frightened Akka and me with her total breakdown; nothing, it seemed, could stop her weeping. But in a few days, her equanimity almost restored, she began preparing herself for the career of a medical social worker. (Deshpande *Binding Vine* 79)

While she may have been upset at not being able to become a doctor, she is strong enough mentally to decide to be a medical social worker. She does not want to give up the medical field. She is determined to continue in the same field if not as a doctor, then as a social worker or a nurse. Vaana works in a hospital. She has been asked to help in not transferring Kalpana who has been raped and brought to the hospital for treatment. Kalpana has been informed that she will be transferred to another hospital as they are short of beds. Urmila has been assisting Kalpana in her treatment and fighting publicly the case of rape. Since Vaana is working in the same hospital, where Kalpana is admitted, she has been asked to help. Urmila says:

> Vaana's getting ready to leave. She's surprised to see me, smiles, then seeing my face says, 'It's about Kalpana, I suppose."
>
> "You know about it. You know they're throwing her out." She's embarrassed, I can see that.
>
> "They're not throwing her out, they're just transferring her to a suburban hospital. Look, I spoke to the AO—they need the bed, there are just fifteen in that ward, she's been here four months already. And there's nothing more they can do for Kalpana here. She needs nursing, that's all. That's just as good in the other place."
>
> "What about the mother? How can she go there everyday?" "You can't expect them to think of that. Be reasonable. Urmi." [...] "You don't know what you're saying, Vaana. Not a terrible thing for the girl to die?

> You think the mother can see it that way? You know nothing about it, you shouldn't talk."
>
> She flinches as if I've struck her, then controls herself with an effort. "I'm just doing a job here, you know I can't do a thing. I spoke to the AO, but once these people take a decision [...] It's no use your quarrelling with me, Urmi. If I could do anything to help, I would."
>
> "I know, but it seems so unfair. Pushing a girl like that around. Not enough beds!"
>
> "Would you like to see the AO yourself? I warn you, though, it's no use. I have enough experience of administrators." (Deshpande *Binding Vine* 166-167)

Vaana tries to justify the hospital administration whereas Urmila tries to find fault with it.

Before Kalpana is raped, she has been working in a shop. It is not a career for her but a job. However, she feels she is leading an independent and self-satisfied life. Her mother Sakuthai explains this about her daughter who she admires:

> She is very smart, that's how she got that job in the shop. Kalpana even learnt how to speak English. People in our *chawl* used to laugh at her, but she didn't care. When she wants something, she goes after it, nothing can stop her. "She's stubborn, you can't imagine how stubborn she is." Pride gives way to resentment. "And she's secretive, she never tells me anything. She didn't even tell me how much her pay was, can you imagine that? Me, her own mother. As if I was going to take her money away from her! I don't want anything. All I ask is that she help me out. She does, I'm not saying she doesn't, but she grumbles. And can you believe it, she gives her father money more easily than she gives me. She doesn't grumble at that, even though she knows he will use it for gambling. He has that *matka* madness. It makes me furious. I don't understand her [...]." (Deshpande *Binding Vine* 92)

Had Kalpana not been raped and that too by her own relative she would have succeeded in her life. However, there is no information about what happens to Kalpana in the novel.

Unlike the characters discussed earlier, Mikki in Shobha De's *Sisters* (1992) has a love marriage. However, her marriage and career are interconnected. She has been forced to choose business as her career as her father is killed in an accident. She is the only daughter of Seth Hiralal, the proprietor of Hiralal Industries. In fact, Mikki has been studying in the United States of America for her M. B. A. degree. She has to give up her studies in order to take up her father's industrial business. She is summoned and handed over the charge of Hiralal Industries by her father's personal secretary, Ramanbhai. As soon as she takes up her father's industries, Mikki asks Ramanbhai to brief her about the industries. He says:

> I appreciate your method of trying to start at the bottom and I agree it is the best way to understand any business. But your case is different. You have been thrown into an unusual situation on the death of your great father. This changes the picture. You don't have time on your hands for apprenticeship. Had you been a son, your father might have taken you into his confidence from a young age and guided you properly from the beginning. But as a daughter, all he wanted for you was a good husband—that is all. Your training, if there was one, was to become an obedient daughter-in-law in some prominent business family [...]. *Beti*, the problem is nobody takes you seriously [...] why waste time with solicitors and accountants? What will they tell you? Nothing. They will give you a cup of tea, compliment you on your nice dress and send you home. My advice is—leave these serious matters to me. I am there to handle them. Trust me. I will guard your interests like a father. But you will make things difficult for yourself if you do things without consulting me." (De *Sisters* 30)

Mikki is right in asking Ramanbhai to brief her about the industries as she has no prior experience in business. Even

Ramanbhai "appreciates" Mikki for her keen interest. He in fact tries to give her a lecture about the risks in business. He suggests that business is not meant for women and so her father has not provided any training for her, as she is his only daughter. Mikki quietly listens to Ramanbhai and replies very carefully and tactfully:

> Thank you for your advice, Ramankaka. I appreciate and value your words. But I'd like you to hear a few of mine now. I can't change my sex, unfortunately. That is the one thing all of you will have to accept. But I can change just about everything else [...] and I intend to. Fate has left me in my father's shoes. Had I been the son he never had but constantly longed for, perhaps I might have had more success with the likes of you. I don't expect you or the others to give up your prejudices—but I want you to know that I will not let that stand in my way. This is going to be my show and I intend running it on my terms. If these old solicitors aren't prepared to talk turkey with me, I'll sack them. That goes for the accountants and anybody else who wishes to treat me like a simple-minded, spoilt little girl out to play at being a businesswoman. My genes are the same as my father's even if my gender isn't. I'm determined not to let the companies go by default. I will learn whatever I have to and I will hire whoever I think fit. (De *Sisters* 30-31)

Mikki does not lose her temper with Ramanbhai for his "advice." Rather, she hits back at him and his accountants. While she thanks him for his concern, at the same time she asks him to "listen" to her "words." She tells him that she "cannot change her sex" as a response to Ramanbhai's point that she was not her father's son to look after the business. However, everyone will have to "accept" her as their boss. She warns them of consequences if they do not realize that she has taken over now.

Although she claims she would look after her father's business, she hands over all her business deals to Binny whom she loves and marries. In fact, he pretends that he is interested in her but his main aim is to seize all her property and make her dependent on him. He is successful in his mission. Mikki is madly in love with him and does whatever he asks her to do. Binny puts conditions on Mikki about taking over Hiralal Industries in order to marry her: "[…] I'm prepared to take on Hiralal Industries with all its current liabilities on two conditions. The first—that you marry me. The second—that you relinquish complete rights in all your father's affairs to me—and that includes properties and any other assets my lawyers will come up with." (De *Sisters* 56)

In effect, he wants to take over both the industries and her self. Mikki's main intention is to marry Binny and not to bother whether the industry can be converted into a profit making industry or not. I agree with E. Satyanarayana's comments on Mikki's marriage:

> Despite being warned, Mikki marries Binny. It is indeed surprising to note that unlike Shobha De's other women-heroes who generally tend to free themselves from the clutches of married life, Mikki deliberately gets into wedlock. Though she has been enamoured of the life of freedom, she is not averse to being a wife, but what she does not like is the inhuman subordination of the woman and confining her to four walls of the kitchen. What with her education in America and progressive thinking, Mikki gives in to Binny whom she loves very much. (148)

In order to marry Binny, Mikki is ready to do anything. Binny also knows about it. He has a calculating mind. He is successful in his plan. She informs her colleagues and personal secretary: "[…] There will be an immediate transfer of funds to ride over the present emergency, and thereafter, we shall be looking at a future take-over. I'll be convening a board of meeting tomorrow, followed by a general meeting soon after the motion is passed. Mr. Malhotra will be in full control [...] and I cannot think of placing the companies built up by my dear father in better hands." (De *Sisters* 88)

I think Mikki is not a successful businesswoman. In order to overcome temporary problems of finance, she is "transferring the funds" to Mr. Malhotra. He will control Hiralal Industries thereafter. Mikki is very firm in her decision although Shanay and Ramanbhai protest against handing over Hiralal Industries to Binny. She says:

> [...] "We are discussing my father's companies and their future. As it turns out my marriage is linked to both. I'm sorry you feel this way, Ramankaka, but the decision is mine and I strongly believe it's in everybody's interests." [...]
>
> Mikki regarded him coolly, "Thank you for your concern and all you've done for my family, Ramankaka. I want you to know that I value you and your advice at all time. And now if you'll excuse me [...]" She walked off leaving him to stare after her retreating back. (De *Sisters* 89)

She is unfair to handover the industry to Binny Malhotra for the sake of her marriage. As a proprietor she has every right to take a decision, which she strongly believes in but which is in everybody's interest.

Gudiya in Namita Gokhale's *Gods, Graves and Grandmother* (1994) falls in love with Kalki and though she does not get the consent of Phoolwati who has been Gudiya's guardian, initially, she has a love-cum-arranged marriage. Phoolwati had promised Gudiya's grandmother that she would look after Gudiya and see to it that she does not lead an unhappy life:

> Phoolwati looked concerned. "What's bothering my Gudiya?" she asked worriedly, still waving the wads of notes in her podgy hands. "Arre, Gudiya, you are born to be a princess—you have your grandmothers (sic) blessings—tell Phoolwati what you want, Gudiya, and she will get it for you. Just test your Phoolwati for once." [...]
>
> "Tell me what's worrying you, Gudiya Rani," She cajoled. "I promised your dead grandmother that I would look after you. You wanted that wretch Kalki,

> you got him! Whatever happens, I will keep my promise. Now tell me, why are you sad?"
>
> "How can I explain, Phoolwati," I sighed. "I never thought that being in love could make a person unhappy."
>
> "Are you talking about that Zero-Hero?" she asked contemptously. "I wish you had fallen in love with a real man, Gudiya." "I love Kalki," I said irritably. "And my name is Pooja. Why can't you remember that?"
>
> "How I wish you could have married a rich man," she continued wistfully. "Rich men are different." (*Gods* 128)
>
> We were married within a week. It should have been the happiest day of my life. The entire temple premises were bedecked with swaying toranas of tender mango-leaves. [...] We got married in the mid-afternoon. (Gokhale *Gods* 164)

Therefore, she consents to the marriage, though reluctantly.

Gudia is a school dropout. Kalki lures her before marriage. He even finds out that there are no parents living with her except Phoolwati with whom she is living. He takes her to "a marriage party" and makes love to her:

> He ripped open my kurta and fondled me with fierce passion. He pummelled my breasts until I cried with pain, and then moved his attentions downwards. When he entered me I let out a fierce cry of pain. He put his hand over my mouth and told me untenderly to shut up, didn't I know there were people around? [...] When we were finished he wore a satisfied smile on his face. "Liked it?" he asked complacently. "Girls always do." (Gokhale *Gods* 120)

As a result of this, she becomes pregnant. She comes to know this fact only after four months of pregnancy. This is a very advanced stage to abort the foetus. After marriage she leads a miserable life. She offers all her jewels to her husband so that he could meet some music directors and have a career. In other words, she has been cheated and exploited in the name of love.

Nisha in Shobha De's *Sultry Days* (1994) is in love with Deb but does not marry him as he does not believe in the institution of marriage. On the other hand, she remains unmarried and continues to concentrate on her career.

Nisha has also chosen her career as an ad agent on her own. She takes up the job to be independent financially. She says:

> I took up a job with a mediocre ad agency straight after college. Just because I'd graduated with English honours and didn't really want to study any further, I had decided to go out and get myself a job, any job. And as everybody knows, when there's nothing better going, join advertising. If your bullshit sells—nothing like it. If not, you can still get by. Not shine as a supernova, but crawl along, jumping from one agency to the next, till you join the huge firmament of senior mediocrities like yourself. By then, you at least have the ad jargon mastered and several cute tricks under your belt. (10)

I think what Nisha does is the right thing. Any "educated" woman should not wait for a big job in the initial stages. I don't mean to say that one should not have the idea of getting a good job. But a beginning has to be made. Nisha does not "want to" continue after graduating with English honours. Nisha is like Anjali in *Socialite Evenings*. She is of the opinion that after graduation there is no necessity to study further. It is better to take up "a job" immediately after graduation. I agree with her view, especially, if a person is not interested in higher studies. She is also of the view that if a person does not get "any job," it is better to take up an "advertising" job. She is practical enough to do so. The ad agency that she joins may not be good but there is always a chance of finding a better one. What is important is gaining experience in any field. Based only on one's own experience there are chances of getting better opportunities.

Nisha is not only happy with her mediocre job but is also content with her pay. She expresses this to a marketing guy Anil Bhandari who is back in India from the US hoping to pay back to his country by working in India. Anil and Nisha talk about their careers:

> "[...] I wanted to come back home and set up my own shop. Hell, I decided, if I was going to bust my ass, I might as well do it for myself [...] but let's not talk about me. What about you? What's a nice girl like you doing in a sloppy ad agency?"
>
> "Frankly, I don't know. I kind of enjoy it. It's not too demanding. The pay's OK. The people are fine. I have enough time to do other things [...] you know, see plays and stuff." (De *Sultry* 83)

Nisha is very frank with Anil about her career and her feelings about it. She gives the impression that she is working to her capacity. She is not embarrassed about her mediocre and "sloppy agency" job. She is not interested in the type of agency but in doing the job and "enjoying" it.

At the same time, Nisha has also undertaken writing in the Sunday supplements of a newspaper. She is interested in doing different things. She does not hesitate to write and is aware of the money she gets out of writing:

> Writing for Sunday supplements was fine. And fun. But it didn't fetch me too much money. And money was what I needed. Badly. Besides, freelancers are the real pariahs of journalism—nobody pays them either on time or sufficiently. Yet, everybody needs them. I had assignments galore. I even got to travel [...] Well, mainly to pick places the staffers didn't want to go to. It was enjoyable [...] but hardly rewarding in monetary terms. But I went along for the ride, covering abandoned monuments, abandoned wives, abandoned pets and abandoned dreams. Something was clearly wrong—I was working harder than ever before in my life, but my bank balance was dismally low. And horror of horrors, the importance of money had begun to dawn on me [...] finally. (De *Sultry* 182-183)

She is also aware that "freelance writers" are treated like "pariahs" in the field of journalism. She accepts all the pain in writing. Moreover, she enjoys travelling that the work entails. Earlier she was not worried about the money she earned but now she is. She needs to earn money too.

As a Sunday supplement writer she becomes famous. However, there is a drastic turn in her career—from journalism to selling basmati rice to Arab countries. Even if she is offered a huge amount for her journalism, she does not want to take up journalism as she has a flourishing rice business:

> I also discovered to my utter surprise that I had business sense. This was by accident. A school friend showed up unexpectedly from Dubai. "Can you supply basmati rice and chick peas to a few grocers there?" she asked. Rather a strange enquiry addressed to someone who was neither a farmer nor a shopkeeper. Recklessly, I agreed. And that's how I became a trader. Did it really represent much of a progression from being a lowly ad agency hack? Not really. But selling chickpeas to the Arabs was more fun than selling cigarettes to the locals. (De *Sultry* 183)

She has changed her career from ad agency to selling chickpeas to Arabs. Is this a progression? Yes it is. Moreover, she is enjoying her new career of selling chickpeas.

Even as she continues with this new business, Amar and Parthiv ask her to work for *Bharat* newspaper. Nisha accepts it only on condition that she be given independence, that she be allowed to continue her business and that she be given a great deal of money:

> Amar continued smoothly, "How much are you making selling rice [...] five grand? Ten grand? We can make you an offer you can't refuse." "Fine," I said. "But I'd still want to continue to sell my rice." "Why?" Parthiv asked.
>
> "Because I enjoy it [...] and I like being my own boss. If I consider joining you at all, I'd prefer to work out some sort of a loose arrangement. Maybe you could consider a retainer. I don't want to give up my business [...] and in case you are interested, it makes me a great deal of

> Yashwantbhai lured at their first meeting, scratching his groin thoughtfully, "Politics [...] women's issues [...] you are the right person. You could head our Special Cell. It is a good job. Good pay. We will look after your daughter's education [...] everything. Also you will be protected." (De *Sultry* 161-163)

Although she wants to continue her job, she cannot do so as there are two daughters to be looked after by her. It is very difficult to look after children as a divorcee. Hence she has to quit the job. But luckily she enters politics with the help of Yaswhantbhai who needs "a woman" to fetch votes by raising "women's issues" and becoming popular. She has been assured hat her children's "education" will be taken care of. She will e paid a "good" and handsome salary. Above all she "will be rotected," as she is a lonely woman in Nagpur.

Pramila divorces her husband only because she has married boring husband. She has everything in her life—a well-settled usband, children, house and a happy life. However, she does ot find pleasure in her life. She feels that her husband is a oring person and takes up writing in order to find some leasure in life:

> Married to a boring mechanical engineer from Pilani at an early age, Pramila strained against the kind of life he had to offer. In quick succession, she produced a boy and two girls, after which she considered her duty towards her husband over and done with. (De *Sultry* 160)

ie main reason why Pramila feels bored with her husband las is that she is married at a very early age. Perhaps she is t even a graduate. In addition to getting married at a very rly age, she has three children even before she can get used to r life. This is a bad indication of their married life. Maybe, r husband should have given her some time to enjoy her life, en her enough time for her to settle down in her life. If a fe has a child one after the other and has no other cupation, she may have this kind of a bored life. She is icating that all that her husband wanted is children and hing else.

> money." Amar and Parthiv exchanged glances. "W
> a package in mind actually. Plus, a fancy desigr
> You would be features editor with complete c
> The only people you'd be reporting to is the two
> [...] "Why not eight profiles over three month
> you?"
>
> "That sounds reasonable [...] and I'm interestec
> *Sultry* 209)

Nisha has risen to the level of being able to
"editorship," for the job of editing is very prestigio
reason is that the "editor" has more power than ar
person in the publication department. Unless Nisha is
to continue her "business" she will not accept the d
Amar and Parthiv. Moreover, she would like to di
workload and the kind of work.

In the same novel, Pramila, on the other hand
arranged marriage. She takes up writing poetry
politics as a career. She finally divorces her husban
she is bored with that life. She in fact takes up this
on her own but to find some change in her life. She
feeling bored with her marital and materialistic life.
not find her life meaningful. She tries to find som
through writing poetry. She in fact leaves her hu
children in order to flourish in her career. She writ
publishers. Later on she gets a job. She writes a le
husband:

> She had found a job in a Marathi fortnight
> staying as a paying guest in Dadar. [...] The j
> away for long hours [...] applying for leave
> and staying home to look after the little
> searching frantically for a substitute maid.
>
> Her bosses were understanding but they cou
> privileges endlessly to accommodate Pramila
> It was time for her to look around and mov
> she promptly did. [...] It was at this point t
> into her through Yashwantbhai, who w
> induct her into politics [...] "We need wom

On the contrary, Vilas her husband, wants to provide everything to his wife before she asks for it. He feels that he is being good to his wife and children. He is trying to please his wife and children but she thinks the other way round. The narrator says:

> Unfortunately, Vilas had different ideas about holy matrimony. He saw them putting down roots in Nagpur, drawing from his provident fund to buy a bungalow there. He wanted to see his son to follow in his footsteps and become a PWD engineer when the time came for him to retire. For his daughters he could only foresee a stable middle-class marriage to doctors (preferably g. p.'s with a "decent" practice) or lawyers. As for Pramila—why, she had everything a woman could ask for—a husband with a 'solid' job, security, lovely children, a moped of her own and all the time in the world to pursue her interests, join the local Mahila Mandal, attend *haldi-kumkums*, organize Sarvajanik Ganapati festivals and show off her latest sari brought by him from Bombay while on "tour." Yet, Pramila was wilting. He thought she was ill. She was, but not in the way he assumed. (De *Sultry* 160-161)

Vilas believes in the institution of marriage. He considers marriage as "holy matrimony." Once a person is married, he is bound to it throughout his life. He feels it is his duty to look after his family. He feels that in spite of all that he has provided Pramila, she is not happy with her married life.

As a result of this boredom, she has taken up writing to find some meaning in her life. However, she does not reveal to her husband that she is writing poetry. As soon as the children go to school, she starts scribbling on papers. Pramila reminds us of Jaya in *That Long Silence* as far as her writing is concerned. Pramila writes "intense", "erotic" and enraged poetry in a pseudonym and gets it published through the pulp publishers. She does get money and thinks of leaving for Bombay. She leaves never to return.

After a few months, Vilas and his mother receive a letter from Pramila informing them about her newly found job and about her being a paying guest at Dadar. She enquires about her children and her husband. She also informs in the letter that she is planning to visit Nagpur very soon. The narrator explains as to why she is in Nagpur a year after her departure:

> Nearly a year after her departure, Pramila went back to Nagpur. Vilas was stony-faced and hostile. The youngest child ran and hid behind the grandmother, while the older two rushed eagerly towards her and asked for presents from Bombay. Pramila was in Nagpur on a specific mission. She wanted a divorce. And the children. Vilas was stunned. His mother wasn't. "Give her the divorce and keep the children," she advised. Vilas consulted his lawyer friend. "Your mother is right," he said. But Vilas was adamant. "I want her," he moaned. They arrived at a compromise. "Take the girls," the mother screamed. "The son is ours. He bears our name." And so it was that after battling for ten days, Pramila took the train back to Bombay with two very frightened little girls with her. (De *Sultry* 161-162)

The reason is that she wants "a divorce" from her husband. Why should she ask for a divorce? What wrong has he done her? He neither quarrels with her nor beats her up. The reason should be justifiable. Look at Vilas's reaction to her request. He is "stony-faced and hostile" and stunned. Vilas's mother asks him to divorce her without any hesitation. Why don't they think about children? How will they grow up when their parents are divorced? If the couple is incompatible or has an unhappy sexual life or if the husband is a wife-beater or a drunkard, then there is a reason for asking for divorce. There is no complaint of that kind against Vilas. However, Vilas is willing to divorce her, though reluctantly. At least to me Pramila's reasons are not justifiable.

Unlike Pramila, Aparna in Shobha De's *Snapshots* (1995) has a love marriage with Rohit who is an architect. Aparna is working as an Accounts Supervisor in an ad agency. Basically, she is not a housewife but a career woman.

Aparna has chosen her career on her own as an Accounts Supervisor. Although she is career-oriented, her husband does not encourage his wife. He has an ego that he is the bread-earner. Even if his wife works he expects her to behave like a housewife and do whatever he asks her to do. She finds it problematic to cope with both married life and career. She finds it very difficult to lead a peaceful life, as her husband is not cooperative. He is a typical patriarchal person. She does not hesitate to argue with her husband. She cannot be taken for granted. When her husband says that he brings home the bread, Aparna reminds him that she also does the same thing. Rohit walks out of Aparna's life without taking divorce legally. He does not understand that his wife also has a career to take care of. He expects his wife to be a traditional housewife:

> One morning, Rohit asked for his coffee and while she showered, he casually packed. When she emerged from the bathroom, she found him dressed and ready to leave. She towel dried her hair and asked unsuspectingly,
>
> "Going somewhere?"
>
> "Yes," Rohit replied, lighting a cigarette.
>
> "You didn't tell me, Baroda again?" Aparna continued.
>
> "Yes," he said coolly.
>
> "How long?" she asked looking for something in her wardrobe. "For good," he replied picking up his bag. [...]
>
> "It is," he said ducking. "Watch me while I leave." And with those words he'd picked up his Samsonite and walked out of her life. No explanations. No apologies. (De *Snapshots* 19)

Rohit does not give any "explanations" as to why he is walking out of Aparna's life. Nor does he apologize for leaving unexpectedly. He assumes that he can walk out of her life at any time he feels comfortable. Aparna misses Rohit and feels a shock.

> The shock of his absence had led (sic) to a depression she had thought she would never pull herself out of. For four days she hadn't dared to leave their smart, stark, impersonally efficient flat. She'd remained in bed with the Japanese lantern swinging maddeningly over her head. She couldn't eat. Or drink. Or smoke. Or think. Or even mourn. She missed him so deeply, so physically, every bit of her being ached. (De *Snapshots* 19)

Rohit walking out of her life has made her think as to why he has left her like that. She goes back to a time when both of them think of having a kid and then postponing it, as both of them are career oriented. She recalls an incident about forgetting to buy a wine bottle:

> "Where's the wine?" he'd asked.
>
> "I forgot. I'm sorry, but I forgot. I was so rushed at the office today—the secretary had bunked—and I had to get the presentation ready for those blasted new batteries—you know, the new account I was telling you about last week?"
>
> Rohit had stared at her coldly. "Fuck you. And fuck your new account. When I tell you to make sure there's wine in the fridge, baby, you bloody well make sure there's wine in the fridge, baby, you bloody well make sure there's wine in the fridge. Now, if you know what's good for you, you'll get your ass out of here. Go to the Club and pick the fucking bottles up." (De *Snapshots* 21-22)

How can he be so rude to his wife if she forgets to buy the wine, as she is busy at office? Look at his reaction to her forgetting to buy wine for him. He uses filthy language and four-letter words. Look at Rohit's authoritarian attitude.

Apart from this, she also recollects the arguments that used to take place quite often between them. About one of them, she says:

> [...] "I thought you were the New Man. I expected you to care and share. But you're like any other husband. The same old double standards. The same hypocrisies."

> Rohit would smile back sadistically, "Too bad you miscalculated. Sure I have double standards I bring home the bread. You cook. Easy." Aparna would retort furiously, "Don't forget I bring home the bread too. I am a serious career person. When we married, you respected my priorities. You knew what you were getting into. If you'd wanted a housemaid, you should have married one." (De *Snapshots* 22)

As Jasbir Jain says in her article "Post-Colonial Realities: Women Writing History," Aparna is "rejecting the hegemony of female projections, [she] cross[es] over to occupy a centrality ordinarily withheld from [her]" (65).

Unlike Aparna, Parvati in Namita Gokhale's *A Himalayan Love Story* (1996) has an arranged marriage with Lalit Joshi. Parvati has lost her father at the early age of one. She has been looked after and is educated by her mother's stepbrother Hiranand Joshi. He runs a school and is very particular about Parvati's education. Contrary to her wishes, Hiranand Joshi has chosen a husband for Parvati. She is asked to marry Lalit Joshi and Parvati obliges. She does not say anything negative. She meekly abides by the verdict:

> The year I turned twenty Masterji [Hiranand] told me that I was to be married. He had chosen a boy for me, somebody I already knew, and obviously liked. I thought perhaps he was talking about Mukul Nainwal, who was then studying in Allahabad; but no, Masterji had decided that I was to be married to Mukul's best friend, Lalit Joshi.
>
> It was not that I disliked Lalit. In fact, all in all, I rather liked him. [...] I considered the prospect of marriage to Lalit. It was not likely to be very exciting, but I was hardly in a position to contradict Masterji or his decisions. [...]
>
> The day I was to be married I was ritually bathed with turmeric and sandalwood. I wore a red silk sari and the gold champakali necklace my mother had left me. (34-36)

Why should she hesitate to say whether she would "marry" Lalit or not? Of course, Masterji has provided her education, money and now a marriage alliance. This does not mean she has to follow whatever he suggests. From the above lines, it is clear that she is interested in marrying "Mukul Nainwal" and not Lalit. However, she does not protest or expresses her opinion. She simply obeys him. She has no guts to say that she likes Mukul and would like to marry him. Why can't she "contradict" Masterji's "decision"? It is her life after all. I think it is also wrong on the part of "Masterji." He feels he can dictate terms to Parvati. One has to remember that he runs a school and provides education to children. He has to take Parvati into confidence before he declares his selection of a husband for Parvati. Parvati's position is also critical. She is faced with a moral dilemma. What is her life without Masterji's helping hand? Unable to cope with life, she becomes insane.

Maya too in Shobha De's *Second Thoughts* (1996) has an arranged marriage. She does protest to her mother about the arranged marriage:

> "An arranged marriage? For me? Don't be ridiculous. Besides, I have one more year to go before I finish college," Maya remembered protesting just two months earlier.
>
> "So? Who says you can't finish college and then get married?" her mother had argued.
>
> "Then why do we have to go to Bombay now?" Maya had sulked.
>
> "Because boys like Ranjan get snapped up before you and I can blink our eyes—that's why. Besides, he's available for only two weeks. Something about a big assignment he has to do. His family wants to finalize everything before then. Prodipda was very keen on our meeting the Maliks. Ranjan is quite a catch. Who knows, by the time we get to Bombay, some other lucky girl might have grabbed him. Don't think there are no pretty Bengali girls in that city. Bombay is full of them, I'm told there are thousands and thousands of good

> Bengali families there," Chitra had commented in her characteristic agitated fashion. (3)

There is no one to listen to Maya about her anxiety of not being able to graduate. Look at the attitude of Maya's mother. If there is a good match available, families compete. They feel they may miss a "good chance" for their daughters. This is the case with Maya's parents. On the contrary, Maya is fed up with the talk of her marriage. She is interested only in completing her studies and getting a degree. If the marriage is fixed the parents may ask her to stop her studies. This is Maya's worry. However, her mother assures Maya that she can complete her college education. Look at Chitra using the words "catch" and "grab." How competitive are the mothers for "right" boys! Ranjan wants a wife who can be a traditional Indian wife. He feels that he is earning enough money to support his wife and family. He believes that it is a woman's duty to run a good home. After expressing his view, he asks Maya whether she agrees with him or not. In fact, she does not reveal her views:

> Maya [...] nod[s] dumbly while everybody waited to hear her well-considered views. Finally, it was her uncle who'd intervened to say with a laugh, "Our Maya is very talented. Always getting high marks in school and college. [...]
>
> In any Indian family, the husband's comforts always come first. Everything else follows. But it's good for young girls to have a hobby. Keep them busy also." (De *Second* 11)

I think Maya should have expressed her "views" instead of keeping her "views" to herself. Later on, Maya tells her views to her parents. She should have expressed that she is interested in doing a job as she is "educated" and has a degree in textile designing. My strong view about "educated" women is that they should not forget their education or dump it for family life. They have to do something, not just to earn money but to keep themselves busy.

Maya is married to Ranjan. He is a very orthodox person like his mother. He wants his wife to be at home, whether she is educated or not. In his opinion education is not for women. He does not try to understand his wife. He is busy with his own work. Maya has a neighbour Nikhil Verma who is "four or five years younger than" Maya. However, Maya has an extra-marital relationship with Nikhil Verma, who is unmarried. He makes advances towards her and gives her a gift, exploiting her loneliness. He has no business to try and interfere in her personal life. Life to her is boring. What has he got to do with her life? He has to concentrate on his own studies and future. Interestingly, Maya initially resists his advances and later on accepts them. The affair happens when Ranjan is out of town on office work. Nikhil enters her flat with flowers declaring that it is his birthday. He initially kisses her and later on takes her to her bedroom and has sex with her:

> It was a kiss that involved Nikhil's entire being. A kiss so focused, so complete, I surrendered to its soft urgency even though my mind was on mundanities like the washerwoman showing up earlier than usual. [...] Every bit of me was suddenly alive to the feel of Nikhil's lips, hands, arms, neck, chest, knees, legs. [...] May be I was going crazy. I didn't want to think of consequences. [...] I felt free. Lunatic. Wonderful. [...] I allowed myself to be pushed back on my bed—the bed I shared with Ranjan. I knew we were on Ranjan's side of it by the smell of the bed linen and pillows. I could feel Nikhil's hands under my caftan, pulling it up, up and up. [...] Fifteen minutes later, my eyes were still shut. Nikhil had obviously dressed and gone. [...]. (De *Second* 268-271)

Alka Saxena rightly points out: "After a breezy affair with Nikhil, Maya would have to spend the rest of her life, sometimes clad in her mother-in-law's discarded sarees and dance to the tune of her rigidly conservative husband. Nothing would have been more irksome" (270). The main reason for Maya to think in this manner is Ranjan's indifference to her emotional and sexual desires. One has to blame Ranjan for his lack of understanding about his wife. Ranjan thinks that he is providing everything to his wife. He is providing material things. What about personal care, tenderness, affection, emotional expressions and romantic feelings? That does not mean Nikhil is providing all that. He is only an opportunist exploiting her.

Unlike Maya, Sumitra in Shashi Deshpande's *A Matter of Time* (1996) has a love marriage. Sumitra is loved by Gopal, who marries her. Sumitra is a young eighteen-year old girl and naturally reciprocates his love and marries him. It is an inter-caste and inter-lingual marriage. This kind of a thing is generally possible only in love marriages. Gopal takes the advice of his friends. Gopal feels: "She's not of our caste, she does not speak our language. What will my parents say?" (67). He agrees to marry her only when one of his friends says: "Marry her, the friend said, and he said it over and over again. 'Marry her, she's a good girl, she'll make you a good wife, I am sure of that. Marry her.' [...] So I married Sumi. And I knew I was right, it was my body that told me this truth. I never had any doubts about my feelings for her"(67).

Sumitra has been separated from her husband, Gopal. Gopal is a lecturer in History in a college. There is no legal divorce just like in the case of Rohit and Aparna in Shobha De's *Snapshots* who are not legally divorced but are separated. The reason that Gopal gives to Premi, the younger sister of Sumi, is ridiculous:

> "Why did you do it, Gopal?" [...]
>
> "Why did I do it? I can give you so many answers, but I've begun thinking that the plain truth is that I just got tired."
>
> "Tired? Of Sumi?" [...]
>
> "Well, let me put it this way. I could no longer believe that there is a meaning to my life, a happy culmination waiting for me at the end of it. Can you imagine what living with such a person would be for my children? For Sumi?"
>
> "No meaning to your life?" Premi gets hold of that phrase. "Oh Gopal, what about your children?"

> "For you, it's Nikhil, isn't it? But not for me; to think of being the purpose of my parents' life would have been too heavy a burden on me to carry. Can I then burden my children with that load? No, Premi, the meaning has to be found in your own life." (Deshpande *Matter* 133-134)

He says he is "tired" of his daughters. Is it because he has no male company in the family? One cannot agree with his reason. He cannot give the lack of a male member in the family as the reason. He also says that he does not find any "meaning" to his married "life." Why does he think of giving his daughters an education and getting them married a burden? Moreover, indirectly he points out to Premi that she has only a son, Nikhil to look after whereas he has three daughters. He suggests that his daughters find meaning to their lives on their own. He has to have a solid and logical reason to be separated from his family members. Is he trying to say that he cannot manage his family without a son in his family? He does not even say that he wants to take a divorce from his wife. Nor does his wife demand a divorce. She quietly accepts the separation. She does not even express her anger. The important factor is that he has fallen in love with Sumi and has married her against her parents' wishes. It is a love marriage. However, Sumi's eldest daughter Arundhati cannot tolerate her father leaving them without his support and presence in their house, without even applying for divorce. Aru does suggest the following:

> [...] Aru has no intention of forgetting, no intention of letting Sumi forget, either.
>
> "I think you should see a lawyer," she says to her mother.
>
> "You mean because of Gopal? Devi's been saying that to me, too, she wants me to meet Murthy's cousin who's a lawyer. But I don't see the point of it."
>
> "The point? The point is you've got to do something."
>
> "What ? Get a divorce? I'm not interested."

> "But he owes you, he owes all of us, yes, you especially, he owes you—" lamely, "something. He can't get away like this! He has to give us maintenance."
>
> Sumi laughs, she seems genuinely amused. "Gopal has outsmarted the law. He's given us all that he had. And he has nothing now, not even a proper job. I don't think he's getting more than a bare subsistence from Shankar's press—so Ramesh tells me. So what can the law make him do?" "Sumi, you are making it too easy for him, you're letting him get away with it. He's getting scot-free. It's not right, he must be made to realize what he's done [...]."
>
> "How? By punishing him? Do you want to punish him, Aru? I don't. I'm not interested. I just want to get on with my life." She puts an arm around Aru's shoulder.
>
> "Let him go? Aru, just let him go. This is not good for you." [...] "Let him go? As if he's a—a mere acquaintance or somebody with whom we've had a small misunderstanding? He's our father, Ma, he's your husband. How can you dismiss it so lightly? I don't understand you at all." (Deshpande *Matter* 60-61)

Sumi is "not interested" in getting a "divorce" from Gopal. This indicates that she does not want to be separated from her husband. It is different if Gopal wants to lead a single life. Aru's point is that he has to pay for their "maintenance," for producing them and marrying her mother. Sumi does not want to take any action against her husband. She is not "interested" in punishing him. It seems she still has a liking for him in spite of his deserting her.

Like Sumi, Ammu too in Arundhati Roy's *The God of Small Things* (1997) marries an assistant manager of a tea estate (his name is not given in the novel) for love. He sees Ammu in a wedding reception and proposes to her. Ammu decides immediately and writes a letter to her parents. They don't respond to her letter. However, Ammu does not wait for their consent or for their letter. She goes ahead with an elaborate Calcutta wedding:

> He was a small man, but well-built. Pleasant-looking. He wore old-fashioned spectacles that made him look earnest and completely belied his easy-going charm and juvenile but totally disarming sense of humour. He was twenty-five and had already been working on the tea estates for six years. He hadn't been to college, which accounted for his schoolboy humour. He proposed to Ammu five days after they first met. Ammu didn't pretend to be in love with him. She just weighed the odds and accepted. She thought that *anything*, anyone at all, would be better than returning to Ayemenem. She wrote to her parents informing them of her decision. They didn't reply. Ammu had an elaborate Calcutta wedding. (Roy *God* 39)

Ammu divorces her husband because he drinks excessively. Moreover, Ammu's husband asks her to sleep with and look after his boss. This divorce is justified, as her husband is an alcoholic, a wife-beater and one who is willing to "sell" his wife. No "educated" woman would accept it if her husband crosses his limits. The narrator says:

> Her husband turned out to be not just a heavy drinker but a full-blown alcoholic with all of an alcoholic's deviousness and tragic charm. [...] Ammu was eight months pregnant when war broke out with China. [...] Estha and Rahel were born. [...] By the time the twins were two years old their father's drinking, aggravated by the loneliness of tea estate life, had driven him into an alcholic stupor. (Roy *God* 40-41)

No wife can tolerate an alcoholic husband. He does not take care of his wife even at the stage of "pregnancy." As she does not have her parents' support, it is his responsibility all the more to take care of her.

He knows that he will be sacked for neglecting his duty. However, his boss eyes Ammu and her beauty. He wants to exploit the situation by threatening the husband by asking him to resign from his post. At the same time Mr. Hollick, the boss gives a suggestion by which he may be able to retain his job:

> "You are a lucky man you know, wonderful family, beautiful children, such an attractive wife... An extremely attractive wife..." Over coffee, Mr. Hollick proposed that Baba go away for a while. For a holiday. To a clinic perhaps, for treatment. For as long as it took him to get better. And for the period of time that he was away, Mr. Hollick suggested that Ammu be sent to his bungalow to be "looked after." (Roy *God* 41-42)

Look at how Mr. Hollick tries to exploit Ammu's husband's weakness:

> She said nothing. He grew uncomfortable and then infuriated by her silence. Suddenly he lunged at her, grabbed her hair, punched her and then passed out from the effort. Ammu took down the heaviest book she could find in the bookshelf—*The Reader's Digest World Atlas*—and hit him with it as hard as she could. On his head. His legs. His back and shoulders. When he regained consciousness, he was puzzled by his bruises. He apologized abjectly for the violence, but immediately began to badger her about helping with his transfer. This fell into a pattern. Drunken violence followed by post-drunken badgening. Ammu was repelled by the medicinal smell of stale alcohol that seeped through his skin, and the dry, caked vomit that encrusted his mouth like a pie every morning. When his bouts of violence began to include the children and the war with Pakistan began, Ammu left her husband and returned, unwelcomed, to her parents in Ayemenem. (Roy *God* 42)

Ammu remains silent to his proposal. Her husband loses his temper and "feels uncomfortable and then infuriated" by "her silence." She leaves with her children to her native place. However, Ammu is not welcomed by her parents at Ayemenem.

Virmati in Manju Kapur's *Difficult Daughters* (1998) too has a love marriage with a small difference. She becomes Prof. Harish Chandra's second wife. Virmati protests against her parents' choice of a husband for her. She does reveal the fact that she does not want to marry him. Thus she decides to do her B.T. course so that she can be away from the home and her future husband. She falls in love with an English Professor. She even becomes pregnant before marriage and terminates her pregnancy. She demands that Prof. Harish marry her. He has to marry her as a second wife on the suggestion of a poet friend of his:

> The poet tich-tiched in exasperation. "Bhai, what can they do? Now you get married. Nothing is simpler. A pundit will be arranged—that's all you really need. [...] The next morning a pundit was arranged, and the puja samagri brought. The groom, throwing himself into the spirit of the thing, decided that his bride had to be dressed in something suited to the occasion. [...] In the evening the wedding ceremony proceeded smoothly. The poet's parents did the kanya-daan, the seven pheras were taken, the couple pronounced man and wife. As Virmati rubbed her eyes, watering from the smoke, she knew, rather than felt, that the burden of the past five years had lifted. (Kapur *Difficult* 186)

Before the marriage takes place, Virmati has had sex with Prof. Harish by involving herself in a pre-marital relationship. Harish is already married with children:

> The Professor tightened his grip. His hands inched higher. "Don't," she whispered. "Please."
>
> "Why aren't you mine? And I yours? Body and soul, heart and mind? I worship you, Viru, I want to express it, that's all." The Professor got up and pressed his lips to her throat, her ears, her chin, her lips, murmuring endearments while his breath came faster. He seemed to be in a trance. Dazed, Virmati didn't think it would be fair to bring up the fact of his existing wife and children. But this wasn't right either.
>
> "Then marry me," she said, trying to push him away. "Marry me and make it clear to everybody."
>
> "I will, I will, darling, I will. Just give me time."
>
> His hands held her face, stroked her hair, pushed her against the pillows, wandered lightly over her body, still

> so tight and miserable. They drew light circled on her skin, loosened the drawstring of her salwar, opened the hooks of her Kammez. (Kapur *Difficult* 114)

Professor Harish has taken the initiative in having an affair with her. He loves her passionately and intently. However, Virmati is not willing to participate, as she is a virgin. She does not want to be part of it until he marries her. Harish again brings his romantic words such as "mine" and "yours" and philosophical terms such as "body" and "soul" to convince her. Virmati surrenders to him and loses her virginity. I feel Virmati's parents are responsible for her losing her virginity. She has been forcibly engaged to a canal engineer. In order to escape from this marriage, she goes on to do further studies and gets involved with Prof. Harish.

Virmati unwillingly bows down to her parents' wishes to get engaged to Inderjeet, a canal engineer. However, she is bold enough to say to her parents that she does not want to get married to Inderjeet and wants to go for further studies:

> "I want to study." How weak and fragile that statement sounded, even to Virmati, as it left her hesitant lips, and fell on the skeptical ears of the family. Kasturi hit her. Across her face, from cheek to cheek. "For this, I let you go to college. So that you are ruined permanently? Are you mad?" [...] "*Achcha, achcha,*" Suraj Prakash made neutral noises. "Maybe she was in great difficulty, but she should have come to us, that was her mistake, Why did you do this? Tell us, beti, whatever is in your heart?" "Study," mumbled Virmati like a mantra. She swallowed. "Study [...]" "For such a little thing?" said her father. "You did this for such a little thing?"
>
> "And not marry." Virmati's face twisted. "I don't want to marry." "But why? You know every girl has to go to her own home. This is your right, and our duty. As it is, we have taken our time, not wishing to hurry you. We have let you study, as much as any girl has studied in Amritsar."

> "I know, Pitaji." Oh, why was he so good to her? Why did he speak so gently? She preferred the way the others spoke.
>
> "Then, what is it? The boy, too, is good."
>
> She had to say something. "The boy," she said. "I do not like the boy." (Kapur *Difficult* 79-80)

Later on she goes for further studies as an escape from being close to Inderjeet and falls in love with Prof. Harish and marries him. She does not even hesitate to be a second wife. This itself shows how strong her voice is. She is involved in pre-marital sex, becomes pregnant, and even aborts the foetus. All these decisions are taken on her own.

Virmati marries an English Professor not as a first wife but as a second wife. The reason is that if she marries Inderjeet, who is her parents' choice, she will have to lead a life in a joint family. She knows what a joint family is. She has been in the set-up of a joint family right from her childhood. She does not like the system. She is educated now. She protests against the system. Therefore, she is ready to marry a married man. She feels that being a second wife is not as bad as living in a joint family system. Maybe she will have less work, more privacy and personal satisfaction. She knows the intricacies of a joint family system, especially how difficult it is for women. Further Harish is a lecturer in a college. She expects that she will have a peaceful life, as his first wife is uneducated. She feels that she will be preferred to the first wife. The fact that Harish is interested in Virmati tells us that he may not like his first wife. Perhaps his wife is not educated and cannot discuss or share intellectual ideas with him. Otherwise he would not have shown any interest in her. The ultimate aim of Virmati is to move away from the joint family system. She is a strong advocate of the nuclear family system. There is no doubt about it.

Virmati too has been forced to do her B.T. course and then become a Headmistress of a school in Nahan. The narrator says:

> Virmati was charmed by Nahan. She heard the sounds of the foundry floating up at all hours, and felt herself at one with the working people of the world. She stood in her tiny garden and looked across the valley, turned her head and looked towards the school of which she was headmistress, and sensed her singleness and her power. She was twenty-three and the youngest amongst her staff. Her qualifications, B.A. and B.T. from Lahore, were so impressive that the Maharani had dispensed with the usual interview prior to the appointment. (Kapur *Difficult* 169)

At 23 with B.A. and B.T. qualifications, she is very young to take up the job of Headmistress. This fact itself reveals how lucky Virmati is. The Maharani does not interview Virmati as a regular formality. The Maharani is very impressed with her qualifications. Virmati has to teach apart from her administrative duties:

> Virmati's other major duty in the school was teaching. She taught English Literature and Household to classes IX and X. Household was hygiene, nutrition, domestic management, health care, and enough applied maths to balance a budget. (Kapur *Difficult* 169-170)

Whatever may be the job it does not satisfy her. She works until Harish marries her. She even writes a threatening letter to Harish about marrying her early:

> She wrote to the Professor that she was sick and tired of waiting for him. If he couldn't make up his mind to marry her, then she might as well devote herself seriously to her career. Nahan was not the place to do it. Either in Lahore or, if her family didn't agree, Jullunder. (Kapur *Difficult* 173)

The above lines clearly indicate that she is not career-oriented but is doing the job to pass her time till Harish marries her. Veena Singh rightly says: "She is a B.T., goes for a job but a career is not her goal" (169). Further, Singh says: "Virmati does a professional course but is not career-oriented. She does not think in terms of education and profession as a means to achieving individual freedom" (165). Virmati says straightaway in her letter that she is "sick and tired of waiting" for his call. If at all he has not "made" up his mind to "marry" her, then she "might as well devote herself seriously" in concentrating on "her career." This shows how committed she is to her career! As soon as Harish marries her, she leaves for his home. After the marriage she is not happy as a second wife. Harish treats her specially as a companion not just as a "domesticated" wife. He even asks her to take up either a paid job or voluntary one so as to avoid conflicts with his first wife Ganga. The narrator says:

> Virmati did get a job, but not as a volunteer. Opposite AS College was a primary school, housed on the ground floor of an old building. As before, Virmati's qualifications made her an excellent choice for principal, while marriage added acceptability. Nobody thought much about her youth or beauty now. (Kapur *Difficult* 213)

When an "educated" woman has qualifications there is no dearth of opportunities to "get a job." The only difference is that in the present one she is a married woman and in the earlier one she was unmarried. Thus she has been carrying on with her job out of force rather than out of self-interest.

Ida, the daughter of Virmati is just her opposite. She is married but divorces her husband, as her husband does not allow her to have a child. Veena Singh says: "[T]he forced abortion is also the termination of her marriage" (168). Ida says in the opening of the novel: "The one thing I had wanted was not to be like my mother" (Kapur *Difficult* 1). Look at the daughter's criticism of her own mother. Although Virmati is an "educated" woman and works, she becomes a traditional woman. Geetha Ganapathy-Dore also feels that Ida's "[...] decision to divorce Prabhakar may have been prompted by the fact that he is a successful academic 'like her father'" (42).

Padma in Anjana Appachana's *Listening Now* (1998) is a Ph. D. holder, a lecturer in English. She is not married but has a child from her lover. In fact she could have married Karan, a college lecturer. Unfortunately, the adamant and narrow-minded attitude of Karan's orthodox mother has spoiled their getting married to each other. Karan's mother hides Padma's letters and does not inform Karan about Padma's parents' visit with regard to settling their marriage. In fact, Karan has not been the major hurdle for her marriage. Moreover, without telling Karan and taking his consent his mother has fixed his marriage. Karan says:

> "In the letter she wrote and said that now that I had got into the civil services the time was right to get married. She never got my answer, naturally. So she assumed that it was all right, I was never the best of correspondents. She went ahead with all the arrangements. She sent me a telegram a couple of weeks before I went home, asking me to immediately confirm by which train I was coming. I wondered [...] briefly [...] why a telegram? But [...] I didn't give much thought [...] I sent her a wire with the details of my arrival."
>
> [...] "I told her, I can not get married. My mother collapsed. She has always had a weak heart. The doctor had to be called. My sisters took me to another room and said that I would not only bring dishonour to my family but to the girl's family. They said everyone had come—all her relatives, all ours, all their friends, all ours. About five hundred people were expected for the ceremony that night." (Appachana *Listening* 374)

How can any mother fix a marriage without asking her son or showing the girl to her son? She must be very confident about her son's obligation towards her. Moreover, she goes ahead with the marriage arrangements for her son. Padma's Appa also commits a mistake by saying that if Karan is married then "Padma is married too":

> He [Appa] said, "He asked me, Are you the man Padma wanted to marry? I said to him, Yes, but I am already married and—He did not let me finish. He opened the door and said, Leave. Padma is married too." (Appachana *Listening* 377)

Karan comes in search of Padma to tell her the real situation. In fact Padma is not married but as it is a prestige question he says so, which is one of the reasons why Padma and Karan are separated for thirteen years. In fact, Appa is a very broad-minded person with regard to providing education to his daughters and son. He encourages them to study up to the post-graduation level. He does not bother about the expenses for their studies. It so happens that he makes a mistake in separating Karan and Padma for thirteen years and life long.

Padma has been forced to take up the job of a lecturer in English as her lover deserts her, making her pregnant. Padma has no interest in a career but she works in order to fulfil her responsibility as a single parent to her daughter. She is offered a job in the English Department as soon as she finishes her M. A. At that time she is in love with Karan. She is not sure of her marriage. She wants to marry him first and later on decide what she would like to do. Her Appa also asks her:

> [...] "Why don't you want to take up that lecturership?" For she had been offered one as soon as she finished her M. A., it had been offered to her on a platter. Amma had said to Appa, "If she wants to work she can also do it after she gets married, she can get any job, but she might not get such an offer again." Appa hadn't even looked at Amma. "Why, my child?" he had repeated. (Appachana *Listening* 171)

She has no answer to her Appa's question, as she cannot give a straight answer. Her Appa shares his feelings with her Amma that it is a good "offer." Moreover, she cannot get this kind of a good offer later. Getting a job is not a problem for her. In spite of her Appa's repeated question she does not give the true reason. She keeps quiet. Later on, Karan leaves for his native place and comes back only after thirteen years. Before that, her sister Shantacca and her brother Madhava go to ask Karan's parents about Karan's promise to marry Padma. They get a negative reply and Padma remains unmarried. Meanwhile, she is pregnant and gives birth to Mallika and lives as a single parent, telling the neighbours that her husband has been killed in an accident. Padma takes up a job in a college and has not been enjoying her career as it has been forced on her:

> [...] Padma didn't mix with anyone else, she didn't go out, she never went to her parents' for a holiday, she had no social life at all. All she did was to go to her college, teach, come back, tutor Mallika, take tuitions in the late afternoon, send off Mallika to play, correct papers, prepare for her lectures, spend about an hour or so chatting with Madhu and Anu, then it was Mallika again, and after Mallika slept she would work on her doctorate. On weekends she and Mallika went to the library, and Padma read and slept. How she slept, till nine in the mornings on weekends, Madhu noted disapprovingly. Sometimes, Madhu would ask Padma about her college and the girls she taught and her colleagues, and Padma would tell her an anecdote or two about her teaching experiences and the conversations she had with the other lecturers, but since she never met any of them after she left her college and never spent any time with them unless it was between classes, there wasn't much to talk about. (Appachana *Listening* 61-62)

Although she has told her friends and neighbours about her husband's death in an accident, it is not true. Her lover has deserted her. Naturally she has a guilty feeling about her own life. She has a daughter to look after.

Padma had to give tuitions to provide good education for her daughter. After thirteen years, Karan, the lover of Padma, accidentally meets her. They talk about each other's life and the reasons why they had to be separated. However, in the conversation Karan asks her what career she is planning for Mallika. Padma says:

> "What subjects does Mallika plan to take in the ninth?"
>
> "She isn't sure."
>
> "Isn't she inclined towards the arts?"
>
> "She is. But [...] it isn't practical. Unless she wants to appear for the I.A.S. She will have more options with a science background. She can become a doctor."

> "Is that what she wants?"
>
> "She doesn't know what she wants. I suppose it's what I want for her."
>
> "Sita was telling me she comes first in class."
>
> "She and Prabha—Mrs. Prasad's daughter, yes. One or the other."
>
> "Wouldn't you like Mallika to teach, like you?"
>
> "No."
>
> "You don't enjoy it?"
>
> "I love it."
>
> She saw the surprise on his face and said, "I wouldn't have been able to support myself and a child on the salary. I've managed because my mother has helped support me, and I have [...] the house. Mallika must be [...] self-supporting." (Appachana *Listening* 450)

Thus she could cope with the teaching career. Padma opines: "Mallika must be self-supporting" when she grows up. Teaching career is a noble career unlike any other. I don't agree with Padma here. Money is not everything in life. What is important is mental and moral satisfaction.

Uma in Anita Desai's *Fasting, Feasting* (1999) has an arranged marriage through a matrimonial column in a newspaper. However, she is cheated. This is one of the best examples to show how easily parents of a bride can be cheated in an arranged marriage. This is especially so with matrimonial column alliances. Uma has had no marriage proposals, as she is not good at studies and is a bit dull in her behaviour. Hence her parents give Uma's details along with her photograph in the matrimonial column. They get a response from Harish who claims that he is already married but that he has had no children through his wife. Thus he is interested in Uma. They have been told that Harish "is in pharmaceutical business and earning decent income" (87). In fact, Harish has four children living with his wife in Meerut. He runs an ailing pharmaceutical factory. In order to save his pharmaceutical factory he marries Uma. By marrying Uma he gets a dowry and with that money he saves his factory. J.P. Tripathi observes: "The tragedy of a girl rejected by many parties in marriage is pathetically drawn in the case of Uma. She is drawn into another deceitful marriage with Harish, an already married man with children, for the sake of a dowry, after this marriage she is considered a blighted 'illiterated' girl" (19). Uma is cheated by Harish. She neither has a job nor is she divorced from Harish.

In this decade there are arranged marriages like that of Malini, Amrita, Devi, Maya, Parvati and Uma, love-cum-arranged marriages like that of Urmila, Gudiya and love marriages like that of Mikki, Aparna, Sumi, Ammu and Virmati. Malini has a career but gives it up on the request of her husband. Mikki undertakes a business career left behind by her father after his demise in an accident and is cheated. Amrita is a die-hard model and tries to dedicate herself and to concentrate on her career. Urmila is a college lecturer. Nisha is a columnist, a challenging career for women. Pramila is a creative writer and enters politics. Aparna is an accounts supervisor. Maya could have chosen textile designing as a career but her husband does not encourage her and he wants his wife to be at home. Virmati does not consider a job as seriously as her marriage. In fact, she works out of necessity. Padma has a job of teaching and remains unmarried as a single parent with a daughter born outside marriage. There are separation cases in the sense that women do not divorce legally but leave their husbands and lead their lives. Devi leaves not only her husband but also her lover and goes to her mother, emphasizing a strong mother-daughter bond. Aparna is left by her husband. Her husband walks out on her just like that. How uncertain married life is in the 1990s! Sumi is also left by her husband for not having a son and does not look after his three daughters. What an escape from family responsibilities! Ammu's divorce is completely justified. Her husband is a rogue asking his wife to sleep with his boss in order to retain his job.

WORKS CITED

Appachana, Anjana. *Listening Now*. New Delhi: India*Ink*, 1998.

De, Shobha. *Starry Nights*. New Delhi: Penguin, 1991.

——. *Strange Obsession*. New Delhi: Penguin, 1992.

——. *Sisters*. New Delhi: Penguin, 1992.

——. *Sultry Days*. New Delhi: Penguin, 1994.

——. *Snapshots*. New Delhi: Penguin, 1995.

——. *Second Thoughts*. New Delhi: Penguin, 1996.

Desai, Anita. *Fasting, Feasting*. New Delhi: Vintage, 1999.

Deshpande, Shashi. *The Binding Vine*. New Delhi: Penguin, 1992.

——. *A Matter of Time*. New Delhi: Penguin, 1996.

Ganapathy-Dore, Geetha. "Impossible Reconciliation in Manju Kapur's *Difficult Daughters*." *Commonwealth Essays and Studies* 23.1 (2000): 35-42.

Gokhale, Namita. *Gods, Graves and Grandmother*. New Delhi: Orient, 1994.

——. *A Himalayan Love Story*. New Delhi: Alka, 1996.

Hariharan, Githa. *The Thousand Faces of Night*. New Delhi: Penguin, 1992.

Jain, Jasbir. "Post-Colonial Realities: Writing Women History." *Interrogating Post-Colonialism: Theory, Text and Context*. Ed. Harish Trivedi and Meenakshi Mukherjee. Shimla: IIAS, 1996.161-176.

Kapur, Manju. *Difficult Daughters*. New Delhi: Penguin, 1998.

Roy, Arundhati. *The God of Small Things*. New Delhi: India*Ink*, 1997.

Roy, Evangeline Shanti. "Shashi Deshpande's *The Binding Vine*: A Quest for the Anchor of Life." *Littcrit* 27.1&2 (2001): 77-78.

Satyanarayana, E. "The Dialectics of Self-Assertion: the Liberated Woman in Shobha De's *Sisters*." *Critical Studies on Indian Fiction in English*. Ed. R.A. Singh and V.L.V.N. Narendra Kumar. New Delhi: Atlantic, 1999. 145-151.

Saxena, Alka. "*Second Thoughts*: A Slice of Urban Life." *The Fiction of Shobha De*. Ed. Jaydipsinh Dodiya. New Delhi: Prestige, 2000. 259-271.

Singh, Veena. "How Difficult are Difficult Daughters? *Sunlight on a Broken Column* and *Difficult Daughters* as Female

Bildungsroman." *Contemporary Indian Literature: Positions and Expositions*. Ed. Santosh Gupta. Jaipur: Rawat, 2000. 161-175.

Tikkha, Neelam. "Lesbian Relationships in *Strange Obsession*." *The Fiction of Shobha De*. Ed. Jaydipsinh Dodiya. New Delhi: Prestige, 2000. 220-226.

Trikha, Pradeep. "A New Voice in the Indian Fiction: Githa Hariharan." *Indian Women Novelists Set III: Vol. 6*. Ed. R.K. Dhawan. New Delhi: Prestige, 1995. 9-12.

Tripathi, J.P. "*The Binding Vine* and Indian Ethos." *The Fiction of Shashi Deshpande*. Ed. R.S. Pathak. New Delhi: Creative, 1998. 150-154.

——. "Anita Desai's *Fasting, Feasting*: Continuity and Experiment." *Indian English Literature Since 1950 (Vol.2)*. Ed. Charu Sheel Singh. New Delhi: Anmol, 2001.15-29.

Vijayasree, C. "Re-Visionist Myth-Making: A Reading of Githa Hariharan's *The Thousand Faces of Night*." *The Post Modern Indian English Novel: Interrogating the 1980s and 1990s*. Ed. Viney Kirpal. New Delhi: Allied, 1996. 176-181.

Conclusion

7

In my dissertation I have examined the "educated" Hindu women characters in the Indian English Women's novels written from 1947 to 1990s and seen how they tackle the three issues of "marriage", "career" and "divorce" in their daily lives. I am sure such a study will be useful to readers, "educated" women in general, and to men who are also a part of the above issues. I am of the strong opinion that women have to be "educated" irrespective of their parents' capability. When parents can give birth to a girl child, it is their moral duty to make their daughter "educated."

Coming to the issue of marriage, "educated" women may go through love marriage, love-cum-arranged marriage or arranged marriage. In the above three types of marriages, love marriage is agreeable to the couples but not to the parents. A long standing marriage depends on how the couple leads and lives its life. So love marriage is the best marriage from the couple's point of view. Leila in *Cry,* Simrit in *The Day*, Devi in *A Situation,* Tara in *Clear Light*, Saru in *The Dark*, Indu in *Roots*, Paro in *Paro*, Anjali in *Socialite*, Aasha Rani in *Starry*, Aparna in *Snapshots*, Ammu in *The God*, Sumi in *A Matter* and Virmati in *Difficult* have love marriages. I do support this marriage, as this is the ultimate goal of lovers falling in love. In this context, I would like to give one example. In most of the films, irrespective of language, religion, caste, or nation, the theme is based on love leading to marriage. But love-cum-arranged marriage is the best from the couple's point of view as well as from the parents' point of view. Devaki and Kusum in *A Time*, Pinky in *A Situation*, Tara in *Clear Light*, Urmila in *The Binding*, Gudia in *Gods,* have love-cum-arranged marriages. Among these, except Gudia the other three characters are happy with their marriages. I strongly advocate this type of marriage. In the above two types of marriages, first of all there should be two lovers either for love marriage or for love-cum-arranged marriage. Then the third type of marriage is the most common type of marriage. It has been a "times immemorial" type of marriage. Rukmani in *Nectar*, Premala in *Some Inner*, Uma in *This Time,* Pramila in *Sultry Days*, Maya in *Strange*, Monisha in *Voices,* Gauri in *Storm*, Sita in *Where Shall*, Manasi in *Alphabet*, Geeta in *Inside*, Priya and Paro in *Paro*, Jaya in *That Long*, Karuna in *Soicialite*, Malini Arora in *Starry Nights*, Devi in *The Thousand*, Amrita in *Strange*, Parvati in *A Himalayan*, Maya in *Second* and Uma in *Fasting* have arranged marriages. Parents and some women prefer arranged marriage. Sometimes, even boys prefer to go for this kind of marriage. I think the reason behind this type of marriage is that the couple is the responsibility of the parents of both sides. In case of disputes, differences, clashes or misunderstandings, parents from both sides will enter and try to solve them or to dissolve the married life of the couple. Whether one recommends this type of marriage or not, it will continue to dominate as far as marriage is concerned.

However, I stand for an uninterrupted and peaceful marriage. To me this is represented in a love-cum-arranged marriage. Such a couple is really lucky as there will not be any problems with regard to their married life. The second choice will be love marriage. There is a responsibility on both the man and the woman in a love marriage. They have to retain their love throughout their lives. It is challenging as they may or may not have the support of their family members. To me the last option would be an arranged marriage. Even if there are problems there are parents to intervene and set right the problems.

I hypothesized that as the decades progressed from 50s to 90s there will be lot of love and love-cum-arranged marriages, but surprisingly the total number of arranged marriages are more than the love or love-cum-arranged marriages. Among the novels I have looked at, there are six love-cum-arranged marriages, twelve love marriages and twenty arranged marriages.

The next issue is of career. As I have already mentioned, "educated" women should have a career of their own choice. One should never listen to or blindly follow someone else's suggestion with regard to career. Of course, one can listen to suggestions. Ultimately, the decision should be one's own. Job is not a career for Veena in *A Time,* Nita in *This Time*, Shree in *Forever*, Indu in *Roots*, Priya in *Paro*, Karuna in *Socialite,* Kalpana in *The Binding*, Mikki in *Sisters*, Pramila in *Sultry*, Virmati in *Difficult* and Padma in *Listening*. These women do jobs out of compulsion. And a career is not a job for Amla in *Voices*, Leila in *Cry,* Simrit in *The Day*, Geeta in *Inside*, Ila Das in *Fire*, Jaya in *That Long* and Aparna in *Snapshots* as they do jobs out of their interest and not for their parents' sake or for their husband's sake. Career is a passion for Manasi in *Alphabet*, Devi in *A Situation*, Bim in *Clear Light*, Saru in *The Dark*, Sonali in *Rich*, Anjali in *Socialite,* Amrita in *Strange,* Urmila in *The Binding,* Vaana in *The Binding* and Nisha in *Sultry Days*. In these novels, if we look at the number of career women who have opted for their work on their own, there are sixteen, whereas women who have chosen jobs but not careers are just nine. As far as the issue of career is concerned, my hypothesis is correct that there will be more career women than women who have jobs. Career is one's own dream. These women put as much effort as they can in order to make their dreams come true.

I have hypothesized that many educated women would choose modelling as their career but there are not more than two in my study. Another surprise to me in this study is that the second highest number, four, is of educated women opting for writing as a career. I have not expected these many women opting for writing. However, as per my expectation, the highest number of educated women, that is six, have taken up teaching.

The last issue is that of divorce. As I have suggested it should be the last resort. It should not be due to an emotional break down as in the case of Rashmi in *This Time* who does not understand her husband's busy schedules with his business. Her parents' disapproval of Rashmi's divorce is a strong point for Dalip. Devi in *The Thousand* leaves Mahesh and elopes with Gopal and ultimately goes back to her mother. She lives neither with Mahesh nor with Gopal.

On the other hand Rohit in *Snapshots* leaves his wife for illogical reasons. Gopal in *A Matter* leaves Sumitra as he is unable to look after his daughters. Sociologists like Judith S. Wallerstein and Joan B. Kelly have conducted a study and presented to us the effects of divorce on children. Simrit and Som in *The Day* and Pramila and Vilas in *Sultry* are examples to show the effect of divorce on their children. If there are no children it is not such a problem as it happens between Arjun Mitra and Uma in *This Time,* Jaya and Sarla in *Clear Light* with their husbands.

Divorce takes place mainly due to an extra-marital relationship as in Priya and B.R. in *Paro*, Karuna and her husband in *Socialite*. In the case of Anjali in *Socialite,* it is mainly due to extra-marital relationships between her husband and her friends. B. R. divorces his wife Paro in *Paro* because she is involved in an extra-marital relationship with "Bucky" Bandipur.

I do not mean to say that one has to adjust to any kind of adverse situations and that one should not hesitate to punish a man who has no human values as Nila in *Cry,* Shree in *Forever* and Ammu in *The God* do. In the interesting case of Ida, in *Difficult,* she divorces her husband for not allowing her to retain her pregnancy.

The divorce may also lead to a possibility of another marriage as it happens with Saroj in *Storm* who leaves her husband and goes to live with Vishal. Even in this, one should be very cautious. The first experience should not be repeated. One ought to make sure that the divorce will not create any problem in the second marriage. Virmati in *Difficult* is a different case as she marries Prof. Harish and becomes his second wife. Harish married Virmati without divorcing his first wife although it is illegal. Virmati does not mind whether

Harish has a wife already. She is ready to accept being a second wife. Similarly, Mira in *The Binding* marries Kishore's father to become his second wife.

I had hypothesized the reasons for divorce as follows: emotional break down, extra-marital relationship, punishing the husband, second marriage etc. I have not found a single case of divorce not happening without a problem between the couple. I thought I would find more than one but surprisingly I did not come across a single case. The best examples for this are couples like Premala and Kitsamy in *Some Inner* and Gautama and Maya in *Cry*. This could be the result of an understanding between the husband and wife. Moreover, they are educated.

The educated women who take divorce from their husbands do not regret the outcome, because they find that there is so much in life apart from married life. Married life is not everything. One can do a lot of service even as a single woman or as a single parent.

Afterword

Although I have restricted myself to look at novels from 1947 to 1990s, I am aware of novels like Shashi Deshpande's *Small Remedies* (2000) and *Moving on* (2004), Jaishree Mishra's *Ancient Promises* (2000), and *Accidents Like Love and Marriage* (2001), Nayantara Sahgal's *Lesser Breeds* (2003), Githa Hariharan's *In Times of Siege* (2003), Manju Kapur's *A Married Woman* (2003), Anita Desai's *The Zigzag Way* (2004) published in 2000 and after.

I am sure some of the issues I have dealt with in this thesis have a place in the 2000s' novels. Research is a never-ending discovery. It is a continuous process. There can be no stagnation. As long as there are serious researchers, that is "passionate academic" researchers, they will continue to look at recent developments and consolidate on their findings.

Select Bibliography

Primary Sources

Appachana, Anjana. *Listening Now*. New Delhi: India*Ink*, 1998.

Das, Kamala. *Alphabet of Lust*. 1976. New Delhi: Orient, 1978.

De, Shobha. *Socialite Evenings*. 1988. New Delhi: Penguin, 1989.

——. *Starry Nights*. New Delhi: Penguin, 1991.

——. *Sisters*. New Delhi: Prestige, 1992.

——. *Strange Obsession*. New Delhi: Penguin, 1992.

——. *Sultry Days*. New Delhi: Penguin, 1994.

——. *Snapshots*. New Delhi: Penguin, 1995.

——. *Second Thoughts*. New Delhi: Penguin, 1996.

Desai, Anita. *Cry, the Peacock*. 1963. New Delhi: Orient, 1995.

——. *Voices in the City*. 1965. Delhi: Orient-Hind, 1968.

——. *Where Shall We Go This Summer?* 1975. Delhi: Orient, 1994.

——. *Fire on the Mountain*. 1977. New Delhi: Allied, 1990.

——. *Clear Light of Day*. New Delhi: Allied, 1980.

——. *Fasting, Feasting*. 1999. London: Vintage, 2000.

Deshpande, Shashi. *The Dark Holds No Terrors*. New Delhi: Vikas, 1980.

——. *Come Up and Be Dead*. Ghaziabad: Vikas-Tarang, 1983.

——. *Roots and Shadows*. 1983. New Delhi: Orient-Disha, 1996.

——. *That Long Silence*. 1988. New Delhi: Penguin, 1989.

——. *The Binding Vine*. New Delhi: Penguin, 1992.

——. *A Matter of Time*. New Delhi: Penguin, 1996.

Dutt, Toru. *Bianca Or The Young Spanish Maiden*. 1878. Ed. Subhendu Mund. New Delhi: Parachi, 2001.

Gokhale, Namita. *Paro: Dreams of Passion*. 1984. New Delhi: Penguin, 1999.

——. *Gods, Graves and Grandmother*. New Delhi: Rupa, 1994.

——. *A Himalayan Love Story*. New Delhi: Alka, 1996.

Hariharan, Githa. *The Thousand Faces of Night*. New Delhi: Penguin, 1992.

Kapur, Manju. *Difficult Daughters*. New Delhi: Penguin, 1998.

Markandaya, Kamala. *Nectar in a Sieve*. 1954. Bombay: Jaico, 1996.

——. *Some Inner Fury*. 1955. Bombay: Jaico, 1957.

——. *Two Virgins*. 1973. London: Chatto & Windus, 1974.

Mehta, Rama. *Inside the Haveli*. 1977. New Delhi: Penguin, 1996.

Narsimhan, Raji. *Forever Free*. Delhi: Hind, 1979.

Nikambe, Shevanthibai M. *Ratanbai: A Sketch of a Bombay High Caste Hindu Young Wife*. Ed. Eunice de Souza. New Delhi: Sahitya Akademi, 2003. Rpt. of London: Marshall, 1895.

Roy, Arundhati. *The God of Small Things*. New Delhi: India*Ink*, 1997.

Sahgal, Nayantara. *A Time to be Happy*. 1958. New Delhi: Sterling, 1975.

——. *This Time of Morning*. 1965. Delhi: Orient-Hind, n.d.

——. *Storm in Chandigarh*. 1969. Delhi: Orient-Hind, n.d.

——. *The Day in Shadow*. 1971. Delhi: Penguin, 1991.

——. *A Situation in New Delhi*. New Delhi: Himalaya, 1977.

——. *Rich Like Us*. London: Heinemann, 1985.

Saraswati, Pundita Ramabai. *The High Caste Hindu Woman*. 1888. New Delhi: Inter-India, 1984.

Satthianadhan, Krupabai. *Kamala: The Story of a Hindu Life*. Ed. Chandani Lokuge. 1894. New Delhi: OUP, 1998.

——. Saguna: *First Autobiographical Novel in English by an Indian Woman*. Ed. Chandani Lokuge. 1895. New Delhi: OUP, 1998.

Secondary Sources

Full Length Books

Bai, K. Meera. *Women's Voices: The Novels of Indian Women Writers*. New Delhi: Prestige, 1996.

Chaudhary, J.N. *Divorce in Indian Society (A Sociological Study of Marriage, Disruption, and Role Adjustment)*. Jaipur: Printwell, 1988.

Deena, Sahab. *Mourya Women in India*. Allahabad: Chugh, 1988.

Devi, Shakuntala. *Women's Status and Social Change*. Jaipur: Pointer, 1999.

Gore, M.S. *Urbanization and Family Change*. Bombay: Popular, 1969.

Parameswaran, Uma. *Kamala Markandaya*. Jaipur: Rawat, 2000.

Pathania, Usha. *Human Bonds and Bondages: The Fiction of Anita Desai and Kamala Markandaya*. Delhi: Kanishka, 1992.

Rao, V.V. Prakasha and V. Nandini Rao. *Marriage, The Family and Women in India*. New Delhi: Heritage, 1982.

Ross, Aileen D. *The Hindu Family in its Urban Setting*. Toronto: U of Toronto P, 1961.

Sandhu, Sarabjit K. *The Image of Woman in the Novels of Shashi Deshpande*. New Delhi: Prestige, 1991.

Sebastian, Mrinalini. *The Novels of Shashi Deshpande in Post-Colonial Arguments*. New Delhi: Prestige, 2000.

Seshadri, Vijayalakshmi. *The New Woman in Indian-English Women Writers Since the 1970s*. Delhi: B. R., 1995.

Srivastava, Sharad. *The New Woman in Indian English Fiction: A Study of Kamala Markandaya, Anita Desai, Namita Gokhale and Shobha De*. New Delhi: Creative, 1996.

Uma, Alladi. *Woman and Her Family: Indian and Afro-American—A Literary Perspective*. New Delhi: Sterling, 1989.

Zelliot, Eleanor. *From Untouchable to Dalit: Essays on the Ambedkar Movement*. New Delhi: Manohar, 1992.

Articles

Abraham, John E. "Feminism and our Fiction." *Feminism and Indian English Fiction*. Ed. P.M. Nayak and S.P. Swain. Bareilley: PBD, 1996. 20-27.

Acharya, Shanta. "Problems of Self in the Novels of Anita Desai." *Indian Women Novelists Set I: Vol. II*. Ed. R.K. Dhawan. New Delhi: Prestige, 1991. 50-67.

Adhikari, Madhumalathi. "Changing Values of Anita Desai's Major Women Characters." *Indian Writing Today*. Ed. C.S. Visweswara Rao. New Delhi: IAES, 1996. 113-121.

——. "Enclosure and Freedom: Arundhati Roy's *The God of Small Things*." *Explorations: Arundhati Roy's The God of Small Things*. Ed. Indira Bhatt and Indira Nityanandam. New Delhi: Creative, 1999. 39-46.

——. "Power Politics in *The God of Small Things*." *Arundhati Roy: The Novelist Extraordinary*. Ed. R.K. Dhawan. New Delhi: Prestige, 1999. 41-48.

——. "*Snapshots*: A Post-Colonial Text." *The Fiction of Shobha De*. Ed. Jaydipsinh Dodiya. New Delhi: Prestige, 2000. 237-242.

——. "The Equation of Power in *Snapshots*." *The Fiction of Shobha De*. Ed. Jaydipsinh Dodiya. New Delhi: Prestige, 2000. 252-258.

——. "Decoding Mythical Patterns in R.K. Narayan, Anita Desai and Shashi Deshpande." *Indian English Literature Since 1950*. Vol.2. Ed. Charu Sheel Singh. New Delhi: Anmol, 2002. 44-55.

Agarwal, Chandra P. "Configurations in Ashes: Twentieth Century Indian Women Writers." *Indian Literature* 34.4(1991): 132-144.

Agarwal, Madhavi Lata. "Anita Desai: Alienation in *Voices in the City*." *POETCRIT* 27.1 (2004): 60-63.

Agarwalla, Shyam S. "Three Modern Versions of the Draupadi Myth: R. K. Narayan, Mulk Raj Anand and Rama Mehta." *Feminism and Literature*. Ed. Veena Noble Dass. New Delhi: Prestige, 1995. 214-218.

——. "The Anger in *The God of Small Things*." *Arundhati Roy: The Novelist Extraordinary*. Ed. R.K. Dhawan. New Delhi: Prestige, 1999. 266-277.

Ajayan, C. "A Segment of Existence: Arundhati Roy's *The God of Small Things*." *Journal of Literature and Aesthetics* 5.2 (1997): 97-99.

Akhtar, Nasim. "Loneliness as a Theme in *Voices in the City*." *The Quest* 11.2 (1997): 30-32.

Alam, Qaiser Zoha. "Namita Gokhale's *Gods, Graves and Grandmother*." *Indian Writings in English Vol. II*. Ed. Manmohan K. Bhatnagar. New Delhi: Atlantic, 2001. 187-202.

Alcock, Peter. "Rope, Serpent, Fire: Recent Fiction of Anita Desai." *Journal of Indian Writing in English* 9.1 (1981): 15-34.

Ali, Syed Mashkoor. "Markandaya's *A Handful of Rice* and Malamaud's *The Assistant*: A Comparative Study." *Indian Women Novelists Set II: Vol. III*. Ed. R. K. Dhawan. New Delhi: Prestige, 1993. 135-144.

Amaniddin, Syed. "Anita Desai's Technique." *Indian Women Novelists Set I: Vol. II*. Ed. R.K. Dhawan. New Delhi: Prestige, 1991. 214-225.

Ambekar, K.P. "Symbolism in *Where Shall We Go This Summer?*" *Indian Women Novelists Set I: Vol. III*. Ed. R.K. Dhawan. New Delhi: Prestige, 1991. 201-206.

Amin, Amina. "Imagery as a Mode of Apprehension in Anita Desai's Novel." *Indian Women Novelists Set I: Vol. II*. Ed. R. K. Dhawan. New Delhi: Prestige, 1991. 226-238.

——. "Text and Counter-text: Oppositional Discourse in *The God of Small Things*." *Explorations: Arundhati Roy's The God of Small Things*. Ed. Indira Bhatt and Indira Nityanandam. New Delhi: Creative, 1999. 18-28.

——. "Breaking Laws, Crossing Forbidden Territory: An Analysis of *The God of Small Things*." *Arundhati Roy: The Novelist Extraordinary*. Ed. R.K. Dhawan. New Delhi: Prestige, 1999. 104-111.

Anand, T.S. "*Where Shall We Go This Summer?* Anita Desai's Stance Against Negativism." *The Fiction of Anita Desai*. Ed. R. K. Dhawan. New Delhi: Bahri, 1989. 96-107.

——. "*Paro*: A Psychological Approach." *Indian Women Novelists Set II: Vol. I*. Ed. R.K. Dhawan. New Delhi: Prestige, 1993. 205-212.

——. "The Flight from the Virtuous Stereotype: A Study of *Storm in Chandigarh*." *Indian Women Novelists Set II: Vol. IV*. Ed. R.K. Dhawan. New Delhi: Prestige, 1993. 157-162.

Appasamy, S.P. "*The Golden Honeycomb*: A Study of Princely Indian By Kamala Markandaya." *Journal of Indian Writing English* 6.2 (1978): 56-62.

Argyle, Barry. "Kamala Markandaya's *Nectar in a Sieve*." *Ariel* 4.1 (1973): 35-45.

Arora, Neena. "'Woman Made Woman'—A Feminist Reading of Nayantara Sahgal's *This Time of Morning* and *A Situation in New Delhi* and Doris Lessing's *Martha Quest* and *The Grass is Singing*." *Indian Women Novelists Set II: Vol. IV*. Ed. R.K. Dhawan. New Delhi: Prestige, 1993. 65-85.

Arora, Nina. "*Rich Like Us*: A Note." *Recent Commonwealth Literature*. Ed. R.K. Dhawan. New Delhi: Prestige, 1989. 130-132.

——. "An Analytical Study of *Sisters*." *The Fiction of Shobha De*. Ed. Jaydipsinh Dodiya. New Delhi: Prestige, 2000. 216-219.

Arora, V.K. "Form and Technique in Nayantara Sahgal's Novels." *Literary Endeavour* 1.3 (1980): 41-52.

——. "Anita Desai's Fiction: A New Dimension." *Indian Literature* 24.2 (1981): 44-54.

——. "Contemporary Politics: Its Portrayal in the Novels of Nayantara Sahgal." *Critical Response to Indian English Fiction*. Delhi: Mittal, 1985. 108-121.

——. "The Literary Aesthetics of Anita Desai's Fiction." *Critical Response to Indian English Fiction*. Delhi: Mittal, 1985. 143-156.

——. "Portrayal of Man-Woman Relationship in the Novels of Nayantara Sahgal." *Critical Response to Indian English Fiction*. Delhi: Mittal, 1985. 122-133.

Asthana, R.K. "Tradition and Modernity in *Inside the Haveli*." *Indian Women Novelists Set I: Vol. IV*. Ed. R.K. Dhawan. New Delhi: Prestige, 1991. 192-201.

Awasti, Kamal N. "The Forgotten Men: A Study of Anita Desai's Male Characters." *Indian Women Novelists Set I: Vol. II*. Ed. R.K. Dhawan. New Delhi: Prestige, 1991. 177-190.

——. "The Quest for Identity in the Novels of Shashi Deshpande." *Quest for Identity in Indian English Writing*. Ed. R.S. Pathak. New Delhi: Bahri, 1992. 95-111.

——. "An Archetypal View of Relationships in *Possession*." *Indian Women Novelists Set II: Vol. III*. Ed. R.K. Dhawan. New Delhi: Prestige, 1993. 43-50.

Bai, K. Meera. "Husband and Wife Alienation in the Novels of Nayantara Sahgal and Anita Desai." *Indian Women Novelists Set I: Vol. I*. Ed. R.K. Dhawan. New Delhi: Prestige, 1991. 167-176.

——. "Method and Narrative Techniques in Kamala Markandaya's *Nectar in a Sieve*, Anita Desai's *Cry, the Peacock*, Nayantara Sahgal's *A Time to be Happy* and Ruth Jhabvala's *Heat and Dust*." *Indian Women Novelists Set I*: *Vol. I*. Ed. R.K. Dhawan. New Delhi: Prestige, 1991. 177-203.

——. "From Adolescence to Womanhood: Kamala Markandaya's *Two Virgins*, Ruth Jhabvala's *To Whom She Will* and Santha Rama Rau's *Remember the House*." *Indian English Literature: Since Independence*. Ed. K. Ayyappa Paniker. New Delhi: IAES, 1991. 91-97.

——. "Feminism as an Extension of Existentialism: Women in Indian English Fiction." *Indian Women Novelists Set III*: *Vol. I*. Ed. R.K. Dhawan. New Delhi: Prestige, 1995. 26-32.

Balasubramanian, P.S. "Women's Education." *Quest for Gender Studies*: *A Critique of the Status of Women in India*. Madras: T.R., 1991. 69-77.

Bala, Suman and Subhash Chandra. "Manju Kapur's *Difficult Daughters*: An Absorbing Tale of Fact and Fiction." *50 Years of Indian Writing*. Ed. R.K. Dhawan. New Delhi: IAES, n.d. 105-110.

——. "Women in the Novels of Shashi Deshpande: An Introduction." *Women in the Novels of Shashi Deshpande*. Ed. Suman Bala. New Delhi: Khosla, 2001. 9-17.

Baliga, Jaya. "Being and Becoming: The Quest of Three Women in *Some Inner Fury*." *Indian Women Novelists Set II*: *Vol. II*. Ed. R.K. Dhawan. New Delhi: Prestige, 1993. 187-196.

——. "*Nectar in a Sieve*: A Study in Indian Social Values." *Indian Women Novelists Set II*: *Vol. II*. Ed. R.K. Dhawan. New Delhi: Prestige, 1993. 106-111.

Bande, Usha. "Mother, Daughter and Daughter's Daughter—A Study of Shashi Deshpande." *Mothers and Mother-Figures in Indo-English Literature*. Ed. Usha Bande. Jalandhar: ABSP, n.d. 134-141.

——. "Quest for Wholeness in Anita Desai's *Where Shall We Go This Summer?*" *Journal of South Asian Literature* 2.22 (1987): 87-94.

——. "I Search, I Find": Valmiki's Quest in Kamala Markandaya's *Possession.*" *Osmania Journal of English Studies* 25 (1989): 73-81.

——. "Is Sita Mad?" *Indian Literature* 33.5 (1990): 179-184.

——. "Amla-Dharma Love—An Enigma in *Voices in the City.*" *Indian Women Novelists Set I: Vol. III.* Ed. R.K. Dhawan. New Delhi: Prestige, 1991. 103-110.

——. "Bad Faith in *Where Shall We Go This Summer?*" *Indian Women Novelists Set I: Vol. III.* Ed. R. K. Dhawan. New Delhi: Prestige, 1991. 190-200.

——. "Childhood in Anita Desai's Novels: A Psychological Interpretation." *Indian Women Novelists Set I: Vol. II.* Ed. R.K. Dhawan. New Delhi: Prestige, 1991. 101-126.

——. "Anita Desai, Arun Joshi and Anasakti Yoga." *Indian Women Novelists Set I: Vol. II.* Ed. R.K. Dhawan. New Delhi: Prestige, 1991. 239-250.

——. "Father-Daughter Relationship in Anita Desai's *Cry, the Peacock* and *Where Shall We Go This Summer?*" *Contemporary Indian English Fiction: An Anthology of Essays.* Ed. K.N. Awasthi. New Delhi: ABS, 1993. 18-25.

——. "Politics and Passion: A Theological Perspective in *A Situation in New Delhi.*" *Indian Women Novelists Set II: Vol. IV.* Ed. R.K. Dhawan. New Delhi: Prestige, 1993. 211-217.

——. "Mothers and Mother-Figures in Anita Desai's Novels." *Critical Studies on Indian Fiction in English.* Ed. R.A. Singh and V.L.V.N. Narendra Kumar. New Delhi: Atlantic, 1999. 28-34.

Banerjee, Uma. "An Existential Approach to Maladjustment of Marital Relations in Anita Desai's Novels." *Indian Women Novelists Set I: Vol. II.* Ed. R.K. Dhawan. New Delhi: Prestige, 1991. 155-176.

——. "Sarojini: The Unconvincing Middle-class Wife in *A Silence of Desire.*" *Indian Women Novelists Set II: Vol. II.* Ed. R.K. Dhawan. New Delhi: Prestige, 1993. 247-252.

Bano, Jammela. "*The Nowhere Man*—A Tragedy?" *Indian Women Novelists Set II*: *Vol. III*. Ed. R.K. Dhawan. New Delhi: Prestige, 1993. 187-201.

Barat, Urbashi. "From Victim to Non-Victim: *Socialite Evenings* as a Version of Kunstlerroman." Ed. Jaydipsinh Dodiya. New Delhi: Prestige, 2000. 119-128.

——. "The Medium is the Message: A Study of *Snapshots*." *The Fiction of Shobha De*. Ed. Jaydipsinh Dodiya. New Delhi: Prestige, 2000. 243-251.

Barbato, Louis R. "The Arrow in the Circle: Time and Reconciliation of Cultures in Kamala Markandaya's *Nectar in a Sieve*." *Ariel* 22.4 (1991): 7-15.

Barbuddhe, Satish. "The Plight of Modern Indian Women in *That Long Silence*." *Women in the Novels of Shashi Deshpande*. Ed. Suman Bala. New Delhi: Khosla, 2001. 106-110.

Barche, G.D. "Indu: Another Sisyphus in *Roots and Shadows*." *Indian Women Novelists Set I*: *Vol. V*. Ed. R.K. Dhawan. New Delhi: Prestige, 1991. 111-117.

——. "Facets of Feminism in Indian English Fiction." *Indian Women Novelists Set III*: *Vol. I*. Ed. R.K. Dhawan. New Delhi: Prestige, 1995. 9-17.

——. "*The Dark Holds No Terrors*: Assertion of the Feminine Psyche." *Feminism and Indian English Fiction*. Ed. P.M. Naik and S. P. Swain. Bareilley: PBD, 1996. 84-90.

——. "Facets of Feminism: *Roots and Shadows, Cry, the Peacock* and Temporary Answers." *Feminism and Indian English Fiction*. Ed. P.M. Nayak and S.P. Swain. Bareilley: PBD, 1996. 91-96.

——. "*Inside the Haveli* and *The Nowhere Man*: A Study in the Upanishadic Principle." *Contemporary Indian Writings in English*. Ed. Jaydipsinh Dodiya. New Delhi: Atlantic, 1998. 9-20.

——. "Arundhati Roy's *The God of Small Things*: Juxtaposition and Parellelism." *Littcritt* 25.1&2 (1999): 29-41.

——. "Deconstructing the Deconstruction in the Roy's *The God of Small Things.*" *The Critical Studies of Arundhati Roy's The God of Small Things.* Ed. Jaydipsinh Dodiya and Joya Chakravarty. New Delhi: Atlantic, 1999. 37-48.

——. "Maya: Another Eve in *Second Thoughts.*" *The Fiction of Shobha De.* Ed. Jaydipsinh Dodiya. New Delhi: Prestige, 2000. 272-280.

Barnabas, Simon G. "Ayemenem and the Ayemenem House: A Study of the Setting of *The God of Small Things.*" *Arundhati Roy: The Novelist Extraordinary.* Ed. R.K. Dhawan. New Delhi: Prestige, 1999. 296-306.

Barua, Geeta. "Rise and Fall of a Star: *Starry Nights.*" *Indian Women Novelists Set III: Vol. I.* Ed. R.K. Dhawan. New Delhi: Prestige, 1995. 96-102.

Bhaduri, Seema. "History, Social Dynamics and the Individual in *The God of Small Things.*" *Arundhati Roy: The Novelist Extraordinary.* Ed. R.K. Dhawan. New Delhi: Prestige, 1991. 194-207.

Bharat, Urbasi. "The search for selfhood in the Patriarchal Enclosure: Women in Marriage in Kate Chopin's *The Awakening*, Anita Desai's *Voices in the City* and Nayantara Sahgal's *The Day in Shadow.*" *Indian Women Novelists Set III: Vol. I.* Ed. R.K. Dhawan. New Delhi: Prestige, 1995. 54-66.

——. "Great Stories and Small Ones: Arundhati Roy's *The God of Small Things.*" *Explorations: Arundhati Roy's The God of Small Things.* Ed. Indira Bhatt and Indira Nityanandam. New Delhi: Creative, 1999. 69-82.

——. "History, Community and Forbidden Relationships in *The God of Small Things.*" *Arundhati Roy: The Novelist Extraordinary.* Ed. R.K. Dhawan. New Delhi: Prestige, 1999. 84-99.

Bharucha, Ferheiz C. "*Paro: Dreams of Passion*: Meaning through Mediocrity." *Indian Women Novelists Set II: Vol. I.* Ed. R.K. Dhawan. New Delhi: Prestige, 1993. 213-219.

Bharucha, Nilufer E. "Inhabiting Enclosures and Creating Spaces: The Worlds of Women in Indian English Literature in English." *Ariel* 29.1 (1998): 93-107.

Bhasin, Kamal. "From Modernity to "Purdah': Geeta's Acculturation in Rama Mehta's *Inside the Haveli.*" *Women in Indo-Anglian Fiction: Tradition and Modernity.* Ed. Naresh K. Jain. New Delhi: Manohar, 1998. 114-127.

Bhat, Yashoda. "*Nectar in a Sieve*: A Novel of Change in Rural India." *Commonwealth Quarterly* 13.35 (1987): 4-8.

Bhatnagar, P. "Indian Womanhood: Fight for Freedom in *Roots and Shadows.*" *Indian Women Novelists Set I: Vol. IV.* Ed. R.K. Dhawan. New Delhi: Prestige, 1991. 118-129. (Also published in *Indian Women Novelists in English.* Ed. Birendra Pandey. New Delhi: Sarup, 2001.)

——. "Voice in *Voices in the City.*" *Indian Women Novelists Set I: Vol. III.* Ed. R.K. Dhawan. New Delhi: Prestige, 1991. 129-140.

——. "The Theme of Man-Woman Relationship in the Novels of Anita Desai." *Indian Women Novelists Set I: Vol. II.* Ed. R.K. Dhawan. New Delhi: Prestige, 1991. 143-154.

——. "Pursuit of Art: A Study of *In Custody.*" *Indian Women Novelists Set I: Vol. IV.* Ed. R.K. Dhawan. New Delhi: Prestige, 1991. 102-113.

——. "Search for Identity: A Study of Shashi Deshpande's *The Dark Holds No Terrors.*" *The Quest* 15.1 (2001): 50-57.

Bhatnagar, Vinita Dhandial. "Locating the Absent Mother: A Reading of Anita Desai's Novels." *Reading in Indian English Literature: Nation, Culture and Identity.* New Delhi: Harman, 2001. 106-123.

Bhatt, Indira. "*That Long Silence*: A Study." *Indian Women Novelists Set I: Vol. V.* Ed. R.K. Dhawan. New Delhi: Prestige, 1991. 156-162.

——. "*Voices in the City*: A Study of Monisha's Flight." *Indian Women Novelists Set I: Vol. III.* Ed. R.K. Dhawan. New Delhi: Prestige, 1991. 141-146.

——. "*Voices in the City*: Loneliness and Despair." *Between Spaces of Silence*: *Women Creative Writers*. Ed. Kamini Dinesh. New Delhi: Sterling, 1994. 95-99.

——. "Shobha De's *Sultry Days* and Gita Mehta's *A River Sutra*: A Study in Orientalism." *Indian Women Novelists Set III*: *Vol. I*. Ed. R.K. Dhawan. New Delhi: Prestige, 1995. 67-77.

——. "Shashi Deshpande's *The Dark Holds No Terrors*: A Study in Guilt Consciousness." *Indian Women Novelists Set III*: *Vol. 4*. Ed. R.K. Dhawan. New Delhi: Prestige, 1995. 41-50.

——. "Heart of Darkness." *Explorations*: *Arundhati Roy's "The God of Small Things."* Ed. Indira Bhatt and Indira Nityanandam. New Delhi: Creative, 1999. 98-102.

——. "Victims and Victimizers." *Explorations*: *Arundhati Roy's "The God of Small Things."* Ed. Indira Bhatt and Indira Nityanandam. New Delhi: Creative, 1999. 136-141.

Bhavani, J. "*Nirdvandva*: Individuation and Integration as the Heroine's Quest in Shashi Deshpande's Fiction." *Indian Women Novelists Set III*: Vol. 4. Ed. R.K. Dhawan. New Delhi: Prestige, 1995. 20-31.

Bose, Brinda. "In Desire and in Death: Eroticism as Politics in Arundhati Roy's *The God of Small Things*." *Ariel* 29.2 (1998): 59-72.

Budholia, O.P. "City as Protagonist: Anita Desai's *Voices in the City* and *In Custody*." *Indian English Literature Since 1950: Vol. 2*. Ed. Charu Sheel Singh. New Delhi: Anmol, 2002. 62-70.

Chadha, Ramesh. "*Heat and Dust* and *The Coffer Dams*: A Comparative Study." *Journal of Indian Writing in English* 10.1&2 (1982): 24-30.

Chakravarty, Joya and Indravadan Purohit. "Issues in *The God of Small Things*." *The Critical Studies of Arundhati Roy's "The God of Small Things."* Ed. Jaydipsinh Dodiya and Joya Chakravarty. New Delhi: Atlantic, 1999. 149-153.

Chakravarthy, Radha. "Figuring the Maternal: "Freedom" and "Responsibility" in Anita Desai's Novels." *Ariel* 2.29 (1998): 75-92.

Chanda, Tirthankar. "Cross-Cultural Interaction in *Nectar in a Sieve*." *Indian Women Novelists Set II*: *Vol. II*. Ed. R.K. Dhawan. New Delhi: Prestige, 1993. 120-129.

——. "Sexual/Textual Strategies in *The God of Small Things*." *Commonwealth*: *Essays and Studies* 20.1 (1997): 38-44.

Chandra, N.D. "The Poetics of Feminism in Anita Desai's *Cry the Peacock*." *Recent Indian Literature in English*: *A Cultural Perspective*. Ed. Mithilesh K. Pandey. New Delhi: Anmol, 1999. 48-57.

Chandra, Subhash. "Family and Marriage in Shobha De's *Socialite Evenings*." *Indian English Literature*: *Since Independence*. Ed. K. Ayyappa Paniker. New Delhi: IAES, 1991. 27-33. (Also published in *The Fiction of Shobha De*. Ed. Jayadipsinh Dodiya. New Delhi: Prestige, 2000. 142-148.)

——. "City in the Novels of Kamala Markandaya, Anita Desai and Shashi Deshpande." *Indian Women Novelists Set I*: *Vol. I*. Ed. R.K. Dhawan. New Delhi: Prestige, 1991. 157-166.

——. "Silence No More: A Study of *That Long Silence*." *Indian Women Novelists Set I*: *Vol.V*. Ed. R.K. Dhawan. New Delhi: Prestige, 1991. 147-155.

——. "The Beat Hero in *Voices in the City*." *Indian Women Novelists Set I*: *Vol. III*. Ed. R.K. Dhawan. New Delhi: Prestige, 1991. 122-128.

——. "Art in a Sieve: A Study of *Nectar in a Sieve*." *Indian Women Novelists Set II*: *Vol. II*. Ed. R.K. Dhawan. New Delhi: Prestige, 1993. 130-139.

——. "Crisis of Values in *A Handful of Rice*." *Indian Women Novelists Set II*: *Vol. III*. Ed. R.K. Dhawan. New Delhi: Prestige, 1993. 87-93.

——. "The New Woman" in Namita Ghokale's *Gods, Graves and Grandmother.*" *Indian Women Novelists Set III*: *Vol.* 6. Ed. R.K. Dhawan. New Delhi: Prestige, 1995. 13-20.

——. "Semiotics of Feministic Discourse in Shashi Deshpande's *That Long Silence.*" *Symbolism in Indian Fiction in English.* Ed. Ramesh K. Srivastava. Jalandhar: ABS, 1997. 203-210.

Chandy, Mini. "The Love Laws." *Explorations*: *Arundhati Roy's "The God of Small Things.*" Ed. Indira Bhatt and Indira Nityanandam. New Delhi: Creative, 1999. 83-92.

Chatterjjee, Arundhati. "Rukmani, The Mother Figure in *Nectar in a Sieve.*" *Studies in Indian Fiction in English.* Ed. G.S. Balarama Gupta. Gulbarga: Journal of Indian Writing in English, 1987. 85-92.

Chavan, Sunanda P. "*Inside the Haveli*: Inadequate as a Work of Art." *Indian Women Novelists Set I*: *Vol. IV*. Ed. R.K. Dhawan. New Delhi: Prestige, 1991. 239-248.

Chawla, Nishi. "Beyond Arundhati Roy's 'Heart of Darkness': A Bhaktinian Reading of *The God of Small Things.*" *Arundhati Roy*: *The Novelist Extraordinary*. Ed. R.K. Dhawan. New Delhi: Prestige, 1999. 342-355.

Chellappan, K. "Being and Becoming in Anita Desai's *Where Shall We Go This Summer?*" *Subjects Worthy Fame*: *Essays on Commonwealth Literature*. Ed. A.L. Mc Leod. New Delhi: Sterling, 1989. 1-10.

Chellappan, K. "Self in Time and Place: A Study of Anita Desai's *Clear Light of Day.*" *Essays in Criticism on Indian Literature in English*. Ed. M. S. Nagarajan et al. New Delhi: S. Chand, 1991. 139-144.

Cherlin, Andrew J. "The Consequences." *Marriage Divorce Remarriage*. Cambridge: HUP, 1981. 69-92.

Chhaya, Y.P. "Pearls in an Oyster." *Explorations*: *Arundhati Roy's "The God of Small Things.*" Ed. Indira Bhatt and Indira Nityanandam. New Delhi: Creative, 1999. 120-129.

Chindade, Shirish V. "*Inside the Haveli*: The Epistemology of Eternal India." *Indian Women Novelists Set I*: *Vol. V*. Ed. R.K. Dhawan. New Delhi: Prestige, 1991. 7-15.

Chinneswararao, G.J. "Nayantara Sahgal's *A Situation in New Delhi*." *Commonwealth Quarterly* 3.9 (1978): 154-161.

Chitnis, Suma. "The Sociology of Women's Education: Two Different Issues." *Women's Studies in India: Some Perspectives.* Ed. Maithreyi Krishna Raj. Bombay: Popular, 1986. 59-66.

Choubey, Asha. "*The Day in Shadow*: A Study in Inertia and Submission." *Post-Independence Indian English Fiction.* Ed. Rajeshwar Mittapalli and Alessandro Monti. New Delhi: Atlantic, 2001. 77-87.

Clement, A. "'The Centre Cannot Hold': The Vulnerable World of Anita Desai." *Indian Women Novelists Set III: Vol. I.* Ed. R.K. Dhawan. New Delhi: Prestige, 1995. 213-243.

Conde, Mary. "Forging a New Identity: A Study of *The God of Small Things*." *Arundhati Roy: The Novelist Extraordinary*. Ed. R.K. Dhawan. New Delhi: Prestige, 1999. 166-176.

Coser, Rose Laub. "Reflections on Feminist Theory." *Feminism and Sociological Theory*. Ed. Ruth A. Wallace. New Delhi: Sage, 1989. 200-207.

Dale, James. "Sexual Politics in the Novels of Kamala Markandaya." *World Literature Written in English* 21.2 (1982): 347-355.

Damodar, G. "The Outsiderist Tradition in Joshi and Desai." *Kakatiya Journal of English Studies* 13 (1993): 59-66.

Daruwalla, Keki. "An Intense Book: *That Long Silence* Shashi Deshpande: An Excerpt." *Indian Literature* 34.6 (1991): 30-36.

Das, Bijay Kumar. "Shashi Deshpande's *That Long Silence* and the Question of Reader Response." *Aspects of Commonwealth Literature*. New Delhi: Creative, 1995. 125-132.

Das, B.K. "Shobha De's *Sisters*: An Appraisal." *Changing Faces of Women in Indian Writing in English*. Ed. M.Q. Khan and A. G. Khan. New Delhi: Creative, 1995. 64-70.

——. "*That Long Silence*: An Indian Paradigm of Character Progression." *The Fiction of Shashi Deshpande*. Ed. R.S. Pathak. New Delhi: Prestige, 1998. 126-131.

Dash, Sandhyarani. "A Woman More Sinned than Sinning: A Study of *Starry Nights*." *The Fiction of Shobha De*. Ed. Jaydipsinh Dodiya. New Delhi: Prestige, 2000. 167-173.

Dash, T.R. "Nayantara Sahgal and Feminism." *Feminism and Indian English Fiction*. Ed. P. M. Nayak and S. P. Swain. Bareilley: PBD, 1996. 97-100.

Datta, Vandana. "The Inner Landscape: A Study of Stream of Consciousness in the Works of Anita Desai." *Creative Forum* 10.1-2 (1997): 73-79.

Davees, C.J. "Design in *The God of Small Things*." *Arundhati Roy: The Novelist Extraordinary*. Ed. R.K. Dhawan. New Delhi: Prestige, 1999. 328-337.

Desai, Rakesh N. "The Dialectic of Inside/Outside in Rama Mehta's *Inside the Haveli*." *The Inside View: Native Responses to Contemporary Indian English Novel*. Ed. Rangrao Bhongle. New Delhi: Atlantic, 2003. 138-146.

Deshpande, P. S. "Illusion and Reality in Anita Desai's *Where Shall We Go This Summer?*" *When East Meets West: Indian Thought in Anglo-Indian and Indo-English Fiction*. Ed. Adapa Ramakrishna Rao and M. Siva Rama Krishna. New Delhi: Sterling, 1994. 139-148.

De Souza, Eunice, ed. Introduction. *Ratanbai: A Sketch of a Bombay High Caste Hindu Young Wife*. By Shevanthibai M. Nikambe. 1895. New Delhi: Sahitya Akademi, 2003. 1-14.

Devadawson, Christel R. "From Danzing to Ayemenem: A Look Ahead at Arundhati Roy." *Arundhati Roy: The Novelist Extraordinary*. Ed. R.K. Dhawan. New Delhi: Prestige, 1999. 286-295.

Dharker, Rani. "Girl-Wife-Mother: The Marginalised in the Texts of Shashi Deshpande and Bharati Mukherjee." *Indian-English Fiction 1980-90: An Assessment*. Ed. Nilufer E. Bharucha and Vilas Sarang. Delhi: B.R., 1994. 105-114.

——. "Who's Afraid of the Big Bad Booker? The Making of Small Gods in Our Times." *Rethinking Indian English Literature*. Ed. U.M. Nanavati and Prafulla C. Kar. Delhi: Pencraft, 2000. 140-144.

Dharwadkar, Aparna. "The Exercise of Memory and the Diasporization of Anglophone Indian Fiction." *Arundhati Roy: The Novelist Extraordinary*. Ed. R.K. Dhawan. New Delhi: Prestige, 1999. 161-165.

Dhawan, R.K. "Arundhati Roy: The Novelist Extraordinary." *Arundhati Roy: The Novelist Extraordinary*. Ed. R.K. Dhawan. New Delhi: Prestige, 1999. 11-22.

Dinakar Lal, Premalatha. "Down a Narrow Road in a Wide Car—A Study of The Anglophilas in *The God of Small Things*." *Literary Half-Yearly* 34.1 (1998): 52-58.

Dinesh, Kamini. "*That Long Silence*: The Narrator and the Narrative." *Contemporary Indian Fiction in English*. Ed. Avadesh K. Singh. New Delhi: Creative, 1993. 84-88.

——. "*Fire on the Mountain*: Negation of the Role Model." *Between Spaces of Silence*: *Women Creative Writers*. Ed. Kamini Dinesh. New Delhi: Sterling, 1994. 107-114.

——. "*Fire on the Mountain*: The Contours of the Mind." *Creative Forum* 10.1-2 (1997): 89-96.

——. "*Second Thoughts*: A Critique." *The Fiction of Shobha De*. Ed. Jaydipsinh Dodiya. New Delhi: Prestige, 2000. 281-283.

Dodiya, Jaydipsinh. "Cultural Conflicts in Kamala Markandaya's Novels." *Indian Women Writers*: *Critical Perspectives*. Ed. Jaydipsinh Dodiya and K. V. Surendran. New Delhi: Sarup, 1999. 1-6.

Dodiya, Jaydipsinh and Indravadan Purohit. "Autobiographical Elements in Arundhati Roy's *The God of Small Things*." *Contemporary Indian Writings in English*. Ed. Jaydipsinh Dodiya. New Delhi: Atlantic, 1998. 99-101.

——. "Arundhati Roy—The Woman and the Writer." *The Critical Studies of Arundhati Roy's "The God of Small*

Things." Ed. Jaydipsinh Dodiya and Joya Chakravarty. New Delhi: Atlantic, 1999. 1-8.

Dooley, Gillian. "Attitudes to Political Commitment in three Indian Novels: *Kanthapura, Train to Pakistan* and *Rich Like Us*." *Littcrit* 20.2 (1994): 30-39.

Driesen, Cynthia Vanden. "When Language Dances: The Subversive Power of Roy's Text in *The God of Small Things*." *Arundhati Roy: The Novelist Extraordinary*. Ed. R.K. Dhawan. New Delhi: Prestige, 1999. 365-376.

Drum, Alice. "Kamala Markandaya's Modern Quest Tale." *World Literature Written in English* 22.2 (1983): 323-332.

Dudt, Charmazel. "Past and Present: A Journey to Confrontation." *Journal of Indian Writing in English* 9.1 (1981): 67-73.

——. "Recurring Metaphors in Shashi Deshpande." *The Fiction of Shashi Deshpande*. Ed. R.S. Pathak. New Delhi: Creative, 1998. 219-227.

Dwivedi, A. N. "Failure and Frustration: A Study of Anita Desai's *In Custody*." *Indian Fiction in English: Problems and Promises*. Ed. R.S. Pathak. New Delhi: NBC, 1990. 110-120.

Dwivedi A.N. and Niroj Banerji. "The Narrative Technique of Kamala Markandaya." *Essays in Criticism on Indian Literature in English*. New Delhi: S. Chand, 1991. 124-133.

Fernandes, Marie. "The Outer Weather in Anita Desai's Novels." *Indian English Fiction 1980-90: An Assessment*. Ed. Nilufer E. Bharucha and Vilas Sarang. Delhi: B.R., 1994. 169-184.

Forbes, Geraldine. "Education for Women." *The New Cambridge History of India. IV.2: Women in Modern India*. Cambridge: CUP, 1996. 32-63.

Ganapathy-Dore, Geeta. "Impossible Reconciliation in Manju Kapur's *Difficult Daughters*." *Commonwealth: Essays and Studies* 23.1 (2000): 35-42.

Ganesh, Latha. "Rushdie and Roy." *Explorations: Arundhati Roy's "The God of Small Things."* Ed. Indira Bhatt and Indira Nityanandam. New Delhi: Creative, 1999. 103-112.

Ganguly, Chandra. "*Fire on the Mountain*: An Analysis." *Commonwealth Quarterly* 21(1996): 40-44.

Gaur, Rashmi. "*That Long Silence*: Journey Towards Self-Actualization." *Women in the Novels of Shashi Deshpande.* Ed. Suman Bala. New Delhi: Khosla, 2001. 88-97.

Geeta, P. "Kamala Markandaya—An Interpretation." *Commonwealth Quarterly* 3.9 (1978): 96-103.

——. "Images and Archetypes in Kamala Markandaya's Novels: A Study in Cultural Ambivalence." *Journal of Commonwealth Literature* 26.1 (1991): 169-178.

——. "The Novels of Kamala Markandaya: Reassessing Feminine Identity." *Between Spaces of Silence: Women Creative Writers.* Ed. Kamini Dinesh. New Delhi: Sterling, 1994. 126-138.

George, Jacob C. "The Indian Scenario in the Novels of Kamala Markandaya: An Assessment of Popular Indian Superstitious Beliefs." *Indian Women Novelists Set II: Vol. II.* Ed. R. K. Dhawan. New Delhi: Prestige, 1993. 35-39.

——. "*The God of Small Things*: Humour as a Mode of Feminist Protest." *Arundhati Roy: The Novelist Extraordinary.* Ed. R.K. Dhawan. New Delhi: Prestige, 1999. 71-76.

Ghosal, Madhumita and Mehra M. Major. "*Pleasure City*: The Continuation of Colonial Influence on Independent India." *Indian Women Novelists Set I: Vol. III.* Ed. R.K. Dhawan. New Delhi: Prestige, 1993. 241-245.

Ghosh, Tapan Kumar. "Tomorrow Will Never Die: Arundhati Roy's Tryst with History in *The God of Small Things.*" *Arundhati Roy: The Novelist Extraordinary.* Ed. R.K. Dhawan. New Delhi: Prestige, 1999. 183-193.

Giri, Mehtab. "Women's Education: National Policies and Development." *Women's Development: Problems and Prospects.* Ed. Shain Aleem. New Delhi: APH, 1996. 79-92.

Goel, Kunj Bala. "Anita Desai's Novels: A Study in Verbal Pattern and Psyche." *Indian Writings in English Vol. I.* Ed. Manmohan K. Bhatnagar. New Delhi: Atlantic, 2001. 181-185.

——. "From the Continent to the Island: Imagery as Archetype in Anita Desai's *Bye-Bye Blackbird.*" *Indian Writings in English Vol. I.* Ed. Manmohan K. Bhatnagar. New Delhi: Atlantic, 2001. 173-180.

Goyal, Bhagwat. "Nayantara Sahgal: A Review." *Culture and Commitment: Aspects of Indian Literature in English.* By Bhagwat Goyal. Meerut: Shalabh, 1984. 74-75.

——. "The World of Women Novelists." *Culture and Commitment: Aspects of Indian Literature in English.* By Bhagwat Goyal. Meerut: Shalabh, 1984. 139-142.

——. "Kamala Markandaya's *Nectar in a Sieve*: A Study." *Culture and Commitment: Aspects of Indian Literature in English.* By Bhagwat Goyal. Meerut: Shalabh, 1984. 97-116.

Greenhalgh, Susanne. "Chapter 2: Growing up." *An Introduction to Women's Studies.* Ed. Beryl Madoc-Jones and Jennifer Coates. Oxford: Blackwell, 1996. 16-37.

Gupta, R.K. "Women in Shashi Deshpande's Novels." *POETCRIT* 15.1 (2002): 41-47.

Gupta, Sangeeta. "The Nature of Brother-Sister Relationship: *Untouchable, A Bend in the Ganges* and *A Situation in New Delhi.*" *Indian Women Novelists Set II: Vol. IV.* Ed. R.K. Dhawan. New Delhi: Prestige, 1993. 218-237.

Gupta, Santosh. "Bridging the Polarities of Imagination and Reason in *Clear Light of Day.*" *Indian Women Novelists Set I: Vol. III.* Ed. R.K. Dhawan. New Delhi: Prestige, 1991. 236-250.

——. "Entrapment and Freedom in *Inside the Haveli.*" *Indian Women Novelists Set I: Vol. IV.* Ed. R.K. Dhawan. New Delhi: Prestige, 1991. 219-229.

——. "Bridging in the Polarities of Imagination and Reason in *Clear Light of Day.*" *Indian Women Novelists Set I: Vol. III.* Ed. R.K. Dhawan. New Delhi: Prestige, 1991. 236-250.

——. "The Binding Vine of Relationships in Shashi Deshpande's Novels." *Recent Indian Literature in English: A Cultural Perspective*. Ed. Mithilesh K. Pandey. New Delhi: Anmol, 1999. 89-102.

Guruprasad, Thakur. "And never the Twain Shall Meet: Kamala Markandaya's *The Nowhere Man*." *Indian Women Novelists Set II: Vol. III*. Ed. R. K. Dhawan. New Delhi: Prestige, 1993. 177-186. (Also Published in *Explorations in Modern Indo-English Fiction*. Ed. R. K. Dhawan. New Delhi: Bahri Publications, 1982. 199-207.)

Guttal, Vijaya. "Reading Shashi Deshpande in the Post-Colonial Context." *Haritham* 14 (2002): 73-81.

——. "Shashi Deshpande's *The Binding Vine* and *A Matter of Time*: A Reading in the Post-Colonial Context." *Littcrit* 29.1 (2003): 55-63.

Harish, Ranjana. "*A Situation in New Delhi*: A Novel of Political Dislocation." *Indian Women Novelists Set II: Vol. IV*. Ed. R.K. Dhawan. New Delhi: Prestige, 1993. 185-191.

——. "*The God of Small Things*: A Tale of Mombattis' Brave Struggle." *Arundhati Roy: The Novelist Extraordinary*. Ed. R.K Dhawan. New Delhi: Prestige, 1999. 222-226.

——. "Her Body was her Own: A Feminist Note on Ammu's Female Estate." *Explorations: Arundhati Roy's "The God of Small Things."* Ed. Indira Bhatt and Indira Nityanandam. New Delhi: Creative, 1999. 47-50.

Harishanker, V. Bharathi. "Beyond Black and White: The Use of Doubling in *The God of Small Things*." *Explorations: Arundhati Roy's "The God of Small Things."* Ed. Indira Bhatt and Indira Nityanandam. New Delhi: Creative, 1999. 51-57.

Harrex, S.C. "A sense of Identity: The Novels of Kamala Markandaya." *Journal of Commonwealth Literature* 6.1 (1971): 65-78.

Hashmi, Alamgir. "A Reading of Anita Desai's *Clear Light of Day*." *Explorations* 8&9 3&4 (1981-1982): 72-79.

Hegde, M.G. "*Plans for Departure*: A Study." *Recent Commonwealth Literature Vol. I*. Ed. R.K. Dhawan. et al. New Delhi: Prestige, n.d. 133-141.

Hey, Valerie. "Chapter 4: Girls and Schooling." *An Introduction to Women's Studies*. Ed. Beryl Madoc-Jones and Jennifer Coates. Oxford: Blackwell, 1996. 62-83.

Hubel, Teresa. "The Politics of the Poor and the Limits of Individualism in Nayantara Sahgal's *Rich Like Us*." *Nayantara Sahgal's India: Passion, Politics and History*. New Delhi: Sterling, 1998. 78-96.

Inamdar, F.A. "Image and Symbol Pattern in Kamala Markandaya's Novels." *Indian Wrtings in English Vol. I*. New Delhi: Atlantic, 2001. 155-172.

Indira, C. "The True Voice of Endurance: A Study of Rukmani in Markandaya's *Nectar in a Sieve*." *Feminism and Recent Fiction in English*. Ed. Sushila Singh. New Delhi: Prestige, 1991. 64-71.

Indira, S. "*The Nowhere Man*: A Comparative Study of Anita Desai's *Baumgartner's Bombay* and *The Nowhere Man*." *Indian Women Novelists Set II: Vol. I*. Ed. R.K. Dhawan. New Delhi: Prestige, 1993. 47-55.

——. "Walking the Tight Rope: A Reading of Githa Hariharan's *The Thousand Faces of Night*." *Indian Women Novelists Set III: Vol. IV*. Ed. R.K. Dhawan. New Delhi: Prestige, 1995. 177-182.

——. "Ethel Wilson's *Swamp Angel* and Shashi Deshpande's *The Binding Vine* as Kunstlerroman." *50 Years of Indian Writing*. Ed. R.K. Dhawan. New Delhi: IAES, n.d. 68-75.

Iyengar, K.P.S. "A Note on Anita Desai's Novels." *Banasthali Patrika* 12: 64-69.

Jacob, Asha Susan. "Victims and Survivors: Kamala Markandaya's Indian Women Protagonists." *Post-Independence Indian English Fiction*. Ed. Rajeshwar Mittapalli and Alessandro Monti. New Delhi: Atlantic, 2001. 103-116.

Jain, Jasbir. "The Politics of Hinduism in the Novels of Nayantara Sahgal." *Littcrit* 2.1 (1976): 45-47.

——. "Sexual Relations in the Novels of Sahgal." *Journal of Indian Writing in English* 6.1 (1978): 41-47.

——. "The Political Novel and the Contemporary Scene." *Indian Book Chronicle* 13.2 (1988): 62-65.

——. "The Novels of Kamala Markandaya." *Indian Literature* 18.1 (1990): 36-43.

——. "The Feminist Perspective: The Indian Situation and its Literary Manifestations." *Other Englishers: Essays on Commonwealth Writing*. Ed. Niaz Zanam et al. Dhaka: University Press, 1991. 66-75.

——. "The Use of Fantasy in the Novels of Anita Desai." *Indian Women Novelists Set I: Vol. II*. Ed. R.K. Dhawan. New Delhi: Prestige, 1991. 68-79.

——. "The Feminist Perspective: The Indian Situation and its Literary Manifestations." *Other Englishers: Essays on Commonwealth Writing*. Ed. Niaz Zaman et al. Dhaka: University Press, 1991. 66-75.

——. "Cities and Gardens in the Novels of Anita Desai." *Indian Women Novelists Set I: Vol. II*. Ed. R.K. Dhawan. New Delhi: Prestige, 1991. 199-213.

——. "The Novel as Political Biography: Sahgal's *Rich Like Us* and *Plans for Departure*." *Indian Women Novelists Set II: Vol. IV*. Ed. R.K. Dhawan. New Delhi: Prestige, 1993. 52-64.

——. "Gender and Narrative Strategy." *Between Spaces of Silence: Women Creative Writers*. Ed. Kamini Dinesh. New Delhi: Sterling, 1994. 29-37.

——. "Post-Colonial Realities: Writing Women History." *Interrogating Post-Colonialism: Theory, Text and Context*. Ed. Harish Trivedi and Meenakshi Mukherjee. Shimla: IIAS, 1996.161-176.

——. "Structure as Symbol: Sahgal's *Plans for Departure* and *Mistaken Identity*." *Symbolism in Indian Fiction in English*. Ed. Ramesh K. Srivastava. Jalandhar: ABS, 1997. 124-132.

——. "Positioning the 'Post' in Post-Feminist: Reworking of Strategies." *Indian Feminisms*. Ed. Jasbir Jain and Avadhesh Kumar Singh. New Delhi: Creative, 2001. 80-95.

——. "Towards the 21st Century: The Writing of the 1990s." *Indian Writing in English: The Last Decade*. Ed. Rajul Bhargava. Jaipur: Rawat, 2002. 11-25.

Jameela Begum A. "Glimpses of Indian Women in Kamala Markandaya's Novels." *Commonwealth Quarterly* 13.36 (1987-1988): 17-23.

Jamkhandi, S.R. "The Artistic Effects of the Shifts in Point of View in Anita Desai's *Cry, the Peacock*." *Journal of Indian Writing in English* 9.1 (1981): 35-46.

——. "Old Delhi Revisited: *Clear Light of Day*." *Indian Women Novelists Set I: Vol. IV*. Ed. R.K. Dhawan. New Delhi: Prestige, 1991. 7-13.

——. "They'd Much Rather Step Down from the Pedestal: Women in *The Village by the Sea*." *Indian Women Novelists Set I: Vol. IV*. Ed. R. K. Dhawan. New Delhi: Prestige, 1991. 43-46.

Jandial, Gur Pyari. "The Woman Question in Anjana Appachana's *Listening Now*." *Modern Indian English Fiction*. Ed. T.S. Anand, L.S. Bedi and Hargunjot Kaur. New Delhi: Creative, 2002. 124-128.

Jessewala, Feroza. "Of Cabbages and Kings: *This Time of Morning* and *Storm in Chandigarh* by Nayantara Sahgal." *Journal of Indian Writing in English* 1.5 (1977): 43-50.

Jeyaraju, M.R. and D. Mruthula. "A Nationalist Reading of *The Golden Honeycomb*." *Critical Essays on Indian Women Writing in English*. Ed. A.S. Ratnam. New Delhi: Herman, 1999. 57-66.

——. "Kamala Markandaya's *The Golden Honeycomb* as a Post-Colonial Novel." *Critical Studies on Indian Fiction in English*. Ed. R.A. Singh and V.LV.N. Narendra Kumar. New Delhi: Atlantic, 1999. 108-114.

Jha, G.S. "Artists in Roy's 'God'." *POETCRIT* 15.1 (2002): 3-9.

John, K.K. "A Band of Masqueraders: A Study of Some Characters of Arundhati Roy's *The God of Small Things*." *The Critical Studies of Arundhati Roy's The God of Small Things*. Ed. Jaydipsinh Dodiya. New Delhi: Atlantic, 1999. 119-123.

Joseph, S. John Peter. "Search for Meaningful Co-existence of Tradition and Modernity in Kamala Markandaya's *Nectar in a Sieve*." *New Quest* 145 (2001): 331-344.

——. "Alienation and Rootlessness in the Novels of Kamala Markandaya." *The Quest* 15.1 (2001): 35-42.

Joshi, Madhu. "What the People of India Are Really Like: A Study of *Nectar in a Sieve*." *Indian Women Novelists Set II: Vol. II*. Ed. R.K. Dhawan. New Delhi: Prestige, 1993. 92-105.

——. "An Eloquent Cry of Despair: *Some Inner Fury*." *Indian Women Novelists Set II: Vol. II*. Ed. R. K. Dhawan. New Delhi: Prestige, 1993. 171-186.

Juneja, Anita. "The Struggle for Existence in *A Handful of Rice*." *POETCRIT* 13.2 (2000): 17-20.

Juneja, Purnim. "The East-West Theme: *Some Inner Fury, The Serpent and the Rope* and *A Dream in Hawaii*." *Commonwealth Literature Vol. I*. Ed. R.K. Dhawan. New Delhi: Classical, 1998. 178-197.

Juneja, Renu. "Identity and Feminity in Anita Desai's Fiction." *Journal of South Asian Literature* 22.2 (1987): 77-86.

Jussawalla, Feroza. "*This Time of Morning* and *Storm in Chandigarh*." *Journal of Indian Writing in English* 5.1 (1977): 43-49.

Kalinikkora, Elena J. "The Hindu Woman from London: Kamala Markandaya." *Indian English Literature: A Perspective*. Gaziabad: Vimal, 1982. 149-163.

Kapadia, Novy. "The End of Imagination, the End of a Dream." *Arundhati Roy: The Novelist Extraordinary*. Ed. R.K. Dhawan. New Delhi: Prestige, 1999. 406-418.

Kapur, Usha. "A Probe into Female Individuality: Anita Desai's Successful Attempt at Viewing an Introvert Heroine

Against the Social Backdrop of Calcutta." *Punjab University Research Bulletin (Arts)* 31.1&2 (2000): 25-27.

Kastura, P.S. "Confrontation with Death in Shashi Deshpande's *If I Die Today*." *Indian English Literature: Since Independence*. Ed. K. Ayyappa Paniker. New Delhi: IAES, 1991. 49-54.

Katamble, V.D. "Kamala Markandaya's *CofferDams*." *Littcritt* 11.1&2 (1985): 54-62.

Kerr, David. "A Sense of Proportion: Multiple Perspectives in Nayantara Sahgal's *Mistaken Identity*." *Aspects of Indian English*. Ed. Shantinath Desai. New Delhi: Sahitya Akademi, 1995. 48-56.

Khan, A.G. "Shobha De 'Vatsyayani'." *Indian Women Novelists Set III: Vol. I*. Ed. R.K. Dhawan. New Delhi: Prestige, 1995. 78-82.

——. "*The Thousand Faces of Night*: An Epic 'Capsulized.'" *Faces of Women in Indian Writing in English*. Ed. M.Q. Khan and A.G. Khan. New Delhi: Creative, 1995. 135-145.

——. "Liberated or Libidinous: Women Writing in English." *Indian Women Novelists Set III: Vol. I*. Ed. R.K. Dhawan. New Delhi: Prestige, 1995. 32-38.

——. "Shashi Deshpande's Heroines: Prisoners by Choice?" *The Fiction of Shashi Deshpande*. Ed. R.S. Pathak. New Delhi: Creative, 1998. 198-206.

——. "Wrinkled Youth and Pickled Future: Comparing Githa Hariharan and Arundhati Roy." *Explorations: Arundhati Roy's "The God of Small Things."* Ed. Indira Bhatt and Indira Nityanandam. New Delhi: Creative, 1999. 93-97.

Khan, M.Q. "Depressed Women in Anita Desai's Fiction." *Changing Faces of Women in Indian Writing in English*. Ed. M.Q. Khan and A.G. Khan. New Delhi: Creative, 1995. 42-63.

——. "A Critique of *Fasting, Feasting*." *Critical Endeavour* 7 (2001): 79-87.

Khanna, Shashi. "Chapter V: Appraisal of her novels from the standpoint of Human Relationships. (A) *Cry, the Peacock*."

Human Relationships in Anita Desai's Novels. New Delhi: Sarup, 1995. 58-62.

Kher, Inder Nath. "The Immigrant Experience in Anita Desai's *Bye-Bye Blackbird*." *Journal of Indian Writing in English* 1.22 (1994): 1-9.

Khushu-Lahiri, Rajyashree. "Broken Laws, Shattered Lives: A Study of *The God of Small Things*." *Arundhati Roy: The Novelist Extraordinary*. Ed. R.K. Dhawan. New Delhi: Prestige, 1999. 112-119.

Kinger, Anil. "Feast From the East: Arundhati Roy's *The God of Small Things*." *The Critical Studies of Arundhati Roy's "The God of Small Things."* Ed. Jaydipsinh Dodiya and Joya Chakravarti. New Delhi: Atlantic, 1999. 130-134.

Kirpal, Viney, "How Traditional Can a Modern Indian be: An Analysis of *Inside the Haveli*." *Indian Women Novelists Set I: Vol. IV*. Ed. R.K. Dhawan. New Delhi: Prestige, 1991. 174-191.

——. "The Writer as Historian: *Rich Like Us*." *Indian English Fiction 1980-90: An Assessment*. Ed. Nilufer E. Bharucha and Vilas Sarang. Delhi: B.R., 1994. 161-168.

——. "Post-Modern Strategies in the Indian English Novel." *Littcrit* 22.2 (1996): 21-34.

——. "*Rich Like Us*: Text, Context and Subtext." *Women's Writing: Text and Context*. Ed. Jasbir Jain. Jaipur: Rawat, 1996. 167-179.

——. "What is the Modern Third Novel?" *Journal of Commonwealth Literature* 23.1 (1998): 144-156.

Knapp, Bettina. "Rita to Exit: A Jungian Approach to Anita Desai's *Fire on the Mountain*." *Indian Literary Review* 6.1-3: 27-34.

Kothandaraman, Bala. "Structure in Nayantara Sahgal's *Storm in Chandigarh*." *Osmania Journal of English Studies* 11.1 (1974-75): 27-36.

Kothari, Reena. "The Multiple Power Structure in Ayemenem." *Explorations: Arundhati Roy's "The God of Small Things."*

Ed. Indira Bhatt and Indira Nityanandam. New Delhi: Creative, 1999. 142-154.

——. "Female Bonding: Githa Hariharan's *The Thousand Faces of Night.*" *Indo-English Fiction: The Last Decade.* Ed. Indira Nityanandam and Reena Kothari. New Delhi: Creative, 2002. 41-46.

——. "Difficult(?) Daughters in Manju Kapur's *Difficult Daughters.*" *Indo-English Fiction: The Last Decade.* Ed. Indira Nityanandam and Reena Kothari. New Delhi: Creative, 2002. 105-109.

Kotwal, Deepsheekha. "Gender and Sexual Identity in Shashi Deshpande's *That Long Silence.*" *English Studies in India: A Journal of Literature and Language* 7 (1999): 38-44.

Krishna, Francine. "Anita Desai: *Fire on the Mountain.*" *Indian Literature* 25 (1982): 158-169.

Krishnaraj, Maithreyi. "Motherhood: Power and Powerlessness." *Indian Women: Myth and Reality.* Ed. Jasodhara Bagchi. Calcutta: Sangam, 1995. 34-43.

Krupakar, B. "Race Relations and *The Nowhere Man.*" *Literary Endeavour* 2.2&3 (1981): 21-25.

Kumar, Gajendra. "*Strange Obsession*: A Critical Study." *The Fiction of Shobha De.* Ed. Jaydipsinh Dodiya. New Delhi: Prestige, 2000. 227-232.

Kumar, Sanjay. "Two Aspects of Feminism: The Expressive and the Explosive in Shobha De." *The Fiction of Shobha De.* Ed. Jaydipsinh Dodiya. New Delhi: Prestige, 2000. 51-61.

Kumar Shiv K. "Tradition and Change in the Novels of Kamala Markandaya." *Critical Responses: Commonwealth Literature.* Ed. Dept. of English, Osmania University. New Delhi: Sterling: n.d. 150-158.

——. "The Fiction of Anita Desai: Another View." *The Humanities Review* 3.2 (n.d): 43-46.

Kumar, Sudhir. "Artist as Vamp: A Feminist Approach to Shobha De's *Starry Nights.*" *Indian Women Novelists*

Set III: *Vol. I.* Ed. R.K. Dhawan. New Delhi: Prestige, 1995. 111-125.

Kundu, Rama. "'Journey to the East' Once Again: Anita Desai's *Journey to Ithaca.*" *Post-Independence Indian English Fiction.* Ed. Rajeshwar Mittapalli and Alessandro Monti. New Delhi: Atlantic, 2001. 44-54.

——. "Redefining the Margin: Arundhati Roy." *Post-Independence Indian English Fiction.* Ed. Rajeshwar Mittapalli and Alessandro Monti. New Delhi: Atlantic, 2001. 171-178.

——. "Githa Hariharan. "Intertext, Metafiction and 'Her Story'." *Post-Independence Indian English Fiction.* Ed. Rajeshwar Mittapalli and Alessandro Monti. New Delhi: Atlantic, 2001. 179-189.

Kunjakkam, K.A. "Women's Issues verses National Perspective." *Feminism and Indian Realities.* New Delhi: Mittal, 2002. 364-373.

Kuortti, Joel. "Interrogating Change: Arundhati Roy." *Arundhati Roy*: *The Novelist Extraordinary.* Ed. R.K. Dhawan. New Delhi: Prestige, 1999. 177-182.

Lal, Malashri. "Rama Mehta's *Inside the Haveli*: A Discourse on Gender and Class." *The Law of the Threshold*: *Women Writers in Indian English.* Shimla: IIAS, 1995. 81-103.

Lata, Pushpa. "A Protest Among the Patriarchal in Shobha De's Works." *The Fiction of Shobha De.* Ed. Jaydipsinh Dodiya. New Delhi: Prestige, 2000. 62-68.

Liu, Marcia P. "Continuity and Development in the Novels of Nayantara Sahgal." *Journal of Indian Writing in English* 8.1-2 (1980): 45-52.

Lokuge, Chandani. Introduction. *Kamala*: *The Story of a Hindu Life.* By Krupabai Satthianadhan.1894. New Delhi: OUP, 1998. 1-16.

Madge, V.M. "Towards Masala Fiction—Shobha De's *Starry Nights.*" *Journal of Indian Writing in English* 1-26 (1998): 30-38.

Mahadevan, Usha. "Arundhati Roy's *The God of Small Things*: A Native Response." *The Inside View: Native Response to Contemporary Indian English Novel*. Ed. Rangrao Bhongle. New Delhi: Atlantic, 2003. 83-94.

Mahajan, Anita. "*The Day in Shadow*: A Study." *Indian Women Novelists Set III: Vol. IV*. Ed. R.K. Dhawan. New Delhi: Prestige, 1993. 9-19.

——. "The Theme of Tradition and Modernity in *The Day in Shadow*." *Indian Women Novelists Set II: Vol. 5*. Ed. R.K. Dhawan. New Delhi: Prestige, 1993. 9-19.

——. "*Storm in Chandigarh*: An Assessment." *Indian Women Novelists Set II: Vol. IV*. Ed. R.K. Dhawan. New Delhi: Prestige, 1993. 163-172.

——. "A Conflict between Younger and Older Generations in *Two Virgins*." *Indian Women Novelists Set II: Vol. III*. Ed. R.K. Dhawan. New Delhi: Prestige, 1993. 157-165.

Maini, Darshan Singh. "The Achievement of Anita Desai." *Indo-English Literature: A Collection of Critical Essays*. Ed. K.K. Sharma. Gazhiabad: Vimal, 1977. 215-230.

Maini, Irma. "Anita Desai and the Feminine Sensibility." *Commonwealth Quarterly* 28 (1984): 1-12.

Maitra, Nivedita. "From Feminine to Female: Shashi Deshpande's *That Long Silence*." *The Quest* 17.2 (2003): 46-51.

Mala, R. "Sexual Predicament and Shashi Deshpande's Women." *Indian Women Novelists Set I: Vol. V*. Ed. R.K. Dhawan. New Delhi: Prestige, 1991. 50-59.

Malik, Nazma. "*The God of Small Things*: A Study of English Influence on Indian Culture." *Explorations: Arundhati Roy's "The God of Small Things."* Ed. Indira Bhatt and Indira Nityanandam. New Delhi: Creative, 1999. 168-178.

Mandal, Somdatta. "From Periphery to the Mainstream: The Making, Marketing and Media Response to Arundhati Roy." *Arundhati Roy: The Novelist Extraordinary*. Ed. R.K. Dhawan. New Delhi: Prestige, 1999. 23-37.

Mani, K. Ratna Shiela. "Arundhati Roy's *The God of Small Things*: A Point of View." *The Critical Studies of Arundhati Roy's "The God of Small Things."* Ed. Jaydipsinh Dodiya and Joya Chakravarty. New Delhi: Atlantic, 1999. 9-21.

Mann, Harveen Sachdeva. "'Going in the Opposite Direction': Feminine Recusancy in Anita Desai's *Voices in the City*." *Post-Colonial Literatures*: *Achebe, Ngugi, Desai, Walcott*. Ed. Michael Parker and Roger Starkey. London: Macmillan, 1995. 155-175. (Also published in *Ariel* 23.4 (1992): 75-95).

Manohar, D. Murali. "Women's Voices: Some Indian English Women Novelists of the 1980s." *POETCRIT* 16.2 (2002): 31-39.

——. "Educated" Women: Happy or Unhappy? Selected Novels of Indian English Women's Fiction of the 1990s." *POETCRIT* 17.1 (2004): 48-56.

Manvar, Twinkle B. "Velutha: The Downtrodden in Arundhati Roy's *The God of Small Things*." *The Critical Studies of Arundhati Roy's "The God of Small Things."* Ed. Jaydipsinh Dodiya and Joya Chakravarty. New Delhi: Atlantic, 1999. 124-129.

Marathe, Sunitha and Viney Kirpal. "The Immigrant Experience: A Comparison of Anita Desai's *Bye-Bye Blackbird* and Markandaya's *The Nowhere Man*." *Indian Women Novelists Set II*: *Vol. I*. Ed. R.K. Dhawan. New Delhi: Prestige, 1993. 56-68.

Masih, I.K. "*A Handful of Rice*: A Perspective." *Indian Women Novelists Set II*: *Vol. III*. Ed. R.K. Dhawan. New Delhi: Prestige, 1993. 94-100.

Masilamani, J. G. "Feminism in Anita Desai." *Kakatiya Journal of English Studies* 3 (1983): 25-33.

Mathur, O.P. "The Discourse of Resistance: A Reading of Kamala Markandaya's *Pleasure City*." *Post-Independence Indian English Fiction*. Ed. Rajeshwar Mittapalli and Alessandro Monti. New Delhi: Atlantic, 2001. 117-123.

Maya, D. "Gender, Culture and Text: A Reading of Indian Women's Fiction in English." *Journal of Literature and Aesthetics* (1999): 92-98.

Mathur, O.P. "*Rich Like Us*: The Aroma and the Nausea." *Between Spaces of Silence: Women Creative Writers*. Ed. Kamini Dinesh. New Delhi: Sterling, 1994. 59-65. (Also published with the changed title "The Nausea of Totalitarianism: A Note on Nayantara Sahgal's *Rich Like Us*." *The Modern Indian English Fiction*. New Delhi: Abhinav, 1993. 177-183.)

——. "After Nehru What? A Perspective on *A Situation in New Delhi*." *Indian Women Novelists Set II: Vol. IV*. Ed. R.K. Dhawan. New Delhi: Prestige, 1993. 202-210.

——. "Arundhati Roy's Paradoxical Celebration of Smallness." *Arundhati Roy: The Novelist Extraordinary*. Ed. R.K. Dhawan. New Delhi: Prestige, 1999. 215-221.

——. "Woman 'Empowered'? Representation in Indian English Fiction." *Samyukta* 1.2 (2001): 68-71.

Mehrotra, Charu. "Conflict and Harmony: Pattern of Evolution in Kamala Markandaya's Fiction." *Indian English Literature Since 1950: Vol. 2*. Ed. Charu Sheel Singh. New Delhi: Anmol, 2002. 85-95.

Meitei, M. Mani. "Anita Desai's *Where Shall We Go This Summer?* A Psycho Analytical Study." *Quest for Identity in Indian English Writing Part I: Fiction*. Ed. R.S. Pathak. New Delhi: Bahri Publications, 1992. 48-58.

——. "Feminism and Anita Desai's *Cry, the Peacock* and *Where Shall We Go This Summer?*" *Feminism and Indian English Fiction*. Ed. P.M. Naik and S.P. Swain. Bareilly: PBD, 1996. 43-55.

——. "Projection of Art and Life in *The God of Small Things*." *Arundhati Roy: The Novelist Extraordinary*. Ed. R.K. Dhawan. New Delhi: Prestige, 256-265.

Menon, K. Madhavi. "The Feminist Echo in Kamala Markandaya's Fiction." *Indian Women Novelists Set III: Vol. 3*. Ed. R.K. Dhawan. New Delhi: Prestige, 1993. 229-236.

——. "The Crisis of Feminine: Shashi Deshpande's *That Long Silence.*" *Commonwealth Quarterly* 18.46 (1993): 31-37.

——. "The Vision in Kamala Markandaya's *The Nowhere Man.*" *Commonwealth Quarterly* 13.34: 24-37.

Micheli, Corrado. "The Eccentric Voice of *The God of Small Things.*" *Arundhati Roy: The Novelist Extraordinary.* Ed. R.K. Dhawan. New Delhi: Prestige, 1999. 208-214.

Mishra, Charu Chandra. "Problematising Feminine Discourse: A Post-Feministic Critique of *The Dark Holds No Terrors.*" *Women in the Novels of Shashi Deshpande.* Ed. Suman Bala. New Delhi: Khosla, 2001. 78-87.

Mishra, D.S. "New Voices in Indian English Novels of 80s." *Contemporary Indian Fiction in English.* Ed. Avadesh K. Singh. New Delhi: Creative, 1993. 33-36.

Mishra, Gnaneswar. "The Search for an Idiom: A Study of *Kanthapura* and *Nectar in a Sieve.*" *How Indian is the Indian Novel in English?* Bhubaneswar: Utkal University, 1990. 36-54.

Mishra, Parvati. "The Downtrodden in Kamala Markandaya's *Nectar in a Sieve* and *A Handful of Rice.*" *Ravenshaw Journal of English Studies* 4.2 (1994): 44-49.

Misra, Nirja. "On the Portals of Change: An Analysis of the Purdah Culture in Rama Mehta's *Inside the Haveli.*" *Margins of Erasure.* Ed. Jasbir Jain and Amina Amin. New Delhi: Sterling, 1995. 72-82.

Mohanram, Radhika. "Narrating the Nation-in-Process: Nayantara Sahgal's *Mistaken Identity.*" *Nayantara Sahgal's India: Passion, Politics and History.* Ed. Ralph J. Crane. New Delhi: Sterling, 1998. 141-164.

Mohan, Rajeswari. "The Forked Tongue of Lyric in Anita Desai's *Clear Light of Day.*" *Journal of Commonwealth Literature* 32.1 (1997): 47-66.

Monti, Alessandro. "A(n) (En)Viable Idiom: Lexical Hybridizations and Speech Acts in Arundhati Roy." *Arundhati Roy: The Novelist Extraordinary.* Ed. R.K. Dhawan. New Delhi: Prestige, 1999. 377-384.

——. "Shakti Unleashed in Muppyland: Shobha De and the Making of Modern India." *The Fiction of Shobha De*. Ed. Jaydipsinh Dodiya. New Delhi: Prestige, 2000. 27-33.

——. "Failed Householders: Renouncement and Distributive Strategies in *Fasting, Feasting*." *Post-Independence Indian English Fiction*. Ed. Rajeshwar Mittapalli and Alessandro Monti. New Delhi: Atlantic, 2002. 55-68.

Mujeebuddin, Syed. "Past and Present in Anita Desai's *Clear Light of Day*." *Kakatiya Journal of English Studies* 18 (1998): 34-44.

Mukherjee, Madhusudan. "Why *The God of Small Things* Sells." *Arundhati Roy: The Novelist Extraordinary*. Ed. R. K. Dhawan. New Delhi: Prestige, 1999. 38-40.

Mukherjee, Meenakshi. "The Theme of Displacement in Anita Desai and Kamala Markandaya." *World Literature Written in English* 17.1 (1978): 225-233.

——. "Women Creative Writers in Indian English Literature." *Between Spaces of Silence: Women Creative Writers*. Ed. Kamini Dinesh. New Delhi: Sterling, 1994. 9-19.

Mulcaire, Tom. "*A Situation in New Delhi*: A Point of View." *Indian Women Novelists Set II: Vol. IV*. Ed. R.K. Dhawan. New Delhi: Prestige, 1993. 192-194. (Also published with the changed title, "Nayantara Sahgal's *A Situation in New Delhi*." *The Commonwealth Review* 2.1-2 (n.d): 193-195.)

Mund, Subhendu. Introduction. *Bianca Or The Young Spanish Maiden*. By Toru Dutt. 1878. New Delhi: OUP, 1998. 1-28.

Mutalik-Desai, A.A. "Glint and Sparkle, Love and Death: Reflections on *Come Up and Be Dead*." *Indian Women Novelists Set I: Vol. V*. Ed. R.K. Dhawan. New Delhi: Prestige, 1991. 90-101.

Myers, David. "Contemporary Tragedy and Paradise Lost in *The God of Small Things*." *Arundhati Roy: The Novelist Extraordinary*. Ed. R.K. Dhawan. New Delhi: Prestige, 1999. 356-364.

Nabar, Vrinda. "The Image of India in Anita Desai's *Clear Light of Day*." *Recent Commonwealth Literature*. Ed. R.K. Dhawan. New Delhi: Prestige, 1989. 227-236. (Also published in *Indian Women Novelists Set I: Vol. IV*. Ed. R.K. Dhawan. New Delhi: Prestige, 1991. 14-25.)

——. "The Four-dimensional Reality: Anita Desai's *Clear Light of Day*." *Image of India in the Indian Novel in English 1960-1985*. Ed. Sudhakar Pandey and R. Raj Rao. Hyderabad: Orient, 1993. 102-112.

——. "A Kind of Safety": The Rationalisation of Purdah in Rama Mehta's *Inside the Haveli*." *Margins of Erasure*. Ed. Jasbir Jain and Amina Amin. New Delhi: Sterling, 1995. 60-70.

Naikar, Basavaraj and N. Ramachandran. "Anatomy of Silence in *A Silence of Desire*." *Indian Women Novelists Set II: Vol. II*. Ed. R.K. Dhawan. New Delhi: Prestige, 1993. 237-246.

——. "Joys and Sorrows of Womanhood in *The Binding Vine*." *Women in the Novels of Shashi Deshpande*. Ed. Suman Bala. New Delhi: Khosla, 2001. 122-126.

Naik, M.K. "The Political Novel in Indian Writing in English." *The Indian Novel in English: Evaluation*. Ed. T. Prabhakar Rao. New Delhi: Phoenix, 1995. 20-32.

Naik, M.K. and Shyamala A. Narayan. "A Room of their Own: Women Novelists." *Indian English Literature 1980-2001: A Critical Survey*. Delhi: Pencraft, 2001. 76-115.

Nair, Rama. "The Art of Fiction: A Note on the "Prelude" of Githa Hariharan's *The Thousand Faces of Night*." *Indian Women Novelists Set III: Vol. IV*. Ed. R.K. Dhawan. New Delhi: Prestige, 1995.170-176.

——. "Dissonance and Harmony in Shashi Deshpande's *The Binding Vine*." *Indian Writing Today*. Ed. C.R. Visweswara Rao. New Delhi: IAES, 1996. 152-157.

——. "Of Roses and Rivers: Thematic Symbolism in *The God of Small Things*." *Arundhati Roy: The Novelist Extraordinary*. Ed. R.K. Dhawan. New Delhi: Prestige, 1999. 248-255.

Nanda, Mini. "Power Structure in Nayantara Sahgal's *Rich Like Us.*" *Women's Writing: Text and Context*. Ed. Jasbir Jain. Jaipur: Rawat, 1996. 180-188.

——. "Is there a God of Small Things?" *Contemporary Indian Literature: Positions and Expositions*. Ed. Santosh Gupta. Jaipur: Rawat, 2000. 176-189.

Narayan, Shyamala A. "Nayantara Sahgal's *Rich Like Us*: A Study." *The Indian Novel in English: Essays in Criticism*. Ed. Ravi Nanda Sinha and R. K. Singh. Ranchi: Ankit, 1987. 77-86.

——. "Nayantara Sahgal: An Assessment." *Commonwealth Literature Vol. I*. New Delhi: Classical, 1998. 268-270.

Narendra, M. "The Treatment of Hinduism in Mrs. Sahgal's *A Time to be Happy, This Time of Morning* and *Storm in Chandigarh*." *Critical Studies on Indian Fiction in English*. Ed. R.A. Singh and V.L.V.N. Narendra Kumar. New Delhi: Atlantic, 1999. 134-144.

Nayak, P.M. and Sadanand Misra. "Colonial Consciousness in Markandaya's *A Silence of Desire* and *Possession*." *Creative Forum* 8.1-2 (1995): 71-80.

Nayar, Nandini. "Twin (Un)Certainities—Arundhati Roy's *The God of Small Things*." *The Critical Studies of Arundhati Roy's "The God of Small Things."* Ed. Jaydipsinh Dodiya and Joya Chakravarty. New Delhi: Atlantic, 1999. 81-86.

Nayar, Pramod K. "Of(f) Limits: Arundhati Roy's *The God of Small Things*." *Contemporary Indian Writings in English*. Ed. Jaydipsinh Dodiya. New Delhi: Atlantic, 1998. 81-85.

——. "Cryptosecrets—Arundhati Roy's *The God of Small Things*." *The Critical Studies of Arundhati Roy's "The God of Small Things."* Ed. Jaydipsinh Dodiya and Joya Chakravarty. New Delhi: Atlantic, 1999. 73-80.

——. "Troping Silence: Oversignification and Liminality in *The God of Small Things*." *Arundhati Roy: The Novelist Extraordinary*. Ed. R.K. Dhawan. New Delhi: Prestige, 1999. 234-240.

——. "*Socialite Evenings*: Toward a Feminist Stance." *The Fiction of Shobha De*. Ed. Jaydipsinh Dodiya. New Delhi: Prestige, 2000. 108-118.

——. "The Function of Ecocriticism at the Present (Apocalyptic) Time: Reading Arundhati Roy's *The God of Small Things*." *Interdisciplinary Perspectives on Modernity*. Ed. Sudha P. Pandeya and Prafulla C. Kar. Delhi: Pencraft, 2001. 123-133.

——. "Text-Self World: Interior Monologue in *A Matter of Time*." *Women in the Novels of Shashi Deshpande*. Ed. Suman Bala. New Delhi: Khosla, 2001. 127-135.

——. "Towards a Feminist Proxemics: Kamala Markandaya's *Possession*." *Re-Markings* (2002): 7-17.

Nimavat, Dushyant B. "The Theme of Suffering and Exploitation in Arundhati Roy's *The God of Small Things* and Toni Morrison's Novels." *The Critical Studies of Arundhati Roy's "The God of Small Things*." Ed. Jaydipsinh Dodiya and Joya Chakravarti. New Delhi: Atlantic, 1999. 142-148.

Nityanandam, Indira. "Assimilation or Alienation: A Study of Geeta in Anita Desai's *Voices in the City* and Monisha in Rama Mehta's *Inside the Haveli*." *Indian Women Novelists Set II*: *Vol. I*. Ed. R.K. Dhawan. New Delhi: Prestige, 1993. 69-74. (Note: The character names against the novels are incorrect. The correct names and the titles are: Geeta in Rama Mehta's *Inside the Haveli* and Monisha in Anita Desai's *Voices in the City*.)

——. "Shashi Deshpande's *The Binding Vine*: Silent No More." *Indian Women Novelists Set III*: *Vol. 4*. Ed. R.K. Dhawan. New Delhi: Prestige, 1995. 60-66.

——. "A Search for Identity: *The Thousand Faces of Night*." *Indian Women Novelists Set III*: *Vol. IV*. Ed. R.K. Dhawan. New Delhi: Prestige, 1995. 183-192.

——. "*The God of Small Things*: A Linguistic Experiment." *Contemporary Indian Writings in English*. Ed. Jaydipsinh Dodiya. New Delhi: Atlantic, 1998. 86-92. (Also published in *Explorations: Arundhati Roy's "The God of Small Things."* Ed. Indira Bhatt and Indira Nityanandam. New Delhi: Creative, 1999. 113-119.)

——. "God's Own Country." *Explorations: Arundhati Roy's "The God of Small Things."* Ed. Indira Bhatt and Indira Nityanandam. New Delhi: Creative, 1999. 179-184.

——. "Sorry Spectacles: The Gaze in Arundhati Roy's *The God of Small Things.*" *Explorations: Arundhati Roy's "The God of Small Things."* Ed. Indira Bhatt and Indira Nityanandam. New Delhi: Creative, 1999. 13-17.

——. "Shashi Deshpande: Road to Self-Realization." *Three Great Indian Women Novelists: Anita Desai, Shashi Deshpande, Bharati Mukherjee.* New Delhi: Creative, 2000. 40-62.

——. "Anita Desai: The Inner World." *Three Great Indian Women Novelists: Anita Desai, Shashi Deshpande, Bharati Mukherjee.* New Delhi: Creative, 2000. 18-39.

——. "Three Fold Oppression: Re-reading Arundhati Roy's *The God of Small Things.*" *Indo-English Fiction: The Last Decade.* Ed. Indira Nityanandam and Reena Kothari. New Delhi: Creative, 2002. 85-91.

Orgun, Gun. "The Western Woman in India: Contextualizing *Plans for Departure.*" *Nayantara Sahgal's India: Passion, Politics and History.* Ed. Ralph. J. Crane. New Delhi: Sterling, 1998. 111-124.

Oumhani, Ce'cile. "Hybridity and Transgression in Arundhati Roy's *The God of Small Things.*" *Commonwealth: Essays and Studies* 22.2 (2000): 85-91.

Pabby, D.K. "Women and Society: Element of Dispossession in Margaret Laurence's *The Diviners* and Anita Desai's *Where Shall We Go This Summer?*" *Indian Women Novelists Set II: Vol. I.* Ed. R.K. Dhawan. New Delhi: Prestige, 1993. 32-46.

——. "Plea for a Saner World Order." *Arundhati Roy: The Novelist Extraordinary.* Ed. R.K. Dhawan. New Delhi: Prestige, 1999. 397-405.

Padmanabham, Lakshmi. "Arundhati Roy: An Inside View." *The Inside View: Native Responses to Contemporary Indian English Novel*. Ed. Rangrao Bhongle. New Delhi: Atlantic, 2003. 105-114.

Pal, Adesh. "Ego-Self Crisis in the Fiction of Shashi Deshpande." *Changing Faces of Women: Indian Writing in English*. Ed. M. Q. Khan and A.G. Khan. New Delhi: Creative, 1995. 71-80.

——. "*That Long Silence*: A Study in Displaced Anger." *The Fiction of Shashi Deshpande*. Ed. R.S. Pathak. New Delhi: Creative, 1998. 119-125.

Pal, Shashi. "Alienation to Existentialism: A Study of Anita Desai's Novels." *The Quest* 9.1 (1995): 35-39.

Palkar, Sarla. "Breaking the Silence: *That Long Silence*." *Indian Women Novelists Set I: Vol. V*. Ed. R.K. Dhawan. New Delhi: Prestige, 1991. 163-169.

Pandey, K.M. "Tearing the Veil: *The Dark Holds No Terrors*." *The Fiction of Shashi Deshpande*. Ed. R.S. Pathak. New Delhi: Creative, 1998. 49-57.

——. "Dimensional Depth of Female Consciousness: A Study of *The Binding Vine*." *Women in the Novels of Shashi Deshpande*. Ed. Suman Bala. New Delhi: Khosla, 2001. 111-121.

Pandey, L.U.B. "Art and Vision of Anita Desai." *The Quest* 4.1 (n.d): 18-28.

——. "Dialectics of Authentic Selfhood and Ferocious Assaults of Existenz: A Critical Exposition of Anita Desai's Contribution to Commonwealth Literature." *The Quest* 5.1 (1992): 24-28.

Pandeya, Prabhat Kumar. "The Poly-timbred Voice: Women in *Cry, the Peacock*." *Indian Women Novelists Set I: Vol. III*. Ed. R.K. Dhawan. New Delhi: Prestige, 1991. 36-46.

——. "Knowledge of Blood: A Study of *Two Virgins*." *Indian Women Novelists Set II: Vol. III*. Ed. R.K. Dhawan. New Delhi: Prestige, 1993. 166-176.

——. "Tender, Beautiful and Erotic: Lesbianism in Shobha De's *Starry Nights*." *Indian Women Novelists Set III: Vol. I*. Ed. R.K. Dhawan. New Delhi: Prestige, 1995. 126-136.

——. "Anatomy of Anger: A Study of *Voices in the City*." *Anger in Action: Explorations of Anger in Indian English Writing*. Ed. R.K. Singh. New Delhi: Bahri, 1997. 88-95.

Pandit, M.L. "*The God of Small Things*: A Novel of Childhood Feelings." *Arundhati Roy: The Novelist Extraordinary*. Ed. R.K. Dhawan. New Delhi: Prestige, 1999. 241-247.

Pandit, Nirzari. "Societal Oppression: A Study of *The God of Small Things*." *Explorations: Arundhati Roy's "The God of Small Things."* Ed. Indira Bhatt and Indira Nityanandam. New Delhi: Creative, 1999. 162-167.

Pandit, P. Vijaya Lakshmi. "Obstacles for Women's Education." *Empowerment of Women through Distance Education: A Case of Dr. B. R. Ambedkar Open University*. Hyderabad: Booklinks, 1997. 29-35.

Paranjape, Makarand. "Cultural and Political Allegory in Nayantara Sahgal's *Rich Like Us*." *Indian Writing Today*. Ed. C.R. Visweswara Rao. New Delhi: IAES, 1996. 136-146.

——. "The Crisis of Contemporary India in Nayantara Sahgal's Fiction." *Indo-Anglian Fiction: Tradition and Modernity*. Ed. Naresh E. Jain. New Delhi: Manohar, 1998. 158-177.

Parasuraman, Laxmi. "*Fire on the Mountain*: A New Dimension of Feminine Self-Perception?" *Literary Criterion* 16.3 (1981): 58-64.

——. "The World of Small and Big Things: Transgressions of Rules and Roles in *The God of Small Things*." *Arundhati Roy: The Novelist Extraordinary*. Ed. R.K. Dhawan. New Delhi: Prestige, 1999. 100-103.

Parikh, Bharati A. "Historicizing India in *Rich Like Us*." *The Quest* 6.1 (1992): 11-16.

——. "*Cry, the Peacock*: Unraveling the Psyche." *Osmania Journal of English Studies* 22 (1986): 125-133.

Pathak, R.S. "The Alienated Self in the Novels of Anita Desai." *Indian Women Novelists Set I: Vol. II*. Ed. R.K. Dhawan. New Delhi: Prestige, 1991. 11-49.

——. "Beyond the He-man Approach: The Expression of Feminine Sensibility in Anita Desai's Novels." *Feminism and Recent Fiction in English*. Ed. Sushila Singh. New Delhi: Prestige, 1991. 89-114.

——. "*Paro*: Dreams of Passion or Passion of Dreams?" *Indian Women Novelists Set. II: Vol. I*. Ed. R.K. Dhawan. New Delhi: Prestige, 1993.186-204.

——. "Feminist Concerns in Shobha De's Fiction." *Modern Indian Novel in English*. New Delhi: Creative, 1999. 147-161.

——. "Shashi Deshpande and the Woman Question." *Modern Indian Novel in English*. New Delhi: Creative, 1999. 192-209.

——. "Kamala Markandaya's Sociological Concerns." *Modern Indian Novel in English*. New Delhi: Creative, 1999. 69-80.

Pathania, Usha. "The Filial Ties—A Bane: *Fire on the Mountain*." *Indian Women Novelists Set I: Vol. III*. Ed. R.K. Dhawan. New Delhi: Prestige, 1991. 207-215.

Patil, P.F. "The Theme of Marital Disharmony in the Novels of Anita Desai." *Indian Women Novelists Set I: Vol. II*. Ed. R.K. Dhawan. New Delhi: Prestige, 1991. 127-142.

Patil, Ujwala. "Sexual Violence and Death in Anita Desai's *Fire on the Mountain*." *Studies in Indian Fiction in English*. Ed. G.S. Balarama Gupta. Gulbarga: JIWE, 1987. 61-67.

——. "'The Wheel Turns': Central Theme in *The Village by the Sea*." *Indian Women Novelists Set I: Vol. IV*. Ed. R.K. Dhawan. New Delhi: Prestige, 1991. 47-55.

——. "The Theme of Marriage and Selfhood in *Roots and Shadows*." *Indian Women Novelists Set I: Vol. V*. Ed. R.K. Dhawan. New Delhi: Prestige, 1991. 130-137.

——. "Rejection of Silence in *A Silence of Desire*." *Indian Women Novelists Set II: Vol. III*. Ed. R.K. Dhawan. New Delhi: Prestige, 1993. 17-25.

Patil, Z.N. "Style in *Inside the Haveli*: A Study in Politeness Strategies." *Indian Women Novelists Set I: Vol. V*. Ed. R.K. Dhawan. New Delhi: Prestige, 1991. 16-30.

——. "Indian Kinship Organisation and Taboo Customs as Reflected in *Inside the Haveli*." *Indian Women Novelists Set I: Vol. IV*. Ed. R.K. Dhawan. New Delhi: Prestige, 1991. 230-238.

Paul, Premila. "*The Dark Holds No Terrors*: A Woman's Search for Refuge." *Indian Women Novelists Set I: Vol. V*. Ed. R.K. Dhawan. New Delhi: Prestige, 1991. 60-81.

Paul, Premila and R. Padmanabhan Nair. "Varieties of Loneliness in *Fire on the Mountain*." *Indian Women Novelists Set I: Vol. III*. Ed. R.K. Dhawan. New Delhi: Prestige, 1991. 216-275.

——. "The Personal and the Political Elements in *Clear Light of Day*." *The Novelist and the Political Milieu: A Study of Indian English Fiction*. Ed. Kamini Dinesh and R.A. Joshi. Jaipur: Rachana, 1995. 31-38.

——. "*The Dark Holds No Terrors*: A Call for Confrontation." *The Fiction of Shashi Deshpande*. Ed. R.S. Pathak. New Delhi: Creative, 1998. 30-42.

Picincco, Pier Paola. "The Goddess of Small Things: Some Observations on the Fictional Technique of Arundhati Roy's First Novel." *Arundhati Roy: The Novelist Extraordinary*. Ed. R.K. Dhawan. New Delhi: Prestige, 1999. 319-327.

Pillai, C. Gopinatha. "Aesthetics of Post-Colonial Feminism: A Reading of *The God of Small Things*." *The Critical Studies of Arundhati Roy's "The God of Small Things."* Ed. Jaydipsinh Dodiya and Joya Chakravarty. New Delhi: Atlantic, 1999. 87-92.

Pinto, Robert. "The Cultural Milieu of Arundhati Roy's *The God of Small Things*." *Recent Indian Literature in English: A Cultural Perspective*. Ed. Mithilesh K. Pandey. New Delhi: Anmol, 1999. 103-129.

Pollard, Arthur. "Kamala Markandaya's *The Golden Honeycomb.*" *Journal of Indian Writing in English* 8.1-2 (1980): 22-26.

Pontas, Hilda. "Nayantara Sahgal—A Bibliography." *Literary Endeavour* 1.3 (n.d): 53-69.

Prabhu, Louella Lobo. "*The God of Small Things*—In Perspective." *The Quest* 12.1 (1998): 26-31.

Prakash, Abha. "Beyond Romance: Desai's and Markandaya's Feminist Methodology." *Journal of Indian Writing in English* 27.2 (1999): 37-42.

Prakash, Raveendran. "Becoming Whole: A Reading of Shashi Deshpande's *The Dark Holds No Terrors.*" *Quest for Identity in Indian English Writing.* Ed. R.S. Pathak. New Delhi: Bahri, 1992. 186-191.

Prasad, Hari Mohan. "Sound or Sense—A Study in Anita Desai's *Bye-Bye Blackbird.*" *Journal of Indian Writing in English* 9.1 (1981): 58-66.

——. "The Quintessence of Kamala Markandaya's Art." *Response: Recent Revelations of Indian Fiction in English.* Ed. Hari Mohan Prasad. Bareilley: PBD, 1983. 158-171.

Prasad, Madhusudan. "Anita Desai's *Voices in the City*: A Critical Study." *Littcritt* 7.2 (1981): 46-58.

——. "Anita Desai's *Voices in the City*: A Critical Study." *Indian Scholar* 4.1&2 (1982): 67-91.

Prasad, S.N. "Feminism and Indian English Fiction." *Feminism and Indian English Fiction.* Ed. P.M. Nayak and S.P. Swain. Bareilley: PBD, 1996. 28-36.

Prasad, V.V.N. Rajendra. "Anita Desai and the Wounded Self." *Indian Women Novelists Set I: Vol. II.* Ed. R.K. Dhawan. New Delhi: Prestige, 1991. 80-100.

Pratima, N. "*Where Shall We Go This Summer?* A Critical Approach." *Indian Women Novelists Set I: Vol. III.* Ed. R.K. Dhawan. New Delhi: Prestige, 1991. 179-189.

Radha, K. "Geeta and the Problem of Adjustment in *Inside the Haveli.*" *Indian Women Novelists Set I: Vol. IV.* Ed. R.K. Dhawan. New Delhi: Prestige, 1991. 202-213.

——. "The Hunger and Anger of Ravi in *A Handful of Rice*." *Indian Women Novelists Set II: Vol. III*. Ed. R.K. Dhawan. New Delhi: Prestige, 1993. 126-134.

——. "Humour in *A Handful of Rice*." *Indian Women Novelists Set II: Vol. III*. Ed. R.K. Dhawan. New Delhi: Prestige, 1993. 81-86.

Rai, G. "The Soil and the Roots: A Study of the Novels of Anita Desai." *The Indian Novel in English: Essays in Criticism*. Ed. Ravi Nandan Sinha and R.K. Sinha. Ranchi: Ankit, 1986. 93-107.

——. "Man-Woman Relationship in Nayantara Sahgal's *Storm in Chandigarh*." *Indian Journal of English Studies*. 31 (1992-1993): 56-61.

Rai, Sudha. "Nayantara Sahgal's *Rich Like Us*: The Discourse of the Political Novel." *Women's Writing: Text and Context*. Ed. Jasbir Jain. Jaipur: Rawat, 1996. 189-198.

Rajendra, Susheela P. "Individual Freedom as the Central Motif in *Storm in Chandigarh*." *Indian Women Novelists Set II: Vol. IV*. Ed. R.K. Dhawan. New Delhi: Prestige, 1993. 173-184.

——. "A Journey towards Freedom, from Fear: A Study of the Feminine Sensibility in Nayantara Sahgal's *The Day in Shadow*." *Indian Women Novelists Set III: Vol. 5*. Ed. R.K. Dhawan. New Delhi: Prestige, 1995. 230-236.

Rajeshwar, M. "Anita Desai's *Cry, the Peacock*: The Father's Unconscious." *Indian English Literature: Since Independence*. Ed. Ayyappa Paniker. New Delhi: IAES, 1991. 44-48.

——. "The Trauma of a House-wife: A Psychological Study of Shashi Deshpande's *That Long Silence*." *Commonwealth Quarterly* 43.17 (1991): 41-60.

——. "Myth as Macro-Structure: A Reading of Kamala Markandaya's *A Silence of Desire* and Nayantara Sahgal's *The Day in Shadow*." *Kakatiya Journal of English Studies* 13 (1993): 67-73.

——. "The Inner World of Indian Women: Neurotic Characters in Indian Women Novelists." *Indian Women Novelists*

Set III: *Vol. I*. Ed. R.K. Dhawan. New Delhi: Prestige, 1995. 48-53.

——. "Superstition and Psyche in Anita Desai's *Cry, the Peacock*." *New Perspectives on Indian Writing*. Ed. V.L.V.N. Narendra Kumar. New Delhi: Prestige, 1997. 84-89.

Ram, Atma. "Anita Desai: A Bibliography." *Journal of Indian Writing in English* 9.1 (1981): 93-98.

——. "A View of *Where Shall We Go This Summer?*" *Journal of Indian Writing in English* 9.1 (1981): 74-80.

——. "Anita Desai—A Novelist of Deep Sensibility." *Indian Poetry and Fiction in English*. By Atma Ram. New Delhi: Bahri, 1991. 38-45.

Ramamoorti, P. "My life is My Own: A Study of Shashi Deshpande's Women." *Indian Women Novelists Set I*: *Vol. V*. Ed. R.K. Dhawan. New Delhi: Prestige, 1991. 37-49.

Ramamurti, K.S. "The Indian Woman Novelist Writing in English." *Littcrit*. 4.1 (1978): 33-42.

——. "Kamala Markandaya's *Two Virgins*: A Problem Novel." *Littcritt* 7.2 (1981): 36-45.

——. "Does the Indian Novel in English Have A Future?" *The Indian Novel in English*: *Evaluations*. Ed. T. Prabhakar. New Delhi: Phoenix, 1995. 12-18.

Ramanathan, Suguna. "Where is Christ in *The God of Small Things?*" *Explorations*: *Arundhati Roy's "The God of Small Things*." Ed. Indira Bhatt and Indira Nityanandam. New Delhi: Creative, 1999. 63-68.

Rama Rao, Vimala. "Myth and Folklore in Shashi Deshpande." *The Fiction of Shashi Deshpande*. Ed. R. S. Pathak. New Delhi: Creative, 1998. 207-211.

Ramraj, Victor. "Arundhati Roy's and Salman Rushdie's Postmodern India." *Arundhati Roy*: *The Novelist Extraordinary*. Ed. R.K. Dhawan. New Delhi: Prestige, 1999. 151-160.

Rana, Amar Nath. "Moral Evaluation of Rukmani and Irawaddy in *Nectar in a Sieve*." *POETCRIT* 17.1 (2004): 22-27.

Rani, G. Sheela Swapna. "The Quest that Led to Take Decisions." *The Fiction of Shobha De*. Ed. Jaydipsinh Dodiya. New Delhi: Prestige, 2000. 160-166.

Rani, K. Suneeta. "Shashi Deshpande's *Roots and Shadows* as Modern Indian Woman's Dilemma." *The Inside View: Native Responses to Contemporary Indian English Novel*. Ed. Rangrao Bhongle. New Delhi: Atlantic, 2003. 53-58.

Rani, P. Hari Padma. "The Manifold Use of Simile in Arundhati Roy's *The God of Small Things*." *Critical Studies on Indian Fiction in English*. Ed. R.A. Singh and V.L.V.N. Narendra Kumar. New Delhi: Atlantic, 1999. 152-156.

——. "The Structural Ambiguity of *The God of Small Things*." *Arundhati Roy: The Novelist Extraordinary*. Ed. R.K. Dhawan. New Delhi: Prestige, 1999. 338-341.

——. "The Theme of Marital Discord in Arundhati Roy's *The God of Small Things*." *The Quest* 14.1 (2000): 34-37.

Rani, T. Asoka. "Feminism vis-a-vis Women's Dignity: A Study of Shashi Deshpande's *That Long Silence*." *Indian Writing Today*. Ed. C.R. Visweswara Rao. New Delhi: IAES, 1996. 147-151.

——. "Nayantara Sahgal's *The Day in Shadow*: A Feminist Perspective." *New Perspectives on Indian Writing*. Ed. V.L.V.N. Narendra Kumar. New Delhi: Prestige, 1997. 68-75.

——. "Women in Marriage: Novels of Nayantara Sahgal and Shashi Deshpande." *Critical Studies on Indian English Fiction*. Ed. R.A. Singh and V.L.V.N. Narendra Kumar. New Delhi: Atlantic, 1999. 124-130.

Rao, A.V. Krishna. "Anita Desai's Modernist Novel." *Literary Endeavour* 2.2&3 (1981): 11-14.

——. "Nayantara Sahgal's Recent Fictions of History: A Study." *Essays in Criticism on Indian Literature in English*. Ed. M.S. Nagarajan, N. Ekambaram and A. Natarajan. New Delhi: S. Chand, 1991. 117-123.

——. "Historical Consciousness in the Novels of Nayantara Sahgal." *Indian Women Novelists Set II: Vol. IV*. Ed. R.K. Dhawan. New Delhi: Prestige, 1993. 19-41.

——. "*This Time of Morning*: A Critical Assessment." *Indian Women Novelists Set II*: *Vol. IV*. Ed. R.K. Dhawan. New Delhi: Prestige, 1993. 138-156.

——. "*This Time of Morning*: A Critical Assessment." *Indian Women Novelists Set II*: *Vol. IV*. Ed. R.K. Dhawan. New Delhi: Prestige, 1993. 138-156.

——. "An Analytic Study of *A Time to be Happy*." *Indian Women Novelists Set II*: *Vol. IV*. Ed. R.K. Dhawan. New Delhi: Prestige, 1993. 122-137.

Rao, B. Ramachandra. "Technique in the Novels of Anita Desai." *The Indian Novel in English-Evaluations*. Ed. T. Prabhakar. New Delhi: Phoenix, 1995. 169-182.

Rao, Bhargavi P. "From Purdah to Popular Culture: Anees Jung's *Unveiling India* and Shobha De's *Socialite Evenings*." *Indian Women Novelists Set I*: *Vol. I*. Ed. R.K. Dhawan. New Delhi: Prestige, 1991. 235-241.

Rao, E. Nageswara. "The Fertility Motif in Kamala Markandaya's *Nectar in a Sieve*." *Essays in Criticism on Indian Literature in English*. Ed. M.S. Nagarajan et al. New Delhi: S. Chand, 1991. 134-138.

Rao, K. Damodar. "Penance as Multiple Response in Githa Hariharan's *The Thousand Faces of Night*." *Indian Women Novelists Set III*: *Vol. IV*. Ed. R.K. Dhawan. New Delhi: Sterling, 1995. 159-169.

Rao, K.S. Narayana. "Religious Elements in Kamala Markandaya's Novels." *Ariel* 8.1 (1977): 35-50.

——. "Some Notes on the Plots of Kamala Markandaya's Novels." *The Indian Novel in English-Evaluations*. Ed. T. Prabhakar. New Delhi: Phoenix, 1995. 194-202.

——. "Love, Sex, Marriage and Morality in Kamala Markandaya's Novels." *Osmania Journal of English Studies*. (n.d.): 69-77.

Rao, Susheela N. "England in the Novels of Kamala Markandaya." *Journal of Indian Writing in English* 15.1 (1987): 1-10.

——. "Nature in Kamala Markandaya's *Nectar in a Sieve* and *The CofferDams.*" *Literary Half-Yearly* 36.1 (1995): 41-50.

Rao, Vimala. "*Where Shall We Go This Summer?* An Analytic Study." *Indian Women Novelists Set I: Vol. III*. Ed. R.K. Dhawan. New Delhi: Prestige, 1991. 172-178.

Rathod, Pradipsinh B. "Hunger as a Motif in Kamala Markandaya." *POETCRIT* 14.2 (2001): 10-19.

Ravi, Srilata. "In the Name of the Mother: A Feminist Reading of Githa Hariharan's *The Thousand Faces of Night.*" *50 Years of Indian Writing*. Ed. R.K. Dhawan. New Delhi: IAES (n.d.) 76-93.

Ray, Mohit Kumar. "'Locusts Stand I': Some Feminine Aspects of *The God of Small Things.*" *Arundhati Roy: The Novelist Extraordinary*. Ed. R.K. Dhawan. New Delhi: Prestige, 1999. 49-64.

Razdan, K.B. "Morag and Maya: Women as the Self-Reflexive Amazon in Margaret Laurence's *The Diviners* and Anita Desai's *Cry, the Peacock.*" *English Studies in India: A Journal of Literature and Language* 6 (1998): 22-31.

Reddy, K. Venkata. "A Tryst with Conscience: *A Handful of Rice.*" *Major Indian Novelists: Mulk Raj Anand, R.K. Narayan, Raja Rao, Bhabani Bhattacharya, Kamala Markandaya*. New Delhi: Prestige, 1990. 87-96.

——. "A Change of the Hunger Theme: *Nectar in a Sieve.*" *Major Indian Novelists: Mulk Raj Anand, R.K. Narayan, Raja Rao, Bhabani Bhattacharya, Kamala Markandaya*. New Delhi: Prestige, 1990. 78-86.

Reddy, P. Bayapa. "Rural Life Shaken to its Roots: Kamala Markandaya's *Nectar in a Sieve.*" *Studies in Indian Writing in English*. New Delhi: Prestige, 1990. 61-69.

Riemenschneider, Dieter. "...in the Days When the Love Laws were Made." *Arundhati Roy: The Novelist Extraordinary*. Ed. R.K. Dhawan. New Delhi: Prestige, 1999. 120-131.

Rossenwasser, Ruth K. "Voices of Dissent: Heroines in the Novels of Anita Desai." *Journal of South Asian Literature* 24.2 (1989): 83-116.

Roy, Evangeline Shanti. "Shashi Deshpande's *The Binding Vine*: A Quest for the Anchor of Life." *Littcrit* 27.1&2 (2001): 77-78.

Roy, Sumita. "Paradoxes of Patriarchy: Feminist Motifs." *Between Spaces of Silence*: *Women Creative Writers*. Ed. Kamini Dinesh. New Delhi: Sterling, 1994. 20-28.

Sachidanandan, K. "Sex, Text, Politics: Women's Writing in India: Problems of Reading." *Indian Literature*: *Positions and Propositions*. Delhi: Pencraft, 1999. 34-45.

Sahayan, V. Sam. "Irony as Counterpoint in Anita Desai's Spiritual Quest: A Study of "Scholar Gypsy" in *Journey to Ithaca* and *Fasting, Feasting*." *Modern Indian English Fiction*. Ed. T.S. Anand, L.S. Bedi and Hargunjot Kaur. New Delhi: Creative, 2002. 65-77.

Sahi, Rashmi. "Human Relationship in the Novels of Shashi Deshpande." *Indian Literature* 42.4 (1998): 167-170.

Sahu, Jyotsna. "Art, Matter and Spirit: Kamala Markandaya's *Possession*." *Indian Writing Today*. Ed. C.R. Visweswara Rao. New Delhi: IAES, 1996. 122-124.

Samanta, Soumyajit. "Against Marginalisation of Indian Women: A Feminist Reading of Shobha De's *Socialite Evenings*." *Feminism and Indian English Fiction*. Ed. P.M. Nayak and S. P. Swain. Bareilley: PBD, 1996. 75-90.

Sandhu, Sarabjit. "The Image of Woman in *That Long Silence*." *Indian Women Novelists Set I*: *Vol. V*. Ed. R.K. Dhawan. New Delhi: Prestige, 1991. 138-146.

——. "The Image of Woman in *The Dark Holds No Terrors*." *Indian Women Novelists Set I*: *Vol. V*. Ed. R.K. Dhawan. New Delhi: Prestige, 1991. 82-89.

——. "The Image of Woman in *Roots and Shadows*." *Indian Women Novelists Set I*: *Vol. V*. Ed. R.K. Dhawan. New Delhi: Prestige, 1991. 102-110.

Sarma, M.N. "Nayantara Sahgal's Novels: Some Thematic Concerns." *Journal of Indian Writing in English* 4.1 (1976): 35-44.

Sathupati, Prasanna Sree. "Conflict and Identity in Shashi Deshpande's Novels." *Indian Women Novelists Set III: Vol. 4*. Ed. R.K. Dhawan. New Delhi: Prestige, 1995. 12-19.

Sathyamala, C. "The Emperor's New Clothes: *The God of Small Things*." *Arundhati Roy: The Novelist Extraordinary*. Ed. R.K. Dhawan. New Delhi: Prestige, 1999. 385-396.

Satpathy, Sumanyu. "The Code of Incest in *The God of Small Things*." *Arundhati Roy: The Novelist Extraordinary*. Ed. R.K. Dhawan. New Delhi: Prestige, 1999. 132-143.

Satyanarayana, E. "The Dialectics of Self-Assertion: The Liberated Women in Shobha De's *Sisters*." *Critical Studies on Indian Fiction in English*. Ed. R.A. Singh and V.L.V.N. Narendra Kumar. New Delhi: Atlantic, 1999. 145-151.

Savio, G. Dominic. "View of Nature in Anita Desai's Novels." *Indian Women Novelists Set I: Vol. II*. Ed. R.K. Dhawan. New Delhi: Prestige, 1991. 191-198.

——. "The God of Small and Significant Things." *Arundhati Roy: The Novelist Extraordinary*. Ed. R.K. Dhawan. New Delhi: Prestige, 1999. 227-233.

——. "*Second Thoughts*: A Slice of Urban Life." *The Fiction of Shobha De*. Ed. Jaydipsinh Dodiya. New Delhi: Prestige, 2000. 259-271.

——. "A Women's Heritage of the Commonwealth: A Study of *The Dark Holds No Terrors*." *Women in the Novels of Shashi Deshpande*. Ed. Suman Bala. New Delhi: Khosla, 2001. 59-68.

——. "The Emergence of Bold Heroines in Contemporary Fiction." *Women in the Novels of Shashi Deshpande*. Ed. Suman Bala. New Delhi: Khosla, 2001. 18-27.

Saxena, Alka. "Feminism: Time to Stop Suffering in Silence." *Indian Women Novelists Set III: Vol. I*. Ed. R.K. Dhawan. New Delhi: Prestige, 1995. 18-25.

——. "*Second Thoughts*: A Slice of Urban Life." *The Fiction of Shobha De*. Ed. Jaydipsinh Dodiya. New Delhi: Prestige, 2000. 259-271.

Scott, Julie. "Female Autonomy: Linking the Public and Private Worlds in *Plans for Departure* and *Mistaken Identity*." *Nayantara Sahgal's India: Passion, Politics and History*. Ed. Ralph J. Crane. New Delhi: Sterling, 1998. 126-140.

Sengupta, C. "Juxtaposition of Opposites: A Study of Characters in *Some Inner Fury*." *Indian Scholar* 11.1 (1989): 1-10.

——. "Alienation in Kamala Markandaya's *Some Inner Fury*: A Study of Characters." *Indian Fiction in English: Problems and Promises*. Ed. R.S. Pathak. New Delhi: NBC, 1990. 85-92.

Sengupta, Jayita. "East-West Encounter in the Novels of Kamala Markandaya." *The Quest* 10.2 (1996): 21-28.

Sengupta, S. "*That Long Silence*: Imagery of Death, Decay and Desolation." *The Fiction of Shashi Deshpande*. Ed. R.S. Pathak. New Delhi: Creative, 1998. 212-218.

Sen, Sarbani. "The De Debate: Cultural Politics and De's Novels." *The Fiction of Shobha De*. Ed. Jaydipsinh Dodiya. New Delhi: Prestige, 2000. 21-26.

Seshadri, Veena. "*That Long Silence*." *Literature Alive* 1.4 (n.d.): 4-5.

Sethuraman, Ramachandran. "Writing Across Cultures: Sexual/ Racial "Othering" in Kamala Markandaya's *Possession*." *Ariel* 23.3 (1992): 101-120.

Shah, Nila. "Making Small Things Big: A Reading into *The God of Small Things*." *Contemporary Indian Writings in English*. Ed. Jaydipsinh Dodiya. New Delhi: Atlantic, 1998. 76-80.

Sharad, Paul. "Tradition and Tragedy: Anita Desai and R.K.Narayan." *Commonwealth Review* 2.1-2 (n.d.): 181-192.

Sharadha, Y.S. "The Problem of Marriage and Affirmation of Self in *Roots and Shadows*." *Women in the Novels of Shashi Deshpande*. Ed. Suman Bala. New Delhi: Khosal, 2001. 51-58. (Also Published in *Modern Indian English*

Fiction. Ed. T.S. Anand, L.S. Bedi and Hargunjot Kaur. New Delhi: Creative, 2002. 110-116).

Sharma, B.D. and S.K. Sharma. "Evil in Shashi Deshpande's Novel: *Come and Be Dead*." *Contemporary Indian English Novel*. New Delhi: Anamika, 2001. 135-143.

——. "The Contribution of Women to the Development of the Indian English Novel." *Contemporary Indian English Novel*. New Delhi: Anamika, 2001. 74-81.

——. "Feminism in Nayantara Sahgal's Novels." *Contemporary Indian English Novel*. New Delhi: Anamika, 2001. 68-73.

Sharma, Ghanshiam. "Structural Interplay in *The CofferDams*." *Indian Women Novelists Set II: Vol. III*. Ed. R.K. Dhawan. New Delhi: Prestige, 1993. 145-156.

Sharma, Lalit M. "Fiction Fantasy and Reality: A Study of Anita Desai's Characters." *Contemporary Indian English Fiction (An Anthology of Essays)*. Ed. Kamal N. Awasthi. Jalandhar: ABS, 1993. 25-34.

Sharma, M.N. "Nayantara Sahgal's Novels: Some Thematic Concerns." *The Indian Novel in English-Evaluations*. Ed. T. Prabhakar. New Delhi: Phoenix, 1995. 205-213.

Sharma, R.K. "*That Long Silence*: Long Night's Journey into Day." *The Fiction of Shashi Deshpande*. Ed. R.S. Pathak. New Delhi: Creative, 1998. 107-118.

Sharma, R.S. "Anita Desai's *Where Shall We Go This Summer?* An Analysis." *Commonwealth Quarterly* 3.10 (1979): 50-69.

——. "Nayantara Sahgal on her work: A Conversation." *The Quest* 12.1 (1998): 1-7.

Sharma, S.D. "*Where Shall We Go This Summer?* A Crisis of Conscience and Values." *The Quest* 5.2 (1991): 1-9.

Sharma, Meenakshi. "Riches Galore in a Land of Poverty: Nayantara Sahgal's *Rich Like Us*." *Literary Criterion* 30.3 (1990): 1-15.

Shastri, N.R. "*Where Shall We Go This Summer*: A Critical Study." *Osmania Journal of English Studies* 17 (1981): 83-103.

Shinde, Shobha P. "The Subjugation of Women: An Aspect of the Indian Ethos with Special Reference to *Inside the Haveli.*" *Indian Women Novelists Set I: Vol. IV*. Ed. R.K. Dhawan. New Delhi: Prestige, 1991. 214-218.

Shinde, Suvarna. "Quest for Freedom: A Study of Margaret Laurence's *A Jest of God* and Shashi Deshpande's *A Matter of Time.*" *Women in the Novels of Shashi Deshpande*. Ed. Suman Bala. New Delhi: Khosla, 2001. 136-144.

Shivram, Meenakshi. "Locating the Woman in Post-Colonial Discourse: A Reading of Shashi Deshpande's *The Dark Holds No Terrors.*" *Post-Coloniality: Reading Literature*. Ed. C.T. Indra and Meenakshi Shivram. New Delhi: Vikas, 1999. 179-185.

Shukla, Suresh. "A Carnival from Kerala: *The God of Small Things.*" *Contemporary Indian Writings in English*. Ed. Jaydipsinh Dodiya. New Delhi: Atlantic, 1998. 93-98.

Singh, A.K. "The Element of Protest in Kamala Markandaya." *Contemporary Indian Fiction in English*. Ed. Avadesh K. Singh. New Delhi: Creative, 1993. 117-124.

Singh, Anita. "A Voice After the Long Silence: Shashi Deshpande's *Roots and Shadows* and *That Long Silence.*" *Post-Independence Indian English Fiction*. Ed. Rajeshwar Mittapalli and Alessandro Monti. New Delhi: Atlantic, 2001. 124-128.

Singh, Avadhesh Kumar. "The Element of Protest in Kamala Markandaya." *Contemporary Indian Fiction in English*. Ed. Avadhesh Kumar Singh. New Delhi: Creative, 1993. 117-124.

Singh, Avtar. "Feminine Sensibility in the Novels of Kamala Markandaya: A Study of *Nectar in a Sieve*, *Two Virgins* and *Possession.*" *Creative Forum* 12.1-2 (1999): 15-22.

Singh, Bir Bahadur. "Anita Desai's *Bye-Bye Black Bird* as a Colonial Discourse: A Critique." *Creative Forum* 8.1-2 (1995): 109-113.

Singh Brijaj. "The Fiction of Anita Desai." *The Humanities Review* 3.2 (n.d.): 40-43.

Singh, Chakradhar Prasad. "The Visitor and the Exile: A Study in Anita Desai's *Bye-Bye Blackbird.*" *Response: Recent Revelations of Indian Fiction in English.* Ed. Hari Mohan Prasad. Bareilley: PBD, 1983. 231-240.

Singh, H.A. "The Protagonist in Kamala Markandaya." *Creative Forum* 1.4 (1988): 49-52.

Singh, Manjit Inder. "Of Memory, Story Telling and 'Packaging': *The God of Small Things* and *The Blue Bedspread* as Texts in a Distracting Age." Ed. T.S. Anand, L.S. Bedi and Hargunjot Kaur. *Modern Indian English Fiction.* New Delhi: Creative, 2002. 51-64.

Singh, N.P. "Women in *The God of Small Things.*" *Arundhati Roy: The Novelist Extraordinary.* Ed. R.K. Dhawan. New Delhi: Prestige, 1999. 65-70.

Singh, Pankaj K. "Feminism and Nayantara Sahgal's *The Day in Shadow* and *Rich Like Us*: From the Particular to the Ideological." *Feminism and Recent Fiction in English.* Ed. Sushila Singh. New Delhi: Prestige, 1991. 135-146.

Singh, R.A. "*Rich Like Us*: Point of view on Narrative Strategy." *The Quest* 6.2 (1992): 32-41.

Singh, R.S. "West Meets East: A Study of Kamala Markandaya's *Possession.*" *Image of India in the Indian Novel in English 1960-1985.* Ed. Sudhakar Pandey and R. Raj Rao. Hyderabad: Orient, 1993. 21-35.

Singh, Surender. "Chapter Four: *The Golden Honeycomb.*" *Princely Life in Indian English Writing.* New Delhi: Reliance, 1995. 80-113.

Singh, Veena. "How Difficult are Difficult Daughters? *Sunlight on a Broken Column* and *Difficult Daughters* as Female Bildungsroman." *Contemporary Indian Literature: Positions and Expositions.* Jaipur: Rawat, 2000. 161-175.

Sinha, B.P. "Nayantara Sahgal's Novels." *The Quest* 11.2 (1997): 33-34.

Sinha, Lakshmi. "Nayantara Sahgal's *Storm in Chandigarh*: A Search for Values." *Studies in Indian Fiction in English*. Ed. G.S. Balarama Gupta. Gulbarga: JIWE, 1987. 104-109.

——. "Nayantara Sahgal's Sextet: From *A Time to be Happy* to *Rich Like Us*." *Indian Women Novelists Set II: Vol. IV*. Ed. R.K. Dhawan. New Delhi: Prestige, 1993. 42-51.

Sinha, Ravi Nandan. "Anita Desai's *Cry, the Peacock*: The Triumph of the Philosophy of Flux." *New Perspectives on Indian Writing*. Ed. V.L.V.N. Narendra Kumar. New Delhi: Prestige, 1997. 76-82.

Sitesh, Aruna. "Ape in Shashi Deshpande's Novels." *Recent Indian Literature in English: A Cultural Perspective*. Ed. Mithilesh K. Pandey. New Delhi: Anmol, 1999. 195-203.

Sivaramakrishna. M. "From Alienation to Mythic Acceptance: The Ordeal of Consciousness in Anita Desai's Fiction." *Kakatiya Journal of English Studies* 3 (1983): 7-24.

Soumini, P. "The Technique of Focalization in Shashi Deshpande's Novel *A Matter of Time*." *Studies in Contemporary Literature: Critical Insight into Five Indian English Authors*. Ed. R.S. Sharma and S. B. Shukla. New Delhi: Sarup, 2000. 93-110.

Srinivasan, Kannamala. "The Future Memory and the Metaphysics of Technological Space: Text in Flux as Narrative Strategy in *The God of Small Things*." *50 Years of Indian Writing*. Ed. R.K. Dhawan. New Delhi: IAES, n.d. 94-104.

Srivastava, K.C. "The Novels of Kamala Das: The Quest for Identity." *The Indian Novel in English: Essays in Criticism*. Ed. Ravi Nandan Sinha and R.K. Singh. Ranchi: Ankit, 1987. 117-122.

Srivastava, Ramesh K. "Artists in *Voices in the City*." *Indian Women Novelists Set I: Vol. III*. Ed. R.K. Dhawan. New Delhi: Prestige, 1991. 94-102. (Also published as "Voices of Artists in the City" in *Journal of Indian Writing in English* 9.1 (1981): 47-57).

——. "Love and Death in Kamala Markandaya's *Some Inner Fury.*" *Indian English Literature: Since Independence.* Ed. K. Ayyapa Paniker. New Delhi: IAES, 1991. 14-26.

——. "Woman as Possessor: A Reflection of Markandaya's Anti-Patriarchal Rage and Divided Consciousness in *Possession.*" *Gender and Culture.* Ed. Iqbal Kaur. New Delhi: D.K., 1992. 163-178.

——. "The Tulasi and the Thermometer: Juxtaposition of Faith and Science in Markandaya's *A Silence of Desire.*" *Commonwelth Quarterly* 18.44 (1992): 26-45.

——. "Stability and Changing Social Scene in Markandaya's *A Silence of Desire.*" *The Quest* 6.2 (1992): 1-17.

——. "Levels of Colonial Consciousness in *Possession.*" *Indian Women Novelists Set II: Vol. III.* Ed. R.K. Dhawan. New Delhi: Prestige, 1993. 26-42.

——. "Symbolic Triumvirate: Bicycle Chain, Sari and Tin Trunk in *A Handful of Rice.*" *Indian Women Novelists Set II: Vol. III.* Ed. R.K. Dhawan. New Delhi: Prestige, 1993. 68-80.

——. "A Study of *A Handful of Rice.*" *Indian Women Novelists Set II: Vol. III.* Ed. R.K. Dhawan. New Delhi: Prestige, 1993. 101-125.

——. "Raging Inferno and Fumbling Inarticulacy: Limits of Narrative Technique in *Some Inner Fury.*" *Indian Women Novelists Set II: Vol. II.* Ed. R.K. Dhawan. New Delhi: Prestige, 1993. 197-215.

——. "Limitations of Markandaya in *Nectar in a Sieve.*" *Indian Women Novelists Set II: Vol. II.* Ed. R.K. Dhawan. New Delhi: Prestige, 1993. 147-156.

——. "The Mother Figures in Markandaya's *Two Virgins.*" *Mother and Mother-Figures in Indo-English Literature.* Ed. Usha Bande. Jalandhar: ABS, 1994. 95-106.

——. "Symbolism in Markandaya's *Two Virgins.*" *Indian Writing Today.* Ed. C.R. Visweswara Rao. New Delhi: IAES, 1996. 125-132.

——. "Symbolism in Markandaya's *Nectar in a Sieve.*" *Symbolism in Indian Fiction in English.* Ed. Ramesh K. Srivastava. Jalandhar: ABS, 1997. 103-112.

——. "Symbolism in Anita Desai's *Cry, the Peacock.*" *Symbolism in Indian Fiction in Englsih.* Ed. Ramesh K. Srivastava. Jalandhar: ABS, 1997. 136-149.

——. "A Village in Transition: '*Nectar in a Sieve.*' *Commonwealth Fiction.* Ed. R.K. Dhawan. New Delhi: Classical, 1998. 211-227.

——. "Return of Shobha De to the Mainstream New Woman: A Study of *SultryDays.*" *The Fiction of Shobha De.* Ed. Jaydipsinh Dodiya. New Delhi: Prestige, 2000. 233-236.

Subbu, Lalita. "Only an Enema!" *The Indian Literary Review* 4.2 (n.d.): 87-91. (On *Paro*: *Dreams of Passion*)

Sudheer, V.C. "In Search of a Nest: *The Nowhere Man.*" *Indian Women Novelists Set II*: *Vol. III.* Ed. R.K. Dhawan. New Delhi: Prestige, 1993. 202-207.

Sudipta, B. "Women Characters in the Novels of Virginia Woolf and Kamala Markandaya." *Indian Women Novelists Set III*: *Vol. I.* Ed. R.K. Dhawan. New Delhi: Prestige, 1995. 39-47.

Suneel, Seema. "Marriage, a Compromise: A Study of Shashi Deshpande's *The Dark Holds No Terrors.*" *Man-Woman Relationship in Indian Fiction*: *With a Focus on Shashi Deshpande, Rajendra Awasthi and Syed Abdul Malik.* New Delhi: Prestige, 1995. 74-122.

——. "Shashi Deshpande, Rajendra Awasthy and Syed Abdul Malik: Life and Works." *Man-Woman Relationship in Indian Fiction*: *With a Focus on Shashi Deshpande, Rajendra Awasthy and Abdul Malik.* New Delhi: Prestige, 1995. 20-73.

——. "Emergence of New Women in Indian Fiction: A Study of Bharati Mukherjee's *Wife,* Shashi Deshpande's *That Long Silence* and R.W. Desai's *Frailty, Thy Name is (W)oman.*" *Feminism and Literature.* Ed. Veena Noble Dass. New Delhi: Prestige, 1995. 219-228.

Surendran, K.V. "Treatment of 'The Downtrodden' in *The God of Small Things*." *Contemporary Indian Writings in English*. Ed. Jaydipsinh Dodiya. New Delhi: Atlantic, 1998. 66-75.

——. "*The God of Small Things* – A Saga of Lost Dreams." *The Critical Studies of Arundhati Roy's The God of Small Things*. Ed. Jaydipsinh Dodiya and Joya Chakravarty. New Delhi: Atlantic, 1999. 49-72.

Swain, S.P. "*The Dark Holds No Terrors*: Assertion of the Feminine Psyche." *Feminism and Indian English Fiction*. Ed. P.M. Naik and S.P. Swain. Bareilley: PBD, 1996. 84-90.

——. "The Unruffled Stream: Jaya in *That Long Silence*." *Creative Forum* 10.1-2 (1997): 97-103.

——. "Images of Alienation—A Study of Anita Desai's Novels." *Feminist English Literature*. Ed. Manmohan K. Bhatnagar. New Delhi: Atlantic, 1999. 18-42.

——. "Erotic Pornography and Sexuality: A Study of *The God of Small Things*." *Arundhati Roy: The Novelist Extraordinary*. Ed. R.K. Dhawan. New Delhi: Prestige, 1999. 144-150.

——. "*Socialite Evenings*: A Feminist Study." *The Fiction of Shobha De*. Ed. Jaydipsinh Dodiya. New Delhi: Prestige, 2000. 129-141.

Swain, S.P. and P.M. Naik. "*Where Shall We Go This Summer?* Sita's Incarcerated Self." *Journal of Indian Writing in English* 1.22 (1994): 21-27.

Talwar, Sree Rashmi. "A Survey of Contemporary Indian Woman." *Woman's Space: The Mosaic World of Margaret Drabble and Nayantara Sahgal*. New Delhi: Creative, 1997. 134-142.

Tambe, Usha. "Shashi Deshpande as a Feminist and a Novelist." *Indian English Fiction 1980-90: An Assessment*. Ed. Nilufer E. Bharucha and Vilas Sarang. Delhi: B.R., 1994. 115-130.

Taneja, G.R. "Deconstructing Feminism: *Nectar in a Sieve* and the Phenomenon of Change." *Indian Women Novelists*

Set II: *Vol. II*. Ed. R.K. Dhawan. New Delhi: Prestige, 1993. 140-146.

——. "History, Change and Modernity: Markandaya's New Women in *Nectar in a Sieve*." *Women in Indo-Anglian Fiction*: *Tradition and Modernity*. Ed. Naresh K. Jain. New Delhi: Manohar, 1998. 48-55.

Thaggert, Miriam. "Relieving Memories: Evaluating History in Anita Desai's *Clear Light of Day*." *World Literature Written in English* 35.2 (1996): 90-102.

Tharoor, Tilottama. "The Melancholic World of Anita Desai." *The Telegraph* Oct. 21, 1984. 8.

Tharu, Susie. "Is there a tradition of Women's Literature?" *Literary Criterion* 21.1&2 (1986): 103-114.

Tharu, Susie and K. Lalita, eds. Introduction to Krupabai Sattianadhan. *Women Writing in India*: *600 B.C. to the Present Volume I*. Delhi: OUP, 1993. 275-276.

Thomas, O.J. "*Cry, the Peacock*: A World of Life and Death." *The Quest* 9.1 (1995): 16-21.

——. "The Enslaved and the Unsolved: The Characters of Anand and Anita Desai." *The Quest* 12.1 (1998): 39-43.

Thumbo, Edwin. "Kamala Markandaya's *A Silence of Desire*." *Journal of Indian Writing in English* 1.2.8 (1980): 108-136.

Tikka, Neelam. "*Lo! Cus Stand I!*: We are not the Sinners but the Sinned Against." *The Critical Studies of Arundhati Roy's "The God of Small Things*." Ed. Jaydipsinh Dodiya and Joya Chakravarty. New Delhi: Atlantic, 1999. 108-118.

——. "Lesbian Relationships in *Strange Obsession*." *The Fiction of Shobha De*. Ed. Jaydipsinh Dodiya. New Delhi: Prestige, 2000. 220-226.

Tikoo, Prithvi Nath. "Pro-feminine Reforms." *Indian Women*: (*A Brief Socio-Cultural Survey*). By Prithvi Nath Tikoo. New Delhi: B.R., 1985. 104-124.

Tikoo, S.K. "Heroism and Pathos in *Voices in the City*: A Thematic Analysis." *Indian Women Novelists Set I*: *Vol. III*. Ed. R.K. Dhawan. New Delhi: Prestige, 1991. 111-121.

——. "Human Relationships in *Pleasure City*." *Indian Women Novelists Set II: Vol. III*. Ed. R.K. Dhawan. New Delhi: Prestige, 1993. 226-240.

——. "*The Day in Shadow*: An Experiment in Feminist Fiction." *Indian Women Novelists Set II: Vol. IV*. Ed. R.K. Dhawan. New Delhi: Prestige, 1993. 238-252.

Tiwari, Shubha. "The Heroine in *The Dark Holds No Terrors*." *Women in the Novels of Shashi Deshpande*. Ed. Suman Bala. New Delhi: Khosla, 2001. 69-77.

Trikha, Pradeep. "A New Voice in the Indian Fiction: Githa Hariharan." *Indian Women Novelists Set III: Vol. 6*. Ed. R.K. Dhawan. New Delhi: Prestige, 1995. 9-12.

——. "*The God of Small Things*: A Rainbow in the Sky." *Arundhati Roy: The Novelist Extraordinary*. Ed. R.K. Dhawan. New Delhi: Prestige, 1999. 278-285.

——. "Githa Hariharan's *The Thousand Faces of Night*: Straight from a Woman's Life." *Feminism and Literature*. Ed. Veena Noble Dass. New Delhi: Prestige, 1995. 169-173.

Tripathi, J.P. "*The Binding Vine* and Indian Ethos." *The Fiction of Shashi Deshpande*. Ed. R.S. Pathak. New Delhi: Creative, 1998. 150-154.

——. "Anita Desai's *Fasting Feasting*: Continuity and Experiment." *Indian English Literature Since 1950 Vol.2*. Ed. Charu Sheel Singh. New Delhi: Anmol, 2001. 15-30.

——. "Indianness in the Novels of Anita Desai." *Contour* 1.2&3 (n.d.): 1-9.

Tripathi, Nalinabh. "Gender Identity and Inner Space in *The Dark Holds No Terrors*." *The Fiction of Shashi Deshpande*. Ed. R.S. Pathak. New Delhi: Creative, 1998. 43-48.

Tripathi, Nisha. "Search for Identity in Shobha De's *Starry Nights*." *Indian Women Novelists Set III: Vol. I*. Ed. R.K. Dhawan. New Delhi: Prestige, 1995. 103-110.

Tripathi, Prayag D. "Material/Manner, Musicality with Metaphoric Multiplicity: *The God of Small Things*." *Arundhati Roy: The Novelist Extraordinary*. Ed. R.K. Dhawan. New Delhi: Prestige, 1999. 307-318.

Trivedi, Darshana. "Arundhati's Similies." *Explorations: Arundhati Roy's "The God of Small Things."* Ed. Indira Bhatt and Indira Nityanandam. New Delhi: Creative, 1999. 130-135.

——. "Small is Beautiful." *Explorations: Arundhati Roy's "The God of Small Things."* Ed. Indira Bhatt and Indira Nityanandam. New Delhi: Creative, 1999. 185-190.

Trivedi, Nisha. "Search for Identity in *Starry Nights." The Fiction of Shobha De*. Ed. Jaydipsinh Dodiya. New Delhi: Prestige, 2000. 180-186.

Uma, Alladi. "Emancipation While Yet Alive: A Reading of Anita Desai's *Where Shall We Go This Summer?" When East Meets West: Indian Thought in Anglo-Indian and Indo-English Fiction.* Ed. Adapa Ramakrishna Rao and M. Siva Rama Krishna. New Delhi: Sterling, 1994. 134-138.

——. "Suppressed Vitality: Woman Behind the Veil." *Margins of Erasure: Purdah in the Sub-Continental Novel in English.* Ed. Jasbir Jain & Amina Amin. New Delhi: Sterling, 1995. 186-189.

——. "Over-[W]rit[d]ing Body: Shobha De's Novels." *The Post-Modern Indian English Novel: Interrogating the 1980s and 1990s.* Ed. Viney Kirpal. New Delhi: Allied, 1996. 182-187.

Vaidya, Sruti. "The Rejoicing Victim—A Study of Nayantara Sahgal's Simrit." *Victim Consciousness in Indian English Novel.* Ed. Usha Bande. Jalandhar: ABS, 1997. 74-80.

Varalakshmi, S. "The Individual and the Nation: A Study of Nayantara Sahgal's Work vis-a-vis the Canadian Women Writers." *Indian Women Novelists Set II: Vol. IV.* Ed. R.K. Dhawan. New Delhi: Prestige, 1993. 86-98.

——. "Nothing to Lose but Our Chains: Nayantara Sahgal's Women in Their Social Context." *Mapping Cultural Spaces: Post-Colonial Indian Literature in English.* Ed. Nilufer E. Barucha and Vrinda Nabar. New Delhi: Vision, 1998. 359-372.

Varma, Manju. "Short Creatures with Long Shadows." *Explorations: Arundhati Roy's "The God of Small Things."* Ed. Indira Bhatt and Indira Nityanandam. New Delhi: Creative, 1999. 155-161.

Varma, R. M. "The Bi-Cultural World of Kamala Markandaya's Novels." *Some Aspects of Indo-English Fiction.* New Delhi: Jainsons, 1985. 32-66.

Venkatachari, K. "Sense of Life" in Kamala Markandaya's *Nectar in a Sieve.*" *Osmania Journal of English Studies* 9.1 (1972): 55-59.

——. "Kamala Markandaya's *Nectar in a Sieve*: A Study in Romantic Realism." *Kakatiya Journal of English Studies* 3 (1983): 97-106.

Verghese, M.J. "Freedom and Suffering in Arundhati Roy's *The God of Small Things.*" *Explorations: Arundhati Roy's "The God of Small Things.*" Ed. Indira Bhatt and Indira Nityanandam. New Delhi: Creative, 1999. 58-62.

Verma, Meenakshi. "A Glance at Arundhati Roy's *The God of Small Things.*" *POETCRIT* 13.2 (2000): 12-16.

Verma, Prathibha. "Cultural Variation of Speech in Anita Desai's Novel *Bye-Bye Blackbird.*" *The Quest* 3.2 (1989): 19-24.

Verma, R.M. "*Bye-Bye Blackbird*: The Dilemma of Immigration." *Contemporary Indian Fiction in English.* Ed. Avadesh K. Singh. New Delhi: Creative, 1993. 96-104.

Vijayasree, C. "Re-Visionist Myth-Making: A Reading of Githa Hariharan's *The Thousand Faces of Night.*" *The Post-Modern Indian English Novel: Interrogating the 1980s and 1990s.* Ed. Viney Kirpal. New Delhi: Allied, 1996. 176-181.

Vinoba, T. "Small is Beautiful: Arundhati Roy's Universe." *Littcrit* 24.1&2 (1998): 24-34.

——. "*The God of Small Things*: A Post-Modernist Reading." *Kakatiya Journal of English Studies* 19 (1999): 96-103.

Vyas, B.O. "Viscid Voices of the Inner Kingdom." *Journal of Indian Writing in English* 9.1 (1981): 1-14.

——. "Of Concerns, Of Anxieties." *Women in Indo-Anglian Fiction Tradition and Modernity*. Ed. Naresh K. Jain. New Delhi: Manohar, 1998. 29-37.

——. "The Dilemma of the Woman Writer (Appendix)." *The Fiction of Shashi Deshpande*. Ed. R.S. Pathak. New Delhi: Creative, 1998. 229-231.

——. "The Power Within." *Creating Theory: Writers or Writing*. Ed. Jasbir Jain. Delhi: Pencraft, 2000. 205-212.

Gokhale, Namita. "Women's Writes." *Indian Feminisms*. Ed. Jasbir Jain and Avadesh Kumar Singh. New Delhi: Creative, 2001. 40-43.

——. "Gender and Literary Sensibility." *Indian Writing in English: The Last Decade*. Ed. Rahul Bhargava. Jaipur: Rawat, 2002. 64-68.

Hariharan, Githa. "Why I Write." *Kunapipi* 16.1 (1994): 280-281.

Markandaya, Kamala. "One Pair of Eyes: Some Random Reflections." *Literary Criterion* 11.4 (1976): 13-25.

Sahgal, Nayantara. "Meet the Author: Passion for India." *Indian Literature* 32.1 (1989): 79-88.

——. "A Search for Answers." Ed. K. Ayyappa Paniker. New Delhi: Sterling, 1983. 80-88.

——. "Some Thoughts on the Puzzle of Identity." *Journal of Commonwealth Literature* 29.1 (1993): 3-15.

——. "The Schizophrenic Imagination." *Creating Theory: Writers on Writing*. Ed. Jasbir Jain. Delhi: Pencraft, 2000. 104-111.

Walter, Inna. "Shobha De's *Socialite Evenings*: An Imitation Tale from Innocence to Experience." *Fiction of the Nineties*. Ed. Veena Noble Dass and R.K. Dhawan. New Delhi: Prestige, 1994. 47-60.

Wandrekar, Kalpana. "Towards Indian Feminism." *Literary Theory and Criticism: Ruminations*. Ed. A.P. Dani and V.M. Gadge. Delhi: Pencraft, 1998. 200-207.

Want, Lily. "*The God of Small Things*: A Feminist Critique of a Phallocratic Structure." *English Studies in India: A Journal of Literature and Language* (2001): 63-72.

Weir, Ann Lowry. "The Illusions of Maya: Feminine Consciousness in Anita Desai's *Cry, the Peacock*." *Journal of South Asian Literature* 16.2 (1981): 1-4.

William, Hayden Moore. "Some Characters in Markandaya's Novels." *Galaxy of Indian Writings in English*. Delhi: Akshat, 1987. 111-121.

Zaidi, Sishat. "Ecriture Feminine: Anita Desai's *Voices in the City* and *Cry, the Peacock*." *Indian English Literature Since 1950: Vol.2*. Ed. Charu Sheel Singh. New Delhi: Anmol, 2002. 71-77.

Book Reviews

Asnani, Shyam M. Rev. of *A Situation in New Delhi*, by Nayantara Sahgal, New Delhi: Himalaya Books, 1977. *World Literature Written in English* 19.1 (1980): 93-94.

Bordwekar, Sandhya. "Scenario for a Hindi Film." Rev. of *Come Up and Be Dead* by Shashi Deshpande. Vikas, New Delhi. *Indian Book Chronicle* 8.16 (1983): 283.

Geeta, P. Rev. of *A Situation in New Delhi* by Nayantara Sahgal. Penguin, New Delhi. *Literature Alive* 2.2 (1988): 36-38.

Gregory, John M. "Clear Light of Day." Rev. of *Clear Light of Day*, by Anita Desai. *Commonwealth Novel in English* 1.1&2:110-113.

Jha, Subhash K. "Tale from Raj." Rev. of *Plans for Departure*, by Nayantara Sahgal. *The Illustrated Weekly of India* 1 (1986): 61.

Masud, Iqbal. "No Departure from Raj Fiction." Rev. of *Plans for Departure*, by Nayantara Sahgal. *Gentlemen* (1986): 103-105.

Mitra, Sumit. "Subtle Magic." Rev. of *Plans for Departure*, by Nayantara Sahgal. *India Today* 28 Feb.1986: 152-157.

Interviews of Indian English Women Novelists

Abraham, Taisha. "An Interview with Arundhati Roy." *Ariel* 29.1 (1998): 89-92.

Ahluwalia, Kishwar. "The Paro-Techniques of Super Success: An Interview." *Femina* 8-22, 1984: 15,17,77.

de'Souza, Hartman. "I have No Concerns: An Interview with Namita Gokhale." *The Hindustan Times Sunday Magazine* April 29, 1984: 8.

Dickman, Sue. "An Interview with Shashi Deshpande." *Ariel* 29.1 (1998): 129-135.

Gangadharan, Geetha. "Denying the Otherness (Interview)." *The Fiction of Shashi Deshpande*. Ed. R.S. Pathak. New Delhi: Creative, 1998. 251-255.

Geeta, T.N. "An Interview with Shashi Deshpande." *Indian Women Novelists Set III*: *Vol. 4*. Ed. R.K. Dhawan. New Delhi: Prestige, 1995. 9-11.

Holmstrom, Lakshmi. "Shashi Deshpande Talks to Lakshmi Holmstorm." *The Fiction of Shashi Deshpande*. Ed. R.S. Pathak. New Delhi: Creative, 1998. 242-250.

Kumar, Shiv K. "Kamala Markandaya: Replies to the Questionnaire." *Kakatiya Journal of English Studies* 3 (1983): 83-84.

Kuorrti, Joel. "'The Double Burden: The Continual Contesting of Tradition and Modernity': Githa Hariharan interviewed by Joel Kuorrti." *Journal of Commonwealth Literature* 36.1 (2001): 7-26.

Libert, Florence. "An Interview with Anita Desai 1 August 1989. Cambridge. England." *World Literature Written in English* 30.1 (1990): 47-55.

Masilamani, J.G. "Anita Desai: Replies to the Questionnaire." *Kakatiya Journal of English Studies* 3 (1983): 1-6.

Ram, Atma. "Interview with Nayantara Sahgal." *Interviews with Indian English Writers*. Ed. Atma Ram. Calcutta: Writers Workshop, 1983. 45-48.

——. "Interview with Anita Desai." *Interviews with Indian English Writers*. Ed. Atma Ram. Calcutta: Writers Workshop, 1983. 23-33.

RamaRao, Vimala. "In conversation with Shashi Deshpande." *The Fiction of Shashi Deshpande*. Ed. R.S. Pathak. New Delhi: Creative, 1998. 256-259.

Riti, M.D. "There's No Looking Back (Interview)." *The Fiction of Shashi Deshpande*. Ed. R.S. Pathak. New Delhi: Creative, 1998. 238-241.

Sengupta, Pascale. "An Interview with Anita Desai." *Commonwealth Essays and Studies* 10.2 (1988): 43-50.

Thakur, Pallavi. "Defining Feminism: An Interview with Shashi Deshpande." *The Quest* 17.2 (2003): 18-29.

Thornton, Linden. "Arundhati Roy in Interview with Lindon Thornton (October 1997)." *Kunapipi* 19.3 (1997): 178-180.

Varalakshmi, S. "An Interview with Nayantara Sahgal." *Indian Women Writers Set II*: *Vol. IV*. Ed. R.K. Dhawan. New Delhi: Prestige, 1993. 9-18.

Viswanatha, Vanamala. "A Woman's World ...All the way (Interview)." *Literature Alive* 1.3 (1987): 8-14.)

Views of Indian English Women Novelists

Desai, Anita. "The Indian Writer's Problems." *Indian Wom Novelists Set I*: *Vol. II*. Ed. R.K. Dhawan. New De Prestige, 1991. 7-10.

Deshpande, Shashi. "The Writing of a Novel." *Indian Wo Novelists Set I*: *Vol. V*. Ed. R.K. Dhawan. New D Prestige, 1991. 31-36.

——. "Why I Write." *Kunapipi* 16.1 (1994): 270-272.

——. "Where do we Belong? The 'Problem' of Eng India." *Kunapipi* 3 (1997): 65-74.